WHICH? WAY TO
BEAT THE SYSTEM

Contributors

Chapter 1

Bob Gann is Director of The Help for Health Trust, a national registered charity working to improve provision of health information to the public. He has worked as a health care librarian, a writer and editor (largely for the British Medical Association) and advises the NHS Executive on provision of the freephone Health Information Service.

Chapter 2

Michael Hobson has worked in education for over 20 years and currently teaches English at St Thomas More School, Royal Borough of Kensington and Chelsea, London

Chapter 3

Derek Osbourne has been a councillor since 1986 and is Deputy Leader of the Royal Borough of Kingston upon Thames. From 1978 to 1990 he also worked for local authorities and is now a human resources consultant with particular experience in working with councils on consultation and customer care issues.

Chapter 4

Meriel Thorne worked at Consumers' Association for five years, latterly as senior public affairs officer, before joining Midland Bank as acting government affairs manager. Julia Gleig is senior public affairs officer at Consumers' Association.

Chapter 5

Jonquil Lowe is a freelance journalist and former head of the Money Group at Consumers' Association. She is the author of several books on personal finance, including, most recently, *Be Your Own Financial Adviser* (Which? Ltd, 1996).

Chapter 6

Keith Richards is an author, broadcaster and barrister-at-law specialising in consumer law. After working for Consumers' Association for ten years, latterly as senior lawyer, he joined the Association of British Travel Agents as head of consumer affairs.

Chapter 7

Alizoun Dickinson has been a senior manager in personnel for 20 years. She is now a management consultant.

Chapter 8

Sian Morrissey was a senior researcher in the Public Interest Research Group at Consumers' Association for five years and is now a freelance writer and researcher specialising in consumer affairs.

WHICH? WAY TO BEAT THE SYSTEM

CONSUMERS' ASSOCIATION

Which? Books are commissioned and researched by
Consumers' Association and published by
Which? Ltd, 2 Marylebone Road, London NW1 4DF

Distributed by The Penguin Group:
Penguin Books Ltd, 27 Wrights Lane, London W8 5TZ

Consultants: Barry S. Doe, Philip Schofield, Jonquil Lowe, Maurice Frankel,
Alan Mann; (for CA) Louise Gitter, Bob Tolliday, Jo Marsh, Emma Murray,
Lakhbir Purewal

Typographic design by Paul Saunders
Cover design by Ridgeway Associates
The publisher wishes to thank Waddingtons Games for permission to reproduce
the Snakes and Ladders board on the front cover

First edition October 1996
Copyright © 1996 Which? Ltd

British Library Cataloguing-in-Publication Data
A catalogue record for this book is available from the British Library

ISBN 0 85202 625 0

For a full list of Which? books, please write to
Which? Books, Castlemead, Gascoyne Way, Hertford X, SG14 1LH.

Typeset by Business Color Print, Welshpool, Powys, Wales
Printed in England by Clays Ltd, St Ives plc

Contents

INTRODUCTION

DEALING with the major institutions that govern so much of what happens in our everyday lives – the NHS, the local council, the education authorities, the banks, the Inland Revenue, the insurance companies and the DSS, among others – can be endlessly frustrating. Basically, they hold all the cards, because they know the intricacies of how their system works and you probably don't. Outsiders, trying to fight against or achieve something as mere members of the public, can find themselves at a great disadvantage – and vastly more inconvenienced by the time and trouble it takes to resolve a dispute than the monolithic bodies whose attitudes or actions they are challenging.

For years *Which?* has fought for a better deal for consumers, by pushing for major changes through government legislation and by helping individuals sort out problems. Much has been achieved. Much is left to fight for. Meanwhile, consumers still need all the help they can get, and this is what *Which? Way to Beat the System* offers. It explains what your rights are and how to exercise them. For example, in the new NHS system, which so many of us find confusing, it explains how to get the information to which you are entitled, how to find out about waiting lists and different treatment possibilities, how to get second opinions, how to complain and what to do if you or someone close to you appears to have been the victim of medical negligence. It looks at the education system, how to find out what goes on in various schools, what feedback schools must give parents on their children's progress, how to get help if your child has learning difficulties, etc., and how to find out about higher education entitlement and possibilities for grants or special sources of funding. It explains how local and national government works, and how you can raise matters with your local council or get your MP to represent your interests in Parliament. Two areas where complexity so often seems to be the order of the day are the financial institutions and the legal system: woe betide any of us who fail to understand and interpret accurately the rules, regulations and legislation which govern us, for such failures are likely to hit us directly in the pocket; and if we are given bad advice by a legal or financial expert, the prospect of redress may be faint. The chapters on these systems may make the task easier. The book also examines the state of play on employment rights, from both the employee's and the employer's standpoint. And finally it elucidates the intricacies of our public transport system, where performance standards and safety issues are a daily concern.

Each chapter describes the relevant 'system' as it relates to its users, explaining, en route, much of the jargon that can make organisations so difficult for outsiders to penetrate and can cause so much confusion and frustration. Where charters or codes of practice have been established to improve standards and clarify for members of the public what they can expect and what their rights are, these have been incorporated.

Although not intended as a complainers' handbook, the book will show what practical steps can be taken if you feel you are getting, or have had, bad treatment. The 'system', after all, is run by people. People are fallible beings, as recent *Which?* reports on solicitors, railway officials and financial advisers – to name a few – have demonstrated. If those on the inside, whom we regard as the experts, can get things wrong, all the more reason for the hapless individuals on the outside to push, as hard as possible, for a fair deal, even if the system as a whole seems not to be delivering it.

Question-and-answer sections at the end of each chapter illustrate the sorts of problems commonly faced (or queries raised) by individuals and offer some solutions, while sources of further information and advice, indicated in the text by an asterisk (*), are listed in a section at the back of the book.

CHAPTER 1

THE HEALTH SERVICES

THE NATIONAL Health Service is an institution in which we take justifiable pride. For the past fifty years it has endured as a guarantee of free health care delivered primarily through the general practice system. These principles have survived economic crisis and shifting political pressures.

But to many people health service provision has never looked more confusing. The development of the purchaser/provider split (whereby health authorities now 'purchase' health care from NHS Trusts independent of their management) has led to a service which is increasingly fragmented for the consumer. It can be difficult to know who is responsible when things go wrong. Add to that a primary health care system which is largely based on independent contractors and a growing private sector, and what at first glance looks like an admirably simple national health care system comes to resemble a maze.

In the vast majority of cases, health care is delivered professionally and humanely, and patients are satisfied. But when things do go wrong, as they inevitably sometimes do, health care consumers can be left confused, frightened and extremely vulnerable. This chapter provides a map to the health care maze which should help you to get the best out of the system for yourself and your family.

The National Health Service structure

National level

In England the Secretary of State for Health is responsible to Parliament for the provision of health services. The Secretary of

State is assisted by the Policy Board and the NHS Executive. The Policy Board sets the broad strategic direction of the NHS. It is chaired by the Secretary of State and its membership includes people from the NHS, business people, Department of Health officials and ministers.

The NHS Executive deals with operational matters within the strategy set by the Policy Board.

Regional level

As part of the Health Authorities Act 1995, Regional Health Authorities were abolished with effect from April 1996 and replaced by eight Regional Offices of the NHS Executive. The Regional Offices act as outposts of the central NHS Executive with a particular responsibility for the performance of health authorities and with a lead role in areas including public health and NHS research and development.

Health Authorities

Health Authorities (formerly District Health Authorities or DHAs) act as local commissioners or purchasers of hospital and community services.

Some health authorities still manage hospitals and other units but in almost all cases now provision of health care services is carried out by NHS Trusts.

Family Health Services Authorities (FHSAs) were formerly responsible for managing contracts for services provided by GPs, NHS dentists, community pharmacists and opticians. Since April 1996 FHSAs have been merged with District Health Authorities to establish unified Health Authorities.

NHS Trusts

Most hospital and community services are now provided by NHS Trusts. Trusts do not report to Health Authorities; instead, they have a contractual relationship (known as the 'purchaser-provider split').

Community Health Councils

In England and Wales, Community Health Councils (CHCs) operate at a local level as patient watchdogs. Health Authorities have to consult CHCs on substantial changes in services (such as hospital closures) and CHCs have the right to meet Health Authorities once a year.

In Scotland, this monitoring role is carried out by the Local Health Councils, and in Northern Ireland by the Health and Social Services Councils.

Wales, Scotland and Northern Ireland

Health services in Wales, Scotland and Northern Ireland are organised differently from the structure used in England. Responsibility here rests with the Welsh Office, Scottish Office, and Northern Ireland Office respectively.

In Wales it is the Secretary of State for Wales who is ultimately responsible for the provision of health services. The Secretary of State is assisted by the Health and Personal Social Services Policy Board and an Executive Committee. The Executive Committee is chaired by the Director of NHS for Wales, and its membership includes heads of divisions within the NHS Directorate and the Welsh Office Chief Medical and Nursing Officers. There are nine Health Authorities.

In Scotland there are 15 Health Boards, responsible for family health services as well as hospital and community services. In Northern Ireland there are four Health and Social Services Boards, covering social services as well as health care. Consumer interests are represented by Community Health Councils in Wales, Local Health Councils in Scotland and Health and Social Services Councils in Northern Ireland.

Health Authorities and Health Boards

Health Authorities (Boards in Scotland and Northern Ireland) are the bodies responsible for purchasing health care services for their residents. Health Authority functions are:

- assessing the local population's needs for health care
- purchasing services for their residents
- public health.

Health Authorities concentrate on public health and assessment of the needs of the population, contracting and quality assurance, leaving the management of health care services to NHS Trusts.

Each authority comprises a chairman appointed by the Secretary of State, five lay non-executive members appointed by the Regional Office and up to five executive members (senior managers including the Chief Executive and chief finance officer).

Under the Health Authorities Act 1995 the 110 District Health Authorities and 90 Family Health Services Authorities were merged with effect from April 1996 and transformed into about 100 unitary health authorities.

Health Authority meetings

You are entitled to attend most meetings of your Health Authority. Meetings of health authorities are subject to the Public Bodies (Admission to Meetings) Act 1960. This means that any formal meeting of the full authority must be open to the public. A notice of the time and place of the meeting must be posted at the authority's headquarters three working days in advance. The authority may resolve to exclude the public from some meetings or part of a meeting because of the confidential nature of business being discussed.

However, guidance from the Department of Health has made it clear that authorities are expected to conduct their business in as open a manner as is reasonable. The authority will probably delegate some of its functions to committees, sub-committees and task groups dealing with specific issues. The boards of NHS Trusts are obliged to meet in public only once a year.

Primary care

Most health care in the UK is provided through the primary health care system, through independent 'family practitioners'.

These are general practitioners, pharmacists, dentists and opticians.

General practitioners

The general practitioner (GP) occupies a key position in health care in the UK. Most everyday diagnosis and treatment is carried out by the GP. If your condition needs the attention of a specialist it is the GP who must make a referral for NHS treatment. The GP can also act as a way in to the network of community care services.

The GP is the central member of the 'primary care team', a group of professionals from various health disciplines who work from a GP surgery or health centre. Other members of the team may include the district nurse, health visitor, practice nurse, community psychiatric nurse, chiropodist, therapists, social worker, receptionist and medical secretary.

General practitioners are independent self-employed practitioners who can have a contract with the Health Authority (formerly Family Health Services Authority) to provide services within the NHS.

There are just over 28,000 GPs in the United Kingdom, with an average list of 2,000 patients each. The number of GPs has increased (in 1970 there were only 24,000) and the number of patients per doctor is falling (in 1970 it was 2,400). Thirty per cent of all GPs are female, compared to 19 per cent in the mid–1980s (and more than half of all trainee GPs are women).

According to estimates produced by the Office of Health Economics, we visit our GP on average 4.4 times a year.

Choosing a general practitioner

Health Authorities are obliged to provide more information than the Family Health Service Authorities they have replaced about local GP practices (in Scotland the Health Boards do this; in Northern Ireland it is the Health and Social Services Board). Lists of GPs including the doctor's sex, qualifications and year of qualifying, as well as details of surgery opening hours, services provided and arrangements for emergencies, are compiled by

Health Authorities and made available to the public in places like public libraries.

Everybody has a right to a GP, and most people at some stage need to choose a new one. Usually this is because they have moved house, but it may also be because the last doctor has moved, died or retired, or because they are not satisfied with their doctor. Except in an emergency, you need to be registered with a GP before you can receive treatment, so it is important to register with one as soon as you can.

GPs are also required to publish practice leaflets, which must contain specific essential information about the practice and services on offer. The distribution arrangements are for GPs to decide, but, as a minimum, a supply of leaflets should be available at the practice for patients and prospective patients and a copy must be sent to the Health Authority/Board.

From April 1993, Patient's Charter standards have obliged Health Authorities/Boards to act promptly and efficiently to help patients find a GP. If you are not already registered with a GP, the Health Authority should find you one within two working days. If you want to change doctors, you should be sent details of how to change, together with a list of local doctors, also within two working days.

Registering with a GP

In order to receive care from a GP when you want it (rather than in an emergency) you must register and have your name on the GP's list. Take your medical card, which shows your NHS number, along to the practice you have chosen and tell the receptionist you wish to register. If you have lost your card contact your Health Authority/Board for a new one. Some practices have pre-registration interviews, to give you a chance to meet the doctor before deciding whether to register. The GP is not obliged to take you as a patient, although he or she is unlikely to refuse unless the list is full.

When you have registered the Health Authority/Board will send you a new medical card and your medical records will be sent on to your new GP. Children under 16 need to be registered by their parents. Just as you can be registered with a different GP from your spouse, so you can register your children with a different GP from your own. However, it may be easier for a doctor to understand and treat a problem if he or she knows the whole family.

What to do if you need to see a GP when you are away from home

If you are going to be away from home for less than three months (while on holiday or temporary business, for example) you can ask a GP to accept you as a temporary resident. You remain on the list of your own GP but can be treated by the temporary GP, should the need arise. You will not be issued with a medical card and your medical records will not be transferred to your temporary doctor.

If you cannot find a GP willing to accept you, contact your Health Authority/Board. You will probably be given a list of GPs to try and will be asked to contact at least three yourself. If you still cannot get accepted the Health Authority/Board will allocate you to a GP. The GP is obliged to accept you – at least on a temporary basis.

Changing your GP

Most people's need of a new GP arises because they have moved house or because the old GP has moved, retired or died. A small proportion change because they are dissatisfied with the doctor. You can change GP without giving a reason, although the new GP is likely to ask why you no longer wish to be with your present doctor. You no longer need to ask your present GP to be able to leave to register with a new GP. You can simply choose your new doctor, go along to the new surgery and ask to be registered as a patient.

Out-of-hours cover

Ninety-five per cent of contacts between patients and GPs take place during normal surgery hours, but out-of-hours emergency cover is an important part of NHS care. The Patient's Charter

15

confirms the 24-hour nature of the GP service (the right 'to receive emergency care at any time').

In 1994, the government announced changes to the GP contract covering out-of-hours cover. Local GPs can set up primary care centres (PCCs) for out-of-hours treatment.

Patients will still be able to speak directly to a doctor out of hours but they may then:

- be given telephone advice
- be asked to visit the GP the next day
- be asked to go to the primary care centre
- receive a home visit
- be referred to hospital.

In many areas GPs are now forming co-operatives to provide out-of-hours cover.

Removal from a GP's list

A GP can remove a patient from his or her list without needing to give a reason why. If this happens you will receive a letter from your Health Authority/Board telling you this and advising you to find another GP. If you are unable to do so, the Health Authority/Board will help you find a new doctor. You are entitled to receive treatment from the former GP for eight days (from the date of the letter that you have been removed from the list) or until you are accepted by another GP, whichever occurs first.

Prescriptions

The most common form of treatment is a medicine, whether an over-the-counter (OTC) medicine you buy yourself or one prescribed by your doctor. GPs will prescribe only a limited amount of a drug at any one time (usually a month's supply), and many drugs have only a limited shelf-life. So if your treatment is continuous you will need to get repeat prescriptions from your doctor. Your GP will probably be able to give you a repeat prescription card naming the drugs you take regularly. You can then leave this with the receptionist so that your doctor can issue a repeat prescription without your needing to make an appointment to see him. Remember that this will take a day or so, so do not leave it until your last pill to ask for a repeat prescription.

Most GPs have a limit on the number of repeat prescriptions they will issue without seeing you. Your GP may ask you to make an appointment to see him after about six months.

Charges and exemptions

People who fall into the following categories are exempt from prescription charges:

- children under 16 years old
- students under 19 in full-time education
- people over 60
- people on income support and family credit
- people receiving disability working allowance
- war pensioners, for prescriptions relating to their war disablement
- pregnant women
- women who have had a child in the past year
- people with some specific medical conditions, including diabetes, epilepsy, permanent stomas, myasthenia gravis, Addison's Disease and thyroid conditions.

Until October 1995, women were entitled to free prescriptions at 60 and men at 65. However, a European Court of Justice ruling found that the UK age exemption arrangements were inconsistent with Directive 79/7/EEC, which provides for equal treatment of men and women in matters of social security. Men and women are now both entitled to free prescriptions from the age of 60.

Dentists

There are over 18,000 dentists in the UK, most of whom provide some NHS treatment (although not to all sections of the community). Health Authorities (Health and Social Services Boards in Northern Ireland, Health Boards in Scotland) maintain lists of dentists in their area who do NHS work. This dental list is available at the offices of the Authority/Board and at your local

Community Health Council (Health and Social Services Council in Northern Ireland and Local Health Council at Scotland), and may also be found in libraries and offices. The dental list will tell you the names of dentists, qualifications, the address of the surgery, surgery times and other information such as languages spoken, wheelchair access and so on. Dentists are also listed in *Yellow Pages* under 'Dental surgeons'. Since October 1991 all dental practices have been required to have leaflets available for patients giving details of services provided. If you have problems finding a dentist in your area prepared to accept you as an NHS patient, contact your Health Authority/Board for advice.

When making your appointment for dental treatment make sure you tell the dentist that you want to be treated on the NHS otherwise you may find yourself being charged as a private patient. If the practice does provide treatment under the NHS you will be asked to sign a form (FP17A) applying to join the dentist's list as a continuing-care patient. By accepting you on this list the dentist agrees to see you for two years and to provide all necessary treatment under the NHS. The dentist is required to give a treatment plan and estimate of charges before commencing treatment.

Changes announced in June 1996 require both adult and child patients to arrange to have a dental examination at least once every 15 months. If these examinations are not made patients can be deregistered from the dentist's list.

Free dental treatment

Unless you come within one of the categories for free treatment you will have to pay some of the costs of treatment, even if this is carried out under the NHS. Your dentist is entitled to charge you if you fail to keep an appointment without notifying him or her.

You are entitled to free NHS dental care if you are:

- under 18 years old (i.e. up to your 18th birthday)
- under 19 and in full-time education
- pregnant or with a baby under one year
- receiving income support or family credit (or your partner is).

Others on low income may still be able to get help with costs, even if they cannot get completely free treatment. Further details are given in leaflet D11, *NHS Dental Treatment,* available from Benefits Agency (DSS) offices and post offices. If you have already paid and think you are entitled to a refund, ask your local Benefits Agency office for form AG5. Remember, there is a three-month time limit for claiming a refund.

Complaints about dentists

If you are dissatisfied with your treatment, complain first to the dentist. Complaints about the Community Dental Service should be made to the NHS Trust providing the service. It may simply be a matter of correcting earlier work (e.g. an ill-fitting denture) without extra charge. This is stage 1 of the new NHS complaints procedure.

If you are still dissatisfied with the standard of service you can ask the Health Authority/Board for a further review by an independent review panel (stage 2).

The final step is complaint to the Health Service Commissioner (Ombudsman), whose remit is being extended to cover family health service practitioners, including dentists.

If you have a complaint to do with improper personal, ethical or professional behaviour you should contact the General Dental Council,★ which can also deal with complaints about private treatment.

Opticians

You can go to any ophthalmic optician for a sight test; there is no need to register with a particular one. Some dispensing practices also have a sight-tester in attendance. NHS sight tests are free but available only to people:

- under 16
- under 19 and in full-time education
- on income support or family credit (or with a partner who is)
- with a valid exemption certificate (AG2)
- registered blind or partially sighted
- diagnosed diabetic or with glaucoma
- aged 40 or over and the brother, sister or child of a diagnosed glaucoma patient.

Other people have to pay a charge of about £13. However, the charge may vary from one optician to another so it is worth shopping around.

Obtaining glasses

When you have had your eyes tested, the sight-tester must give you either a prescription or a statement that you do not need glasses. If a prescription for glasses is needed the sight-tester is required to give you this immediately following the sight test.

You can then use the prescription to obtain glasses either from the optician who examined you or by taking it to another registered optician or supplier of glasses. There is now a wide range of glasses available in department stores and spectacle shops, but if you go to one of these your prescription must not be more than two years old. These suppliers are not allowed to supply glasses to children under 16 or lenses for partially sighted or registered blind people (only registered opticians may do so). The prices of frames are usually clearly marked but make sure you ask about the complete cost, including the kind of lenses you are having.

Some people are eligible for vouchers to help with the cost of buying new spectacles. Those who qualify are:

- under 16
- under 19 and in full-time education
- on income support or family credit (or have a partner who is), or
- a holder of a valid exemption certificate (AG2).

You may also be entitled to a voucher if you need a particularly powerful or complicated lens. If you are entitled to a voucher, tell the optician when you sign the sight-test form. You can choose glasses that cost more than the voucher and pay the extra yourself.

Complaints about opticians

If you have a complaint about the standard of service given within the NHS by an optician you should complain in the first instance to the practice concerned, under stage 1 of the new NHS complaints procedure. If you are still dissatisfied, you have the option of asking the Health Authority/Board for an independent review (stage 2 of the new procedure).

If the complaint is about the optician's conduct you should contact the General Optical Council.★

In January 1993 the Optical Consumer Complaints Service (OCCS)★ was launched as an independent body which tries to settle complaints from members of the public who are not satisfied with optical services. It publishes a leaflet explaining how the complaints service works.

Giving blood

The National Blood Service★ is dependent on voluntary unpaid blood donors. About 2.4 million donations are collected from 1.8 million donors every year. Without them many medical and surgical procedures could not take place, and many lives could not be saved. In November 1995 the government launched a new extension to the Patient's Charter covering blood donors' rights and the standards they can expect from the National Blood Service.

If you give blood you have rights which guarantee that:

- each collection session is supervised by an experienced nurse or doctor
- sterile, disposable blood collection equipment is used for each donor and never re-used
- all staff are specially trained and follow strict procedures
- all information about donors is kept strictly confidential
- donors have access to their records
- interviews about the state of donors' health will be carried out in private
- donors will receive information about the procedures involved
- donors will know the names of staff by their name badges and the person in charge of their session will be clearly identified
- blood taken will be used for the benefit of patients and will not be sold
- donors have the right to complain about any of the services they receive from the National Blood Service, to have their

complaint acknowledged within two working days and to receive a full written reply within 20 working days.

In addition you can expect to:

- receive about two weeks' notice of a donor session and a personal invitation to attend
- be asked to attend at a location convenient to you which is easy to find and accessible
- attend sessions at convenient times
- spend no more than one hour at a donor session.

You can help the National Blood Service by:

- answering conscientiously all personal and health questions to ensure the safety of the blood supply to patients
- telling your local centre about any illness you develop up to two weeks following donation of blood
- donating regularly: you can expect to be called to a session 2–3 times a year
- making every effort to keep appointments.
- informing the local blood centre of any change of address
- encouraging others to become donors. Ask potential volunteers to call the National Blood Service for more information.

Organ donation

The removal of organs for transplantation is permitted by law if the person who dies has previously indicated willingness to become a donor. Normally this is done by signing a donor card which is kept with the individual at all times. Hospital staff will always consult the relatives about possible donations, and if there is any objection it is unlikely that the organs will be used, but there is no legal requirement to obtain permission from the deceased person's relatives before donation can take place. Also, the person in charge of the body should try to ensure that the donor's consent was not withdrawn after he or she signed the card.

If there is no donor card, the hospital staff may ask the relatives whether there is any objection to removal of organs for donation. Decisions have to be made quickly if the organs are to be of any use, which is why it is important for everyone to discuss the matter with their relatives well before the possibility of organ donation arises.

In 1994 a national computerised databank of potential donors was set up. In addition to carrying donor cards, potential donors can now register their personal details confidentially with the Department of Health,★ to assist medical staff in search of organs for transplantation. If the DVLC★ at Swansea is notified that someone is a potential donor, this can be printed on the individual's current driving licence. Otherwise, potential donors should contact the Register by post. The scheme does not replace donor cards, but should greatly improve the speed at which information can be obtained by hospitals and enable many more transplants to take place.

Should a coroner be involved, his or her consent must be obained before organ donation takes place.

In addition to donation of organs by someone who has died, some organs, such as kidneys, may be given by live donors. The Human Organ Transplants Act 1989 was passed to prohibit commercial dealings in human organs and this now places restrictions on live donor transplants between people who are not genetically related. All proposed transplants between a living donor and someone to whom he or she is not related now have to be approved by the Unrelated Live Transplant Regulatory Authority (ULTRA).

Waiting for hospital treatment

Although most treatment is provided in primary care settings many of us go into hospital at some stage in our lives. For hospital treatment under the NHS you will need a GP to refer you to a specialist. The specialist is usually a consultant, whom you will see first of all in the outpatient department at the hospital (or you may see a member of his or her team such as a registrar). Some consultants also see patients in smaller community hospitals or health centres. In the NHS today a routine non-urgent appointment with a consultant almost always involves joining a waiting list. Reducing waiting lists has been a key element of the government's Patient's Charter initiative.

Rights under the Patient's Charter

Patient's Charter rights relevant to waiting times are:

- *to be given detailed information on local health services including waiting times*
  Your local health authority/board will make sure that all local NHS hospitals publicise current maximum admission times
- *to be guaranteed admission by a specific date no later than eighteen months from the day when your consultant first places you on the waiting list*
  Your Health Authority/Board will be responsible for ensuring that the guaranteed times are met, if necessary by offering you treatment in an alternative hospital
- *that your operation should not be cancelled on the day you are due to arrive in hospital*
  If, exceptionally, your operation has to be postponed twice you will be admitted to hospital within one month of the date of the second cancelled operation.

Many Health Authorities/Boards have set their own maximum waiting times which improve on the Patient's Charter standard. Since April 1994 all Health Authorities/Boards have had to adhere to a new maximum waiting time of 18 months. Although the Patient's Charter has not led to a major reduction in the total number of patients on waiting lists (just over 1 million in 1996) it has led to a dramatic fall in long waits. In 1990, 200,000 people had been waiting over a year for admission to hospital – 70,855 of them for over 2 years. By September 1995 the number waiting over a year had dropped to 27,900 (less than 3 per cent of all patients on the waiting list). Forty-two patients had been waiting over 18 months, in breach of the Patient's Charter guarantee. The average time on a waiting list has fallen since 1991 from more than nine months to four months.

Since April 1995 a Patient's Charter standard has required that all first outpatient appointments should take place within 26 weeks of referral, 9 out of 10 patients being seen within 13 weeks. By June 1995 97 per cent of patients were being seen within 26 weeks and 85 per cent were waiting less than 13 weeks.

Joining a waiting list

The procedure is as follows:

(1) your GP writes to the consultant, asking for an appointment and giving details of your condition which the consultant will use to classify you as routine, 'soonest' or urgent

(2) the consultant then writes to you with an appointment date for this outpatient clinic

(3) you attend the consultant's outpatient clinic and the consultant decides whether admission to hospital is necessary. You may not see the consultant at the clinic, but a registrar on his or her team

(4) if you do not need admission, you will be treated as an outpatient or referred back to your GP

(5) if you do need to go into hospital (perhaps for an operation) the consultant decides how urgent admission is, and puts you on his/her inpatient waiting list. Under the Patient's Charter this must be within 18 months

(6) after a further wait (depending on the urgency of the problem) you are admitted to hospital for treatment

(7) following treatment you are discharged from hospital and cared for by your GP.

There may be follow-up appointments at the consultant's outpatient clinic.

Finding the shortest waiting time

All Health Authorities/Boards collect information about their waiting times for treatment and make quarterly returns to the Health Departments. Many Health Authorities/Boards also produce bulletins showing the waiting times of their own consultants and distribute them to local GPs. Since June 1994 waiting time information has also been published as part of the NHS performance tables. If you are faced with a long wait for treatment in your own district:

• first, go back to your own GP and ask him/her to consider referring you to another hospital where the waiting time is shorter. If your condition worsens, your GP may write to the original hospital to ask that you be seen more quickly

• make enquiries to find out where the shortest waiting lists are.

If your GP does not have this information you can:

(1) telephone the Health Information Service.★ You will be automatically routed to your nearest point of contact, which will have details of waiting times in your part of the country. Staff should also be able to tell you whether your Health Authority/Board has contracts with hospitals outside the district. There is also a National Waiting List Helpline at the College of Health★

(2) check which hospital consultant has the shortest waiting list, and think about how far you would be prepared to travel

(3) ask your GP to consider referring you to a consultant in that district. Even if you do the homework for your GP, you will still have to ask him or her to contact the consultant to find out whether you can be taken on as an NHS patient. If your GP is a fundholder this should be reasonably straightforward (however, even fundholding GPs have their own contacts, and these are usually with local hospitals). If not, the GP will need to help you get the agreement of your Health Authority to an extra–contractual referral (ECR)

(4) make clear to your own local hospital whether you are able to go in at very short notice if there is a vacancy. Many hospitals have a short notice list. This means that you could take up a vacancy if someone else was unable to accept the date offered for going into hospital. As the hospital has very little time to fill the bed you could be telephoned and offered admission, even at a few hours' notice.

Outpatients

You may need to visit the outpatient department at the hospital for a number of reasons:

• for examination by a consultant on referral from your GP
• for hospital treatment on an outpatient basis (i.e. without having to stay in hospital)

- for assessment and care in a nurse clinic
- for follow-up appointments after discharge from hospital.

If your GP feels you should see a consultant at the hospital you will see him first in his outpatient clinic. Depending on the seriousness of your condition, you will probably have to join an outpatient waiting list before you can see the consultant. The hospital will write to you nearer the time with details of your appointment. You should also be given information about how to find the outpatient department. The amount of time which patients spend in the waiting room in outpatients, and the environment in which they wait, have given rise to a number of complaints in the past. Many hospitals are now tackling these problems as part of their quality drives. The Patient's Charter sets a national standard for the time patients should wait in an outpatient clinic. You will be given a specific appointment time and will be seen within 30 minutes of it. Patient's Charter monitoring shows that about 88 per cent of outpatients are seen within the Patient's Charter standard of 30 minutes.

The Patient's Charter also now sets a standard by which everyone should get their first outpatient appointment within 26 weeks and nine out of ten people within 13 weeks.

Consent to treatment

When you go into hospital treatment cannot be carried out without your consent. A mentally sound adult has the right to give or refuse consent to be examined or treated. Examining or treating patients without their consent is a form of assault. The only exceptions to this are:

- if a person has a notifiable disease
- if a person has been detained under the Mental Health Act 1983.

The *Guide to Consent for Examination or Treatment* (NHS Management Executive, 1990) recommends that there should be written consent for any procedure carrying any substantial risk or substantial side-effect, including general anaesthesia, surgery, certain forms of drug therapy (e.g. cytotoxic drug therapy) and therapy using ionising radiation. A model consent form has been agreed by the Department of Health, the BMA, the Medical Defence Union and the Medical Protection Society. The form is evidence that the procedure has been explained, that the patient understands the nature and purpose of the proposed treatment, and of the patient's consent to the proposed surgery. Patient and consumer groups argue that patients should be given a copy of their signed consent form. Consent, even in writing, is not valid unless the patient is informed about the procedure and why it is to be performed. The use of standard forms is not compulsory within the NHS, and different forms may be used in private hospitals.

Patients admitted to hospital unconscious

Sometimes patients are admitted to hospital unconscious. In this case the usual practice is to try to contact the next of kin for his/her consent on behalf of the patient. If delay would be dangerous, doctors are entitled to carry out any necessary treatment or operation. However, doctors should not give the patient more extensive treatment than is absolutely necessary to cope with the immediate emergency.

Refusing medical examinations or treatment

You are entitled to refuse all or part of any form of treatment proposed, including drug treatment. Doctors should explain the risks and benefits to enable you to make a decision. If you refuse treatment, this decision must be respected and your decision recorded in the clinical notes. If a Jehovah's Witness refuses to consent to a tissue transplant (including blood transfusion), legally that treatment may not be given.

Parent's right to give/refuse consent for treatment

The law requires parents to give or refuse consent for a child who cannot consent for himself or herself. If a child is in care, or a ward of court, then parents lose this right, although they may be consulted. As soon as a child is able fully to understand (in a doctor's judgement) what is proposed, he or she can give consent on his/her own account.

What to expect if your child goes into hospital

At the very least you should be able to stay with your child as much as possible (this is Department of Health policy). The hospital may provide a chair, mattress or folding bed for you to sleep on. This may not necessarily be next to your child's bed. Most hospitals do not have strictly enforced visiting hours for parents, and you should be able to give your child his or her meals, bath etc. There should be access for parents to washing facilities, use of a sitting room, kitchen, toilets, telephone and restaurant.

Children's ward kitchens often have supplies of breakfast cereals, baked beans etc. for children who do not like hospital food. Provision should be made for children from ethnic minorities who have preferences in relation to food, washing and bathing and clothing. There should also be every encouragement for mothers to breastfeed their baby and space to do so in privacy.

If you are not able to be with your child as much as you would like, tell the ward sister about any food fads, comfort habits, etc. your child has, and whether there are any special words you and your child use. Most hospitals allow children to wear their own clothes as much as possible, and also to bring in their own toys.

Registered sick children's nurses

During their training all nurses gain some experience on children's (paediatric) wards, but some receive additional specialist training to become Registered Sick Children's Nurses. Some hospitals also have hospital play specialists who play with children on the wards, and may also help prepare them for admission or with difficult problems. Hospital-based teachers provide lessons for children of school age. This may be in consultation with the child's school. If your child is going to be admitted to hospital you should be able to arrange a visit to the ward in advance. This should help to make the hospital seem less strange and frightening. Books and leaflets designed to prepare children for hospital are also available.

The Children's Charter

Under the extension to the Patient's Charter, 'Services for children and young people', issued in 1996, you can expect:

- your child to be cared for in a children's ward under the supervision of a consultant paediatrician
- your child to have a qualified, named children's nurse responsible for his or her nursing care
- to be able to stay in the hospital with your child
- (if your child is having an operation and where circumstances permit) to accompany your child into the anaesthetic room and be present until he or she is asleep
- to be told what pain relief will be given to your child
- the NHS to respect your child's privacy, dignity and religious or cultural beliefs
- your child to be offered a choice of children's menus
- to have breastfeeding facilities
- your child to wear his or her own clothes, and have personal possessions
- the hospital to be clean, safe and suitably furnished for children and young people
- all the staff you meet to wear name badges, both for security reasons and so that you know who they are
- your child to have the opportunity for play and to meet other children.
- to have the right for your child to receive suitable education.

Choosing where to have your baby

The choice of where to give birth is not a straight choice between hospital and home. There are other options which offer some of the advantages of home birth, with emergency medical cover quickly to hand. Facilities and policies vary around the UK, and some people may have more choices than others, but basically you can choose between giving birth:

- in a consultant unit in hospital
- in a GP unit in a hospital

- under the domino system
- at home.

The government's Changing Childbirth initiative has emphasised that clinical practice in childbirth should be based on firm research evidence and women should be closely involved in decisions about their own care.

Birth in hospital

The advantage of a hospital birth is that expertise and equipment are at hand in case they are needed. If something goes wrong (for example, if you need an emergency Caesarean delivery), action can be taken immediately and you will not have to be moved. If there is anything wrong with the baby, life-saving equipment is immediately available.

Many hospital maternity units now provide a much more homely and relaxing environment within which to give birth. There may be softer lighting, attractive furnishings etc. and you should be able to prepare a birth plan indicating your choice of birthing position, pain relief and so on.

In a few parts of the UK you have the option of giving birth in a GP unit. This may be part of the hospital's maternity department or a separate unit. Your baby can be delivered by your community midwife, with the assistance of your GP. Some people find this more personal, but you have the hospital facilities if you need them.

Birth in the domino system

'Domino' stands for domiciliary-in-out. The system may also be known as a district bed. Under this system you receive your antenatal care from your community midwife. She gets to know you during pregnancy, accompanies you to hospital and delivers your baby. If all goes well you can go home after about six hours (or after a night's sleep if your baby is born late in the evening).

Birth at home

If you want to have your baby at home you should first talk to your midwife and GP, early in your pregnancy. Most doctors advise against home deliveries for the first baby because it is hard to predict how the birth will go. Although it is your right to have a home birth, you should discuss whether you have any risk factors which make it inadvisable. These would include existing medical conditions such as epilepsy, diabetes, severe anaemia; previous problems in labour, family history of problems such as high blood pressure; or known difficulties for the baby such as breech presentation. If your own GP is unwilling to undertake to care for you during your pregnancy and home delivery, you may be able to register with another GP just for antenatal care, the delivery and postnatal care. You can stay with your usual doctor for the rest of your medical care.

In many areas it can be very difficult to find a GP sympathetic to home births, or with any recent experience of one. In this case you should be able to book directly with your midwife. It is her responsibility to find a doctor to cover if she feels this is necessary. National Childbirth Trust branches usually have the inside knowledge of local views on home birth and it would also be worth contacting your Community Health Council, Local Health Council, Health and Social Services Council or the primary care department of the Health Board.

Maternity Services Charter

In April 1994 the Patient's Charter was extended to maternity services with the publication of the Maternity Services Charter. The Charter lays out key rights and standards including giving the mother:

- the right to choose where her baby is born – at hospital or at home
- the name of the midwife responsible for her midwifery care
- the opportunity to see a consultant obstetrician at least once during her pregnancy

- the opportunity to see a consultant paediatrician if the obstetrician anticipates problems with the baby
- the right to see her maternity records during pregnancy and, if she chooses, to keep them with her
- the right to be given information about local maternity services and an explanation of any treatment proposed, including benefits, risks and any alternatives
- a specific time for appointments, and seeing her within 30 minutes of that time
- the choice of whether to have her partner or a friend or relative with her while she is in labour or giving birth
- the choice of having her baby with her in hospital unless there are clinical reasons why she should not
- the right to have relatives and friends visit her at all reasonable times as long as this does not disturb others.

Participating in clinical trials

Patients may, sometimes unwittingly, be participating in clinical trials (for example, medical research to test the efficiency of a drug in a group of patients with a control group of patients not receiving the drug). The position on consent for medical research varies according to whether the research is expected to benefit the patient or not. Where no benefit to the individual patient is expected, Department of Health guidelines state that a full explanation of the proposed procedure should be given and the patient must feel free to withdraw at any stage. Where research is expected to benefit the patient, although consent should ordinarily be sought, there are sometimes circumstances in which it is inappropriate or even inhumane to explain the details and seek consent (for example, if someone who has a fatal illness does not wish to know this). Every hospital or institution where clinical trials are carried out has its own ethical committee which oversees the conduct of medical research.

Questions to ask if invited to participate in a trial

If you are a potential guinea-pig for a clinical trial, ask your doctor:

- what the purpose of the study is
- what will happen to the results of the research
- whether you can have a copy of the results
- what the known risks and side-effects of the treatment are
- whether you will benefit from taking part in the trial
- what can be done to make you better if you have a problem while taking part
- what you will have to do if you take part; whether you will need lots of blood tests; whether there will be lots of hospital visits or forms to fill
- whether you will be paid; whether the doctor will be paid, and if so by whom and how much
- whether the trial has been approved by a research ethics committee
- why the new medicine is thought to be an effective alternative to existing treatments
- whether you can have time to think about whether to take part
- whether you can have written details to take away with you
- whether you would get compensation if it went wrong for you
- what will happen if you change your mind before the end of the trial and whether rebound effects are likely to occur when you stop
- whether you would be able to continue taking the medicine after the end of the trial if you found it useful
- whether your heart will be monitored after the trial and, if so, for how long.

Discharge from hospital

When you are discharged from hospital make sure you have all the information you need about any medication you are taking, looking after stitches and dressings, how soon you can go back to work, drive a car, and so on. You should also be told whom to contact if you have any problems, and about any self-help support groups relevant to your condition. You may go home with a couple of days' supply of medicine but will probably need to see your GP for a larger supply. The hospital may also give you a letter for your GP, telling him or her about the treatment you have received.

Your rights under the Patient's Charter

The Patient's Charter includes discharge from hospital as one of its National Charter standards. It states that 'before you are discharged from hospital a decision should be made about any continuing health or social care needs you may have'. Your hospital will agree arrangements for meeting these needs with agencies such as community nursing services and local authority social services departments before you are discharged. You, and with your agreement your carers, will be consulted at all stages.

- you should receive a written and verbal explanation before or at the time of admission about what you can expect to happen during your hospital stay
- you should be consulted at all times about plans for your discharge from hospital
- you should be given your own written copy of your discharge plan
- your hospital should make the necessary arrangements for health and social care that you may need when you leave hospital
- you and your family should be made aware of what this after-care may be
- your GP and anyone involved in your care should receive any information they need within 24 hours of discharge (this should include information about your discharge date, diagnosis, treatment, ongoing support, and any follow-up arrangements)
- appropriate transport should be arranged for you to get home
- you should not be discharged into a private nursing home if you or your relatives would have to pay and do not wish to: it is the responsibility of your health authority to arrange this kind of care if you need it.

Discharging yourself from hospital

Although it may not be a very good idea, you can discharge yourself at any time, even against the advice of your consultant. The only exceptions, when you can be compulsorily detained in hospital, are:

- under the Mental Health Act 1983
- if you have a notifiable infectious disease
- if you are unable to look after yourself and have no one else to do so.

If you do discharge yourself you may be asked to sign a form saying you are no longer the responsibility of the consultant. You are not obliged to sign this. If you discharged yourself against the advice of the consultant and needed to be re-admitted the consultant could refuse to treat you. However, he or she would have to refer you to a colleague for any treatment required.

Continuing care arrangements

If a patient has been assessed as not requiring NHS continuing inpatient care, he/she does not have a right to occupy an NHS bed indefinitely. In all but a very small number of cases where patients are placed under Part II of the Mental Health Act 1983, patients have the right to refuse to be discharged from NHS care into a nursing home or residential care home.

In such cases the Social Services department would work with NHS staff and the patient and family to explore alternative options. If these options are rejected, the hospital (in consultation with the Health Authority/Board, Social Services, and where necessary the housing authority) will implement discharge to the patient's home or alternative accommodation, with a package of health and social care. A charge may be made by social services for the social care element.

As a final check before discharge is implemented, a patient, family or carer has the right to ask the Health Authority for a review of the decision not to continue NHS inpatient care. The Health Authority/Board should deal urgently with the request and respond in writing within two weeks.

Health Authorities were required in 1995 to develop local policies making clear the eligibility criteria for continuing health care within the NHS. These were available for public consultation and finalised by April 1996. Health Authorities must now have in place arrangements to handle requests to review decisions on eligibility for NHS continuing care including the use of independent panels. NHS Trusts must have in place arrangements to provide information to patients, families and carers about discharge procedures and local arrangements for ensuring continuing care.

The Patient's Charter

Charter rights

The Citizen's Charter launched by the government in June 1991 introduced a set of initiatives designed to make public services more responsive to consumers and to raise quality standards overall. The Patient's Charter★ puts the Citizen's Charter into practice in the NHS.

As a citizen you already have the following NHS rights:

- to receive health care on the basis of clinical need, regardless of ability to pay
- to be registered with a GP
- to receive emergency medical care at any time, through a GP or the emergency ambulance service and hospital accident and emergency departments
- to be referred to a consultant, acceptable to you, when your GP thinks it necessary and to be referred for a second opinion if you and your GP agree this is desirable
- to be given a clear explanation of any treatment proposed, including any risks and any alternatives, before you decide whether you will agree to the treatment
- to have access to your health records, and to know that those working for the NHS must, by law, keep their contents confidential
- to choose whether or not you wish to take part in medical research or medical student training.

Additional rights were introduced in April 1992:

- to be given detailed information on local health services, including quality standards and maximum waiting times. You will be able to get this information from your Health Authority/Board, GP, Community Health Council, Local Health Council or Health and Social Services Council

- to be guaranteed admission for virtually all treatments by a specific date no later than 18 months from the day when your consultant places you on a waiting list. Most patients will be admitted before this date. (In 1996, 90 per cent are admitted within a year)
- to have any complaint about NHS services (whoever provides them) investigated, and to receive a full and prompt written reply from the chief executive of your Health Authority, Health Board, Health and Social Services Board or general manager of your hospital. If you are still unhappy, you will be able to take the case up with the Health Service Commissioner.

National Charter Standards

The NHS aims to provide nine standards of service to patients under the Charter:

- respect for privacy, dignity and religious and cultural beliefs
- arrangements to ensure everyone, including people with special needs, can use the services
- information to relatives and friends about the progress of your treatment, subject, of course, to your wishes
- emergency ambulances that arrive within 14 minutes in an urban area, or 19 minutes in a rural area
- when attending an accident and emergency department, you will be seen immediately and your need for treatment assessed
- when you go to an outpatient clinic, you will be given a specific appointment time and will be seen within 30 minutes of it
- your operation should not be cancelled on the day you are due to arrive in hospital. If, exceptionally, your operation has to be postponed twice you will be admitted to hospital within one month of the second cancelled operation
- a named qualified nurse, midwife or health visitor will be responsible for your nursing and midwifery care
- a decision should be made about any continuing health or social care needs you may have, before you are discharged from hospital.

In April 1995 the Patient's Charter was extended as follows:

- new national standards for waiting times were set for first outpatient appointments. Ninety per cent of appointments should be within 13 weeks and all within 26 weeks
- the existing 18-month waiting-time guarantee for hip, knee and cataract operations was extended to *all* operations
- a new one-year waiting-time guarantee was given for coronary artery bypass grafts and associated procedures
- a two-hour national maximum for 'trolley waits' – admission to a ward from accident and emergency departments
- a new right to advance notification if a patient is being admitted to a ward for both men and women, with patient preferences for single-sex accommodation being respected wherever possible. Another new standard will specify that toilet and washing facilities should be single-sex
- parents can expect their children to be cared for in a children's ward other than in exceptional circumstances (when a named consultant paediatrician should be responsible for advising on their care)
- a new standard on hospital food, so that, among other things, patients' dietary needs and preferences are respected and a choice of dishes provided
- a new standard specifying that patients receiving home visits from community nurses must be consulted about a convenient time and that the visit should take place within a two-hour time band around that time.

Local Charter Standards

Since April 1992 authorities have had the responsibility to set and publicise clear Local Charter Standards, including:

- first outpatient appointments
- waiting times in accident and emergency departments, after initial assessment
- waiting times for taking patients home after treatment, in cases where the doctor considers that the patient has a medical need for NHS transport
- enabling patients and visitors to find their way around hospitals through enquiry points and better signposting

- ensuring that the staff patients meet face-to-face wear name badges.

You can help the NHS locally through a variety of practical means, such as letting your hospital know if you cannot keep an appointment, by giving blood and by providing feedback on the service.

Primary Care Charter

The original Patient's Charter was extended at the end of 1992 to spell out the rights patients should expect from primary care services. Patients have a right to the following from their GP:

- to be registered with a GP
- to be able to change doctors easily and quickly
- to be offered a health check on first joining a doctor's list
- to receive emergency care at any time through a family practitioner
- to have appropriate drugs and medicines prescribed
- to be referred to a consultant acceptable to them when their GP thinks it necessary, and to be referred for a second opinion if they and the GP agree that this is desirable
- to have access to their health records, subject to any limitations in the law, and to know that those working for the NHS are under a legal duty to keep their contents confidential
- to choose whether or not to take part in medical research or medical student training
- if aged between 16 and 74 and not seen by their doctor in the previous three years, to have the health check to which they are entitled under the existing health promotion arrangements; and to be offered a yearly home visit and health check if 75 years old or over
- to be given detailed information about local family doctor services through their family health service authority's local directory
- to receive a copy of their doctor's practice leaflet, setting out the services he or she provides
- to receive a full and prompt reply to any complaints they make about NHS services.

By the end of March 1995 66 per cent of general practices had their own practice charter, while a further 8 per cent were preparing them.

Family Health Service Standards

The following standards were introduced in April 1993 for family health services:

- if a person is not registered with a GP, the Health Authority must be able to find a GP for that person within two working days
- to help people change doctors easily and quickly, the Health Authority must despatch details of how to change and a list of doctors to anyone who asks, within two working days
- Health Authorities must co-ordinate and publish information about local medical services, including the Health Authorities' own quality standards
- Health Authorities must transfer medical records quickly when a patient changes doctor. (Records which are urgently required should be transferred within two working days, and routine transfers should be completed within six weeks)
- Health Authorities must provide a full and open response to any comments, suggestions or complaints that people make about services.

Mental Health Services Charter

In February 1996 the government issued a consultation version of a new extension to the Patient's Charter covering mental health services.

As well as reflecting existing Patient's Charter rights and standards, it contains some specific new standards for mental health. These should ensure that patients receive:

- an explanation of their diagnosis
- information on the effects of medication, and on alternative treatments
- care in the least restrictive environment appropriate
- information about advocacy and support groups, what to do in

an emergency (including out-of-hours emergencies), supplied in languages and forms other than English where appropriate
- access to independent advocacy services (where such a service exists)
- a named mental health worker (called a key worker)
- time limits for commencing and communicating the outcome of assessments
- information about arrangements for discharge from hospital
- in hospital, the right to wear their own clothes and facilities for private discussion.

These standards are already good practice in many areas, and should be more widely adopted when the new charter is issued following the consultation period.

NHS performance tables

A key part of the Patient's Charter is the publication of information about the standards of service provided by the NHS locally. In June 1994 the government produced its first set of NHS Performance Tables ('league tables') giving 'star ratings' for how NHS Trusts and other hospitals performed on:

- seeing people promptly in outpatient departments
- assessing accident and emergency patients quickly
- giving priority to people whose operations have been cancelled
- allowing people to go home on the same day as their operation (day-case surgery)
- admitting patients from waiting lists
- time taken for ambulances to arrive.

Booklets containing the performance tables have been distributed widely to libraries, hospitals, general practices and so on. They were also reproduced in many national and local newspapers. The tables are published annually, usually in July. Copies are available from the Health Literature Line.★

Complaints about the NHS

The NHS complaints system has traditionally been fragmented and complicated, making it difficult for the patient to complain effectively. The need to settle complaints swiftly and informally was addressed by the 1994 Wilson committee on NHS complaints procedures. The report of the committee ('Being Heard') recommended a simple, unified complaints system for the whole NHS. At the same time GPs, dentists, opticians and pharmacists would be required to operate their own internal complaints procedures. Complaints, according to the recommendations, should be handled informally wherever possible and the complaints mechanism should be separate from disciplinary procedures. Most complaints should be settled within days, and if investigation or conciliation is needed it should happen within three weeks.

A new NHS complaints system, based on the Wilson report, was set up with effect from April 1996. It relates to events on or after 1 January 1996. The key features of the new complaints procedure are:

- rapid 'front-line response' from the person responsible for the service concerned (stage 1)
- recourse to an independent panel if the complainant is still dissatisfied (stage 2). The right to an independent review is not automatic, but the review panel convenor will consider whether the complaint is likely to be resolved in this way before making a decision
- extension of the jurisdiction of the Health Service Commissioner (Ombudsman) to all complaints.

Under the new arrangements, complaints to hospitals, providers of community services and family health services (including general practitioners) will be dealt with in similar fashion at two separate levels, described below.

Stage 1 provides a quick and informal method of complaining direct to the provider of the service. The Trust or general practice will respond to the complaint and endeavour, possibly using conciliation, to provide an answer which satisfies the patient. Most complaints should be answered this way.

Stage 2 provides for independent review if the complaint cannot be answered at stage 1, or if the patient is not satisfied with the response at stage 1. This may include recourse to a three-member independent review panel under an independent lay chairperson: Health Authority panels have in addition a convenor (a non-executive member of the Health Authority or appointed person) plus another independent person appointed by the Secretary of State; NHS Trust panels have in addition a convenor (a non-executive member of the Trust or appointed person) plus a representative of the purchaser (Health Authority or GP fundholder). The decision to convene the panel is taken by a non-executive member of the Trust, or of the Health Authority/Board in the case of complaints involving primary care services.

Patients can refer complaints to the Health Service Ombudsman if they are not satisfied with the response of the NHS or if they are unhappy with a decision not to convene a stage 2 panel.

Making a complaint about family health services

Stage 1 If you have a complaint about family health services, including your general practitioner or any member of the primary care team, you should initially address your complaint to the practice. Practice-based complaints systems will be developed in all family health services. If you would prefer to talk to someone not involved in your treatment, you can telephone or write to your local Health Authority's Complaints Manager. Most complaints should be dealt with at this level, and you should normally receive a full response within 10 working days.

Stage 2 If you are not satisfied with the response at stage 1, you have the option of asking the Health Authority/Board for a further review, which may include the establishment of an independent review panel. The decision on whether to convene a review panel is taken by a non-executive director of the relevant Health Authority/Board, known as a convener.

If you are still dissatisfied with the response to your complaint, or a decision not to convene a review panel, you then have the option of referring the complaint to the Health Service Commissioner (Ombudsman).

Complaints relating to, for example, failure to respond to an out-of-hours call could be dealt with by the above procedure. Complaints relating to the attitude or behaviour of a doctor are still made to the General Medical Council (GMC),★ the professional body with powers to discipline all registered medical practitioners, whether in the NHS or the private sector. It considers complaints about serious failures of care, violent or indecent behaviour, dishonesty etc.

Complaints about family health service practitioners, now often called primary care practitioners, must currently be made no later than one year after the event which caused it (for dentists it is either six months after the end of the treatment which caused the complaint or 13 weeks after you became aware of the cause, whichever is sooner).

The Ombudsman will not usually investigate your complaint if you are also seeking financial redress through the courts. If you do want compensation, you will probably have to take legal action. You must begin this within three years of the date of the incident that gave rise to the complaint. In the case of children, the three-year period does not begin until they are 18, so they have until they are 21 to bring proceedings.

Action for Victims of Medical Accidents (AVMA)★ can supply a list of lawyers with experience in medical negligence cases.

Making a complaint about hospital treatment

Stage 1 Wherever possible, you should tell someone close to the cause of your complaint (e.g. a doctor, nurse or receptionist). If you would prefer to talk to someone not involved in your treatment, you can telephone or write to the NHS Trust hospital's Complaints Manager. The chief executive will ensure that your complaint is investigated by front-line Trust staff. The Patient's Charter guarantees you a prompt response by from the chief executive, and the new complaints guidelines state that you should normally receive a full response within four weeks. Most complaints should be handled at this stage.

Stage 2 If you remain dissatisfied, you have the option of asking for a further review, which may include the establishment of an independent panel by a non-executive member of the NHS Trust board, or convener, as described above, but independent clinical assessors will also be involved in appropriate cases. The panel recommends action to address the complaint.

If you are still dissatisfied with the response to the complaint, or a decision not to convene a stage 2 panel, you can ask the Health Service Commissioner (Ombudsman)★ to investigate.

Community Health Councils (Health and Social Services Councils in Northern Ireland, and Local Health Councils in Scotland) have an important role in publicising the complaints procedure and providing information and support to people with a complaint. Find your local CHC under 'Community' in the phone book.

Making a complaint to the Health Service Commissioner

The Health Service Commissioner (Ombudsman) has been given wide powers by Parliament to investigate complaints about services provided within the NHS. Independent of government and the NHS, he is able to look into certain types of complaint about failures in service or maladministration, such as failure to follow proper procedures, rules or agreed policies; staff attitudes; poor communications; and poor local handling of a complaint. You need to provide some evidence to show that something has gone wrong and that the failure or maladministration has caused you injustice or hardship.

The new NHS complaints procedure extends the role of the Health Service Commissioner as the apex of the two-stage complaints procedure. Patients can complain to the Ombudsman if they are not satisfied with the response to their complaint or if they are unhappy with a decision not to convene a stage 2 independent review panel.

The Health Service Commissioners (Amendment) Bill extends the power of the Ombudsman to give jurisdiction over cases involving clinical judgement and those involving primary care services. This applies to England, Wales and Scotland, for whom the Ombudsman is the same person. The Northern Ireland Commissioner operates under separate legislation. Provisions broadly similar to those contained in the Bill will be introduced under the Northern Ireland Act 1974 and will come into force in late 1996/early 1997.

If you wish to complain to the Commissioner:

- the complaint should first have been made to the NHS Health Authority (or Trust) under the two-stage complaints procedure
- the complaint must be in writing and be supported by all background papers
- the complaint should be made within a year of the incident coming to notice (though the Commissioner may decide exceptionally to waive the time limit)
- the complaint must be made by the person directly concerned or someone suitable to represent that individual.

The Health Service Commissioner can require an NHS authority to produce records or documents, and their staff to give evidence, for the purpose of his investigation. (Note, however, that you will not get an investigation if you have started legal proceedings for compensation.) The Commissioner also arranges for one of his officers to interview the person making the complaint and, if appropriate, other witnesses such as relatives and friends. The procedure is confidential and very informal. The service is free and legal representation is rarely involved.

At the end of his investigation the Commissioner will send you and the NHS authority or trust concerned a written report of his findings. If your complaint, or any part of it, is upheld, the Commissioner will say whether the NHS authority or trust has agreed to remedy any injustice or hardship you have been caused: for example, by offering an apology and agreeing to change policies or procedures. Very occasionally he may recommend reimbursement of a financial loss resulting directly from a failure he has identified.

The Commissioner's work is reviewed by a Select Committee of the House of Commons, which can require an NHS authority or senior members of its staff to appear before the Committee to discuss a particular case.

The Community Health Council will be able to tell you more about the Health Service Commissioner, and may help you to write to him. A free leaflet entitled *How the Health Service Ombudsman Can Help You* can be obtained from his office.

Making a complaint about professional conduct

If your complaint is about improper conduct by a doctor you can complain to the General Medical Council,★ the governing body of the medical profession, which is composed of elected and appointed members of the medical profession and some nominated lay members. The GMC has the power to discipline any doctor who is judged to be guilty of serious professional misconduct. Under the Medical (Professional Performance) Act which came into force in 1996, the GMC was given the power to address concerns about a doctor relating to consistently poor performance, and not just for misconduct.

The GMC publishes a book entitled *Professional Conduct and Discipline: Fitness to Practice* which provides guidance on the disciplinary procedures, describes the types of conduct which may lead to disciplinary proceedings and advises on standards of professional conduct and medical ethics. The ultimate penalty is for a doctor to be struck off the register, which means that he or she can no longer practise; he or she may alternatively be suspended for a period. The GMC also publishes two leaflets for the public entitled *Making a Complaint about the Professional Conduct of a Doctor* and *The Disciplinary Procedures of the General Medical Council*, which should be available from Community Health Councils (Health and Social Services Boards in Northern Ireland and Local Health Councils in Scotland) or direct from the GMC.

Nurses and midwives are governed by a Code of Professional Conduct. Complaints about misconduct that brings their profession into disrepute can be made to the United Kingdom Central Council for Nursing, Midwifery and Health Visiting.★

The fact that Social Services departments have a complaints procedure does not stop you complaining to your local councillor or MP if you prefer. If you feel the complaint relates to maladministration you can complain to the Local Government Ombudsman. A free booklet called *Complaints about the Council: how to complain to your local government ombudsman* contains a complaints form and is available from council offices and Citizens Advice Bureaux, or direct from the Local Government Ombudsman.★

Community Health Councils

Community Health Councils (CHCs) were set up as part of the major re-organisation of the NHS in 1974 and were charged with the duty of representing the local community's interest in the health service. CHCs are central to patient empowerment, providing a channel for representation, consultation and complaint, and an important source of information for the public.

The equivalents in Scotland are Local Health Councils; in Northern Ireland they are called Health and Social Services Councils.

A Community Health Council is made up of lay members with a chairperson and a chief officer (or secretary). The chief officer is a paid employee of the National Health Service. Half the membership is made up of people appointed by the local authority (though they need not be councillors), one-third are appointed by voluntary organisations, and one-sixth by the NHS. CHCs are independent of the Health Authorities/Boards and NHS Trusts which they monitor.

CHCs (or their equivalents in Scotland and Northern Ireland) vary a lot in their everyday activities but there are functions which are common to all:

- taking up complaints
- visiting NHS premises
- consultation on the planning and development of local health services
- provision of information on local services
- monitoring the quality of local services, through consumer surveys etc.

Confidentiality

In 1994 the Department of Health issued guidance on the confidentiality of personal health information. The guidance makes clear that personal health information is protected in the following ways:

- by common law, which applies to all types of information given in confidence
- by the Data Protection Act 1984, in the case of information held on computer
- by the ethical responsibilities of health professionals
- by the contracts of employment of NHS staff, where these contain an express provision on the preservation of confidentiality.

The Code of Practice on Openness in the NHS states that information should be made readily available unless there are good reasons for not doing so. The primary reason would be patient confidentiality.

Security of NHS computer systems

The proposed introduction of a nationwide NHS computer network has led to concerns being expressed about security of confidential clinical information, including personal patient records. Particular concerns have been raised about links being made between the NHS network and the universally accessible Internet.

There is a basic ethical principle, supported by bodies including the General Medical Council and the European Union, that patients must consent to information-sharing. Responsibility for security of personal health records is covered by the Data Protection Act. An EU Directive (adopted 24 July 1995) obliges governments to prohibit the processing of health data except where the data subject explicitly consents.

The British Medical Association has drawn up interim guidelines to help doctors avoid the most common serious mistakes in computer security of clinical information. Principles include control on access to records, deletion of records, communications security, disclosure to third parties, and patient consent. A booklet, *Security in Clinical Information Systems*, is available from the British Medical Association.★

Access to your medical records

You have a right of access to your medical records in whatever form they are held. Section 21 of the Data Protection Act 1984 gives a right of access to health records held on a computer from 1987 onwards. The Access to Health Records Act 1990 has now extended the right of access to manual files. However, this applies only to records made after the Act came into force on 1 November 1991. The Act is not confined to NHS records, but includes those kept in private medicine and the Crown public service (prisons, armed forces etc.).

The Access to Health Records Act does not entitle you to see your medical records immediately on demand. You need to make an application in writing to the holder of the record (general practitioner or, in the case of hospital records, the health authority or NHS Trust). This states that you are the person to whom the record relates or are somebody entitled to apply on this individual's behalf (a parent in the case of children, or a person managing the affairs of someone incapable of doing so).

If the record you wish to see was made within the 40 days immediately before the date of application, access to the record must be granted within 21 days. If the record is older than this the record-holder has 40 days to provide access.

The holder is required to provide access to the record free of charge if it has been added to in the past 40 days. If the entire record is more than 40 days old a charge of £10 can be made. If you would like a copy of the record the cost of photocopying and postage may be charged.

You are entitled to an explanation of any terms which would not be intelligible to a lay person. The doctor or Health Authority/Board holding the record is entitled to deny access to any part of the record if, in their opinion, it would cause serious harm to the physical or mental health of the patient to see it. You can also be denied access to the record if it would cause serious harm to someone else or if the information relates to another identified individual (other than the patient or health professional).

The NHS Management Executive has issued guidance entitled *The Access to Health Records Act 1990: a guide for the NHS* (1992), which includes a model form for patients to use when making an application to see their records.

Access to records prepared for employment or insurance purposes

The Access to Medical Reports Act which came into force in January 1989 gives people the right to see medical reports prepared by their doctor for employment or insurance purposes. If a doctor has been informed that a patient wishes to see a medical report, he or she should refrain from sending the report to the employer or insurance company for 21 days, to allow the patient time to see it. The patient can ask to see the report before it is sent or up to six months after it has been supplied. If the patient believes there are factual inaccuracies he or she may ask for them to be corrected. The doctor is not obliged to make the amendments but if he/she refuses to do so he/she must attach to the report the patient's statement disputing it.

Patient-held records

In maternity and child health services patient-held records are common. The number of mislaid or lost records is no greater than when records are held in hospital or clinic, and the patient-held record is an important support for communication and shared decision-making.

Code of practice on openness within the NHS

The Code of Practice on Openness in the NHS was published in April 1995. It sets out basic principles of public access to information about the NHS. The code covers NHS organisations, as well as family doctors, dentists, opticians and community pharmacists. Its aims are to ensure that people:

- have access to information about the services provided by the NHS, their costs, quality standards, and performance against targets
- are provided with explanations about proposed service changes and have the opportunity to influence decisions on such changes
- are aware of the reasons for decisions and actions affecting their treatment
- know what information is available and where they can get it from.

Copies of the code are available from NHS Trusts and Health Authorities or from the NHS Executive.*

Information available under the code of openness

Apart from some exemptions, NHS Trusts and Authorities must make available the following information:

- what services are provided, the targets and standards set and the results achieved, as well as the cost and effectiveness of services
- details about important proposals on health policies or proposed changes in service delivery
- how health services are managed and provided, and who is responsible
- how the NHS communicates with the public, including details of public meetings, consultations, suggestions and complaints procedures
- how to contact the Community Health Council and the Health Service Commissioner
- how people can have access to their personal health records.

The code recommends that no charge should be made for information in the majority of cases.

Information which may be withheld

NHS Trusts and Authorities must provide information unless it falls into one of the following categories:

- personal information: people have a right of access to their own health records but not normally to information about other people
- requests for information which are 'manifestly unreasonable', too general, or would require unreasonable resources to answer
- information about internal discussion and advice, where disclosure would harm frank internal debate (except where this would be outweighed by the public interest)
- management information, where disclosure would harm the proper and effective management of the NHS
- information about legal matters and proceedings, where disclosure would prejudice the administration of justice and the law
- information which could prejudice negotiations or the effective conduct of personnel management, or commercial or contractual activities
- information given in confidence. The NHS has a common law duty to respect confidences except where this is clearly outweighed by the public interest
- information which would soon be published or where disclosure would be premature in relation to a planned announcement or publication
- information relating to incomplete analysis, research or statistics where disclosure could be misleading or prevent the holder from publishing it first.

Community care

People who in the past would have been cared for in hospitals or long-stay institutions are increasingly cared for in the community. Community care services might include:

- local authority services such as home helps, day centres, meals on wheels etc.
- services provided by voluntary organisations
- provision or adaptation of equipment
- residential care and nursing homes.

Assessment of need

Anyone who thinks they might need community care services can ask for an assessment by their local authority Social Services department. The assessment will identify your capacities and incapacities and areas where you might benefit from support. It will also identify the services, if any, which are to be provided. The assessment will usually be carried out by a qualified social worker.

In most cases GPs or other professionals will be asked, with the person's permission, to provide information about the person being assessed. Where personal information needs to be shared between agencies, you will be told and will be able to withhold your consent.

Local authorities are expected to involve both users and carers fully in the assessment, and to take into account their preferences for the type of care to be provided. If you would like the help of an advocate in this process, the local authority will give details of any local advocacy services.

After the assessment, authorities will generally provide users and carers with a care plan – a written statement of the services to be provided, co-ordinated by a care manager. You should keep in contact with the person responsible for the care plan and make sure he or she is aware of any change in your circumstances.

The Carers (Recognition and Services) Act came into force in April 1996. The Act states that when a person receives an assessment of his/her needs, those providing (or intending to provide) regular or substantial care will also share the right to a separate assessment on request.

Mental health care

Those diagnosed in the 1990s as suffering from a mental illness are far less likely to spend time in hospital than they would have been in the '80s or '70s, and even if they are admitted their stay will be shorter. But despite the moves to care in the community there are still good reasons why some people go into hospital. It may be that careful observation and assessment are required before a course of treatment is decided upon. The patient may feel so distressed and disturbed that hospital care is needed, or may need constant monitoring because of a condition such as anorexia nervosa. There may be no one at home capable of looking after the patient.

Voluntary admission to hospital

The vast majority (as many as 95 per cent) of psychiatric patients are voluntary patients (or 'informal patients'). As a voluntary patient you have a right to refuse treatment and to discharge yourself, although obviously it would be sensible to discuss this with staff first. You may be admitted to one of the old-style psychiatric hospitals or to a department of psychiatry at your local district general hospital. In addition to the treatment you receive from your psychiatrist, there is likely to be a programme of activities including occupational therapy, art and music therapy and group discussions.

Compulsory detention under the Mental Health Act 1983

A small number of patients are compulsorily detained under the Mental Health Act 1983. The Act covers England and Wales, Scotland being covered by the Mental Health Act (Scotland) 1984 and Northern Ireland by the Mental Health Act Order (Northern Ireland) 1986. Detained patients are not free to leave hospital when they wish and are subject to special rules regarding treatment. Applications for compulsory admission can be made by the 'nearest relative' (this may be the person who lives with, or cares for, the person) or an 'approved social worker'. An 'approved social worker' should always be used where possible, not only because such people have received special training in mental health care, but also to avoid any potential adverse effects on the relationship between the patient and the 'nearest relative'. The application must be supported in writing by two doctors.

If you are very worried about the behaviour of someone close to you, or are afraid he/she will harm him/herself or others, your first step should be to contact their GP. If you are unable to do this you can telephone the local social services department. Most have an out-of-hours emergency service. An approved social worker has to make an assessment of the mentally ill person's needs for possible admission to hospital or alternative care needs if requested by a nearest relative. If you are unable to contact the GP or social services you can take the patient to the nearest hospital accident and emergency department and ask to see the duty psychiatrist.

Being 'sectioned'

The main grounds for compulsory admission to hospital are that the person is suffering from a mental disorder of a nature or degree which warrants detention for assessment or treatment, or that the person needs to be detained in the interests of his or her own safety or the protection of others. Depending on the circumstances, the person may be detained under different sections of the Mental Health Act (sometimes referred to as being 'sectioned').

Section 2 Patients can be detained for up to 28 days for assessment, and sometimes followed by treatment. An application can be made by an approved social worker, without the consent of the nearest relative. In Scotland short-term detention is achieved by emergency admission under Section 24 of the Mental Health (Scotland) Act 1984. The patient has a right to appeal to the sheriff for his discharge during the 28-day period. In Northern Ireland the patient can be detained for up to seven days after a report on him has been made by the responsible medical officer or a doctor appointed by the Mental Health Act Commission in Northern Ireland, but only for 48 hours if the report is provided by any other doctor.

Section 3 Patients can be admitted for treatment for up to six months. It can be renewed for a further six months and then for periods of a year at a time by the psychiatrist in charge of the case. The nearest relative's consent has to be obtained by the approved social worker.

Section 4 Patients are admitted under Section 4 only in an emergency: for example, if they are violent or suicidal. The admission is for a maximum of 72 hours, to enable an assessment to be made. An application can be made by an approved social worker without the nearest relative's consent.

Section 5 This may be used to detain voluntary patients whose condition whilst in hospital causes the doctor in charge of treatment to recommend detention for treatment or assessment.

The detention is for a maximum of 72 hours, to enable a proper assessment to be made of the need for further detention. In the Scottish Act Section 25 makes similar provision, except the maximum period of detention arranged by a nurse is only two hours (in England and Wales detention can be made by a nurse for six hours). In Northern Ireland a patient can be detained on doctor's assessment for 48 hours.

Mental health review tribunal

At the end of the period of time stipulated in the relevant section of the Mental Health Act, compulsory patients automatically become informal patients and are free to discharge themselves, unless further steps are taken under the Act. Patients are discharged from hospital to the care of the GP, although there may be continuing outpatient appointments with the consultant psychiatrist. A care programme outlining the patient's health and social care needs should be drawn up by the clinical team and involve the patient and carers. Nearest relatives can apply to have a patient discharged by writing to the hospital managers.

Application can also be made for discharge from compulsory detention through a mental health review tribunal, an independent body consisting of a lawyer, a psychiatrist (from a hospital other than the one where the patient is detained) and a lay person.

Although a mental health review tribunal is not a court of law it helps to be represented by a solicitor. You can get legal aid to pay for advice and representation by a solicitor if your income is below a certain level. Contact your local CAB, MIND or law centre for advice before you proceed.

Following public concern, the Department of Health has issued guidance on the discharge of mentally disordered people and their continuing care in the community. The guidance makes clear that hospital and other staff are responsible for considering, before they discharge a patient:

- whether the patient would present a risk to himself/herself or other people
- whether he or she can be cared for effectively and safely in

the community, if necessary in staffed or supported accommodation.

Making a complaint about mental health care

If you or a relative wish to complain about your treatment or care as a psychiatric inpatient or outpatient, first talk to the staff concerned. If you are unable to sort out the problem informally, put your complaint in writing to the hospital manager or the consultant in charge of your case. Seek advice from your Community Health Council (Local Health Council in Scotland and Health and Social Services Council in Northern Ireland) in framing your complaint. If you are a detained patient, or a relative of one, and are not satisfied with a complaint pursued through these normal channels you can contact one of the following commissions: for patients in England and Wales, the Mental Health Act Commission* (a body set up in 1983 to protect the rights of detained patients); for patients in Scotland, the Mental Welfare Commission for Scotland;* for patients in Northern Ireland, the Mental Health Commission for Northern Ireland.*

Residential care

Changes in arrangements for providing and paying for residential care are one of the most important parts of the NHS and Community Care Act 1990. Since April 1993 local authorities have taken the lead role in arranging and paying for places in homes. The home could be run by the local authority, or a private or voluntary organisation. For individuals to receive financial support from the local authority they must first be assessed as needing care in a home.

In 1995 the total number of residential care homes was 16,300, accommodating 288,000 residents. Places in voluntary and private homes are on the increase (a 4 per cent rise took place in 1992–3), while those in local authority homes are falling (there was a 10 per cent decrease over the same period). The independent sector provides 77 per cent of all places. There were also 4,900 places in 1,650 unstaffed local authority homes for people with mental illness and learning disabilities.

Residential care homes are for people who find it hard to manage alone and need help with personal care (for example, washing, dressing, going to the toilet). Although they do provide some help for residents who fall ill, they cannot usually give long-term, full-time nursing care. Residential care homes are run either by local authority Social Services departments, individuals or private organisations, or voluntary groups like charities or religious orders. Local authorities provide residential accommodation for elderly or disabled people under Part III of the National Assistance Act 1948 (this is why such accommodation is often called Part III accommodation). They can also arrange for people to go into homes run by the voluntary or private sectors. Accommodation for people with learning difficulties or those with, or recovering from, a mental illness is usually provided under the NHS Act 1977.

Nursing homes are for people who need skilled nursing care and cannot be cared for in the community by their GP or district nurse. Qualified nursing staff are available 24 hours a day. There are some health authority nursing homes, but most are run privately or by voluntary organisations.

Some homes offer both types of care (nursing home and residential care home). The main advantage is that you may not have to move if your care needs change, although it will probably mean paying a higher fee if you need more nursing care.

Paying for residential care

Homes of all types vary in what they charge. If you can afford to pay the fees yourself it is still sensible to get your local Social Services department to carry out an assessment of your (or your relative's) needs first. If you find you need help with the fees later on, the local authority can provide this only if it has assessed you (or your relative) as needing residential or nursing care. In the November 1995 Budget the level of assets below which people are eligible for help with the cost of care in residential or nursing homes was doubled from £8,000 to £16,000. Also in 1995 the government announced that local authorities can use only half of a married person's occupational pension towards the cost of care fees. If a spouse remains at home, he or she would have access to the other half.

If you cannot afford the cost of the home and the local authority has assessed you as needing that care, the local authority must carry out a means test to calculate how much you should pay from your income and how much it will contribute. Some people will qualify for income support, which must be claimed from the Local Benefits Agency (DSS) office. This will count towards your contribution towards the cost of the home. The amount which local authorities pay for places in homes varies around the country but the local authority must make sure that there is a suitable home for you at the price it sets.

Housing benefit cannot be claimed on local authority residential home charges. Attendance allowance and the care component of disability living allowance stop after 28 days in residential accommodation.

If you are in hospital and need continuing medical care which the hospital cannot provide, the Health Authority/Board can arrange a placement in a nursing home. You will not be charged fees while you remain a patient of the NHS (although any benefits and state pension will be affected after a time).

You should not be discharged from hospital into a home before a full assessment of your needs has been carried out. Since April 1996 each Health Authority/Board has had to have set criteria by which it decides who should receive continuing care under the NHS. If you are in hospital and believe that your Health Authority's criteria to arrange continuing care in a hospital or nursing home has not been correctly applied to you, you can ask for its decision to be reviewed.

Choosing a home

Some people will enter residential care as a result of an assessment by the local authority. If after assessment the local authority decides the person needs a place in a home it should suggest suitable accommodation.

Some authorities will have a list of preferred providers that they will usually recommend. However, if you do not like the home offered or you have a particular home in mind you can ask the authority to arrange a place in a specific home. It should agree to this provided that:

- the accommodation is suitable for your assessed needs
- there is a place available
- the home is willing to enter into a contract with the local authority
- the home costs no more than the authority would normally pay for residential care for someone with similar needs.

If you want to go into a more expensive home the local authority is obliged to arrange a place so long as you or a third party is able and willing to pay the difference in cost for as long as you will remain living in the home.

Other people will make their own arrangements to enter a private or voluntary home. You and your family should always visit the home to have a look at the care provided before choosing a place. All private and voluntary residential care homes must be registered with the local authority under the Registered Homes Act 1984. They must comply with regulations about the services they supply and local authorities are required to inspect them twice a year (one visit should be unannounced). Since April 1991 local authority homes have also had to be inspected.

Registered nursing homes differ from residential care homes in that they must provide nursing staff, adequate medical, surgical and other equipment, and adequate treatment facilities to meet the care needs of their patients. Registration and inspection of nursing homes are carried out by health authorities, which must inspect each home twice a year.

When you go to visit a home, prepare yourself with a checklist of things to investigate. These might include:

- whether the location is convenient and accessible to shops, transport etc.
- what the fees cover, and whether there is a care plan carrying details of services provided
- whether there is a written contract with residents
- what the staffing levels are, and the qualifications of the staff
- whether the buildings are well maintained and whether there is good access
- how much privacy there is
- how much of your own furniture and personal possessions you will be able to keep with you

- how flexible the routines for mealtimes etc. are
- how many communal rooms there are and what they are used for
- whether there is a residents' committee, so that the views of the residents are taken into account in the running of the home.

Complaining about residential care

A complaint about standards of care in a residential care home or nursing home should initially be made to the person running the home. Registered residential care homes are obliged to operate internal complaints procedures. If you are not satisfied with the response you can complain to the Social Services department of your local authority, which will treat it as a registered complaint under its own procedures. Local authorities and health authorities will liaise over complaints about nursing homes.

Private medicine

If you can afford it, and particularly if you are faced with a long wait for NHS treatment, you might consider seeing a doctor privately. In Britain there are over 200 private acute hospitals and there are about 3,000 pay beds in NHS hospitals. About 500,000 operations are carried out in the private sector (20 per cent of non-emergency surgery in the UK). Thirty per cent of all hip replacement operations are done privately. According to figures from the Independent Healthcare Association the private sector employs 65,000 nurses and has 11,500 acute surgical beds, 2,900 psychiatric beds, 178,000 nursing home places and 167,000 residential home places in 1996. One in 15 of the UK population has private medical insurance.

Pros and cons of private medicine

There are a number of reasons for considering private medical care, but there are also a number of pitfalls.

Qualifications The NHS employs only people who hold recognised qualifications in medicine, physiotherapy, psychology etc. In private medicine this safeguard does not exist. If a GP refers you to a private practitioner you can be confident about his or her status, but if you choose a practitioner yourself you need to be careful to check the qualifications.

Complaints It is much more difficult to pursue a complaint against a private practitioner than against an NHS professional. Private treatment is given on the basis of a contract, and it may be necessary to prove a breach of this contract. However, you could take up a complaint with the General Medical Council, which is concerned with the conduct of all doctors, whether in the NHS or in private practice.

Quality of care Private does not necessarily mean better. Private hospitals and nursing homes often do not have the facilities of an NHS hospital. They may not have intensive care units, there may not be specialist staff (such as an anaesthetist) on call, and you will have to wait for the consultant himself to be called before any treatment can be given. Although personal attention from the consultant is one of the advantages of private health care, this can seem less attractive if you are faced with an unpleasant delay. Consultants in private practice do not have firms of junior doctors to carry out treatment on their behalf.

What you can and cannot expect from the private sector

In general the private medical insurance offered by provident associations such as British United Provident Association (BUPA) and Private Patients Plan (PPP) does not include:

- normal pregnancy and childbirth
- long-term disability or mental illness
- routine dental treatment
- complementary therapies
- cosmetic surgery.

You should compare policies very carefully to see exactly what is covered. A policy which provided for the same level of comprehensive care as the National Health Service would have to be very expensive. Nowadays many people have private medical insurance provided by their employer. It is important to ensure that you know exactly what this covers. Ask to see the full text of the policy and if you have any doubts in your mind about what it means, ask questions.

Private medical treatment should give you:

- a room to yourself, with telephone and television
- a choice of admission date
- visiting permitted at any reasonable hour
- a choice of consultant, who will perform the operation himself
- a shorter wait for non-urgent conditions such as varicose veins, hip replacements and hernias (but if this is your main concern check first whether you could be seen more quickly at another hospital under the NHS).

Finding a private consultant

Most consultants will ask for a GP's letter even if you are consulting them privately, so the right place to start looking for a private consultant is your GP. If you are claiming the cost through a scheme such as BUPA or PPP, a GP referral is essential. Your GP should know of local consultants with a private practice. Most of these work mainly for the NHS and see patients privately as well. The Independent Healthcare Association★ can provide information on private consultants.

Complementary medicine

A national opinion poll carried out in 1985 found that 13 per cent of the population had actually used complementary (or 'alternative', as it is also known) medicine at some time, and although the survey has not been repeated there can be no doubt that its popularity has increased enormously over the subsequent decade. A Department of Health-funded study published in November 1995 indicated that some 40 per cent of GP partnerships in England provide access to some form of complementary therapy for their patients. The most frequently provided therapies are homeopathy and acupuncture, and GP fundholders are more likely than non-fundholders to offer complementary therapies to their patients.

Fundholding general practitioners may directly employ complementary therapists within their practice staff. Non-fundholding general practitioners may employ such therapists subject to their Health Authority's agreement to pay for the service.

Some GPs are trained in one or more complementary therapies themselves (this could be a factor in choosing your GP). Others employ complementary practitioners within the health centre or surgery. If you are lucky enough to have this option you may be able to get free treatment within the practice.

Homeopathy is one type of complementary medicine which is generally available on the NHS. There are several homeopathic hospitals which take NHS referrals from GPs. Beyond this, the use of complementary therapies within hospitals depends to some degree on the interests and attitudes of the medical and nursing staff. However, acupuncture is used for pain relief at an increasing number of hospitals, and osteopathy and chiropractic are now quite widely available on the NHS. Some hospitals use aromatherapy as an alternative to sleeping pills. Some hospital chaplains offer healing by the laying-on of hands.

Choosing a complementary therapist

Most people who consult a complementary practitioner do so on a private paying basis. It is very important to check the credentials of the practitioners before starting any treatment (or parting with any money). While doctors, nurses and certain state-registered professionals such as dentists and physiotherapists must by law have a certain minimum training before they can practise, most complementary therapies fall outside the curricula of medical schools and there are no government requirements for the training of complementary therapists.

Most therapies have their own professional body (for example, the British Homoeopathic Association) and you should check that the practitioner is a registered member. However, these registering bodies do not necessarily stipulate any level of training. Moreover there may be several organisations for a single therapy, all of them claiming to register practitioners and often with scathing opinions of the rival organisations in their field. For many therapies there is no agreement on the training needed to be a competent practitioner and some practitioners are not registered with any organisation. Qualifications such as certificates or letters after a practitioner's name could mean that he or she has had years of training or has simply been on a course lasting a few days.

Untrained or inadequately trained therapists could cause injury, or may fail to notice a problem which should be brought to a conventional doctor's attention.

For advice on finding competent practitioners, or on the registering bodies, contain the British Complementary Medicine Association★ or the Institute of Complementary Medicine.★

Medicines Act 1968

Under the 1968 Medicines Act all new medicines are required to be safe and effective before they can qualify for a licence. Medicines already on the market are gradually being reviewed and the Committee on the Safety of Medicines is now reviewing the safety and effectiveness of herbal remedies; homeopathic remedies are next on the list. Herbalists and homeopaths are concerned that the review procedures for assessing the effectiveness of ordinary remedies are not appropriate for complementary medications and that the review may lead to a reduction in the availability of herbal and homeopathic preparations.

Regulation of complementary therapists

The most popular complementary therapies purchased through the NHS are acupuncture, osteopathy, chiropractic, homeopathy, counselling and hypnotherapy. The regulatory position on each of these is as follows:

- **acupuncture** The British Acupuncture Council★ runs a national register of qualified practitioners and has an ethical and disciplinary code. The profession has also set up an accreditation board, which is looking at all schools of acupuncture. The British Medical Acupuncture Society maintains a register of acupuncturists who are also medically qualified

- **osteopathy** Legislation was passed in 1993 giving osteopaths (and chiropractors) statutory regulation. No one who is not registered with the General Osteopathic Council is allowed to practise as an osteopath. A similar scheme is to operate for chiropractors. For more information contact the Osteopathic Information Service★
- **chiropractic** The British Chiropractic Association★ maintains a register of qualified chiropractors who subscribe to the Association's code of ethics
- **homeopathy** Doctors can take the postgraduate training programme of the Faculty of Homeopaths, an organisation established by a 1950 Act of Parliament. Practitioners without medical degrees can register with several bodies. The Society of Homoeopaths sets standards of three years' training and 18 months' practice under clinical supervision. It has disciplinary and ethical codes. There are also plans to introduce NVQs into homeopathy. Contact the Society of Homoeopaths★ for more details
- **counselling** The British Association for Counselling★ is the umbrella body for membership organisations including Relate and the Samaritans. It also has 11,000 individual members. All members sign up to a Code of Ethics. BAC supports a national register for counsellors with a disciplinary code
- **hypnotherapy** There is little co-ordination in this area, although some hypnotherapy organisations belong to the UK Council for Psychotherapy,★ a new national umbrella body set up to help introduce national standards for training and practice.

Health care abroad

Free or reduced-cost medical treatment is available in European Community countries (and some other countries with reciprocal arrangements) for UK residents who are suddenly taken ill or have an accident during their visit. Only emergency treatment under the state health care system is covered. Before you travel, make sure you obtain a copy of the Department of Health booklet *Health Advice for Travellers* (T5), which gives details of entitlements to health care abroad, immunisation requirements etc. Copies are available from doctors' surgeries, post offices, travel agents etc. or via a Department of Health freephone number.★ The information is also updated on Prestel, to which most travel agents have access.

Medical care in (most of) Europe

To get medical care in most European countries you will need a form E111. The *Health Advice for Travellers* booklet contains an application form for an E111. If you are going abroad only for a short stay and do not plan to live abroad, take the completed form to a post office to be stamped. Then keep the form with your passport and take it with you when you go abroad. You can use the same E111 for as long as you remain resident in the UK. If you need emergency treatment while in a European Union (EU) country make sure you show your E111 form. Sometimes treatment is free, sometimes you may have to pay the full cost and claim a full or partial refund. Claim any refund by applying to the local sickness insurance fund of the country you are visiting, in person or by post. You must enclose the original documents, so keep a photocopy. If you leave your claim until you return to the UK you may face a long wait or lose the money altogether.

If you could not get a refund abroad, write explaining why to DSS Pensions and Overseas Benefits Directorate;★ if you are a resident of Northern Ireland, write to the Primary Care and Practising Development Directorate.★ Enclose your E111, original bills, prescriptions and receipts.

A form E111 covers only temporary stays. If you are going to work in another EU country for more than 12 months, or to work for a foreign employer, the E111 is not appropriate as you should be insured under the social security legislation of the country of your employment. The Department of Social Security can advise.

Since January 1994, Austria, Finland, Iceland, Norway, and Sweden have joined with the member states of the EU to form the European Economic Area (EEA). As a result, reciprocal health care arrangements between EU countries apply to these countries as well.

Non-European Union countries

The UK has reciprocal health agreements with a number of countries outside the European Union. These cover the provision of emergency medical treatment at reduced cost, or in some cases free of charge. You will normally need to produce your UK passport, and in some countries your NHS medical card as well. Remember that the range of medical care outside European Union countries may be less than that provided by the British NHS, and the costs of treatment may not be fully covered by reciprocal agreements. Also remember that the vast majority of countries in the world do not have any sort of reciprocal arrangement with the UK, including the USA, Canada, Switzerland, all of the Middle East, Africa, all of South America, and most of Asia and the Pacific region.

Make sure you have adequate personal health insurance before you go abroad. Policies should cover the cost of flying the sick person home, as well as the costs of local treatment.

Health care for visitors to the UK

The services of the NHS are intended for the use of people resident in the UK regardless of their nationality or origin. It has always been government policy that eligibility to receive free medical treatment relates to residence in the UK, not to nationality or payment of National Insurance contributions. Those who are ordinarily resident here are entitled to use health services as NHS patients without charge. People from a number of other countries are entitled to treatment under European Union regulations and certain other reciprocal arrangements.

A person is accepted as ordinary resident if he or she is lawfully living in the UK for a settled period of time (usually interpreted as six months or more) or has come to the UK with the intention of taking up permanent residence.

UK residents, including those who have recently entered the country intending to take up permanent residence, may apply to a GP for registration for general medical services. It is a matter of discretion for the GP whether to accept any person as a patient, but the Health Authority/Board has the power to find a doctor for patients who are having difficulty registering. Once registered, people from abroad have the same rights to receive treatment and prescriptions as any other patient.

Hospital treatment for visitors to the UK

Under the NHS (Charges to Overseas Visitors) Regulations 1982 visitors to the UK who are not ordinarily resident or covered by reciprocal arrangements are liable to be charged for NHS hospital treatment.

The regulations specifically cover hospital treatment. The treatment of these patients is subject to the same priority as other NHS patients. The beds they occupy are not pay beds. They can obtain drugs prescribed in hospital subject to the same prescription charges as other NHS patients.

Charges do not apply for:

- anyone who has come to the UK to take up permanent residence
- anyone who at the time of their treatment has been in the UK for the previous 12 months
- anyone who has come to the UK for employment, including some students and trainees
- members of HM Forces and other Crown servants
- people working overseas who have had at least ten years' continuous residence in the UK and have either been working abroad for not more than five years or have been taking home leave in the UK every two years
- nationals of the EEA and other countries with which the UK has reciprocal arrangements
- UK state pensioners living abroad (for treatment the need for which arose during the visit)
- treatment in accident or emergency departments
- treatment of certain notifiable diseases and sexually transmitted diseases
- compulsory psychiatric treatment
- community nursing
- ambulance services
- family planning clinics
- HIV testing.

NHS information services

The easiest way to find out more about rights and services is to phone the national freephone Health Information Service.★ Set up in 1992, it links callers through a single number to 23 local health information centres. The freephone number covers England, Northern Ireland and Wales; a similar service★ is available in Scotland.

Callers are automatically routed to their nearest service which provides information on NHS services, waiting times, common illnesses and treatments, complaints procedures, maintaining and improving health and Patient's Charter standards.

The Health Information Service centres have access to extensive collections of health information literature and databases of self-help groups and NHS services nationally and locally.

More detailed information on how the NHS works and how to get the best out of it is contained in the NHS A-Z database, available at most Health Information Service centres or from The Help for Health Trust.★

Questions and answers

Q *I had treatment for a health problem in the 1980s and am now concerned about exactly what happened. Am I entitled to see my medical records?*

A The Access to Health Records Act gives you the right to see your medical records written after November 1991, by applying in writing to the holder of the record (health authority for hospital records or general practitioner for GP records). You have no legal right to see written records made before the start date of 1 November 1991 *unless* your records were held on computer: the Data Protection Act 1984 gives you a legal right to see any computer-held records, including medical records, held from 1 November 1987.

Q *Can I attend my Health Authority's meetings to hear the decisions that are being made on my behalf?*

A You are entitled to attend most meetings of your Health Authority. Meetings of Health Authorities are subject to the Public Bodies (Admission to Meetings) Act 1960. This means that any formal meeting of the full authority must be open to the public. A notice of the time and place of the meeting must be posted at the authority's headquarters three days in advance. However, the authority may exclude the public from some meetings, or parts of them, if the business is confidential. Some important business is also carried out by sub-committees whose meetings are not open to the public. You have less right to hear the business of your local hospital. NHS Trusts are obliged to meet in public only once a year.

Q *My wife got free prescriptions at the age of 60. Will I have to wait until I'm 65 to get mine free?*

A Certain categories of people are exempt from prescription charges (see page 17). Until October 1995 women in the UK were entitled to free prescriptions at 60 but men had to wait until they were 65. Then the European Court of Justice found that the UK age arrangements were contrary to the EU directives providing for equal treatment of men and women in social security matters. Men and women are now both entitled to free prescriptions from the age of 60.

CHAPTER 2

THE EDUCATION SYSTEM

MANY changes have taken place in education in recent years. Promises have been made to deliver greater choice and improved standards, new types of school are being introduced, and parents should now be able to exercise more rights in respect of their children's education. However, getting to grips with the education system in order to achieve what you want from it can be a daunting prospect. The radical innovations of the last few years – the National Curriculum, attainment targets, key stages and so on – have brought with them a raft of jargon that can be very confusing for those outside the system. But if you know your rights, and where to go to get the information and advice you need, you can do a great deal to 'beat' the system when it seems to be thwarting you.

Choices in education are not confined to those entering primary and secondary schools. This chapter also looks at nursery education, the complex decisions confronting pupils at 18+, and the possibilities for entering education later as a mature student.

In addition, there is guidance on all the big issues affecting parents, such as how to choose between different schools – what to look for and how to obtain information; what you can do if your application is refused; what to do if your child is being bullied; how best to educate a child with learning difficulties; what to do if a child in school appears not to be up to standard, or if the teacher is part of the problem.

One word of caution: education in Britain is a hotly debated political issue and the political parties have fundamentally different policies on education. Any change of government will be likely to affect the education system in the shorter or longer term.

The school system

State-funded schools

Schools which offer free education, primary (ages 5–11) and secondary (ages 11–18), are funded by the state, via the local education authorities (LEAs). In some areas there are also middle schools for children aged 8–9 to 12–13. Most are maintained by the LEA, which fixes the school budget. There are an increasing number of self-governing schools (although only two in Scotland) known as grant-maintained (GM) schools, which are independent of the LEA and receive their funding from central government. Some of these schools – both LEA and grant-maintained – are voluntary-aided schools, often known as church schools, which encourage a particular set of beliefs. The 1993 Education Act gives voluntary bodies, including groups of parents working together, the opportunity to set up self-governing schools which receive funding direct from central government.

The vast majority of state-funded schools are day schools, but about 40 state schools offer boarding places. At the latter, which represent the full range of secondary schools, tuition is free but parents have to pay the boarding cost.

Another initiative has been the setting up of technology colleges and language colleges, formed from existing schools but placing special emphasis either on technology, science and mathematics or on modern foreign languages.

Parents have a right to a free school place in a state school for their offspring aged 5–16 and a place at school or college at age 16–18. As a parent (or guardian), you have the right to say which school you would prefer your child to attend, but that does not mean you can insist on a place at a particular school.

LEA and GM schools have admissions criteria – rules that are followed when deciding who will be offered a place, and which must be explained in the school's prospectus. Some schools select children by ability and set examinations to test them. Otherwise, admissions policies must be objective and reasonable: for example, based on the distance between the child's home and the school, or the fact that brothers or sisters already attend the school. Parents have the right to appeal if they are unhappy with a decision concerning selection.

Parents have a duty to make sure that their children are educated, but this does not have to take place at school. They have the option of educating their children at home (see 'Home-based education', page 99).

Independent schools

Independent schools do not receive any direct state income; they are largely funded by the fees paid by parents. Independent schools have a very long history in the UK and the old-established 'public' schools have come to symbolise the traditional approach to education in Britain. But there are all types of independent school, selective and non-selective, boarding and day, large and small, mixed and single-sex. The entrance requirements for individual schools should be detailed in the school's prospectus.

The National Curriculum

The National Curriculum, introduced following the Education Reform Act of 1988, marks a major educational change which will last for many years, because all state schools in England and Wales must follow it. One of its chief aims is to provide consistent content in education across schools in England and Wales. The National Curriculum has major implications for the curriculum in general, for the content of subjects and for testing and examination procedure, so it is as well to become familiar with the jargon and to find out what the policy will mean for your child.

The National Curriculum must be taught in state schools, except those in Scotland. Although it is not compulsory in independent schools, many of them follow it.

In Scotland there is a '5–14 Development Programme' which, although similar to the National Curriculum, allows teachers and schools more discretion in how to apply it. This was introduced in 1991 and should be fully operational by the summer of 1999.

Primary schools and the National Curriculum

In England, all pupils (except for those who may be exempt because they have special needs: see 'Special educational needs', below) must study three core subjects: English, mathematics and science and the other foundation subjects: physical education, design and technology, history, geography, music and art. The curriculum is divided into four age-related key stages, the first two of which take place at primary school. Children take tests at the end of each key stage (ages 7 and 11 in primary school).

Key stage 1
Year 1 (age 5–6)
Year 2 (age 6–7) Key stage 1 tests at end of year 2 in English and maths, marked by class teachers.

Key stage 2
Year 3 (age 8–9)
Year 5 (age 9–10)
Year 6 (age 10–11) Key stage 2 tests at end of year 6 in English, maths and science, marked by external examiners.

(Note that the results of this test do *not* affect what secondary school pupils go to, as decisions on secondary transfer are made by the secondary schools earlier in the year.)

Secondary schools and the National Curriculum

At secondary level the National Curriculum is divided into a further two key stages, 3 and 4. Secondary schools must teach the same subjects as primary schools, plus a modern language, and lessons should take up at least 24 hours a week. At the end of key stage 3, pupils can drop music, art, technology, history and geography.

Key stage 3
Year 7 (age 11–12)
Year 8 (age 12–13)
Year 9 (age 13–14) Key stage 3 tests in English, maths and science, marked by external examiners.

Key stage 4
Year 10 (age 14–15)
Year 11 (age 15–16) Key stage 4 tests are the General Certificate in Secondary Education (GCSE) examinations, marked by external examiners.

Schools are also required to teach religious education but it is *not* one of the National Curriculum subjects.

National Curriculum documents describe what teachers must teach at each key stage, although they do not include detailed lesson plans. Schools approach the content of the National Curriculum in different ways and decide for themselves which books and other materials to use. They do not necessarily have to teach the subjects separately: very few primary schools, for example, divide the week into ten or more subjects. At primary level it is more usual to have a topic-based approach, whereby any topic can be used as a vehicle for delivering science, history, English, and so on.

Parents have the right to a range of information about the curriculum and their children's progress. The National Curriculum sets 'standards of achievement' in each subject for pupils aged 5–14. For most subjects these standards of achievement are assessed according to a range of levels from 1 to 8, 8 being the highest level.

The results for the national tests will be expressed for each subject tested in terms of these levels/standards of achievement, rather than as percentages or pass marks. As a guide:

- typical 7-year-olds should be challenged by the standards at level 2
- typical 11-year-olds should be challenged by the standards set at level 4
- typical 14-year-olds should be challenged by the standards at levels 5 and 6.

(The National Curriculum for music, art and physical education, or PE, does not use levels 1–8. Instead there is a single description of the standard for each area of learning that most pupils can expect to reach at the end of a key stage.)

The Parent's Charter

The Parent's Charter, part of the government's Citizen's Charter initiative, is founded on the principle of opening schools to parent power. It guarantees information on class sizes, teaching methods, examination results, job and college destinations of leavers and other matters. The Charter in England and Wales stipulates that parents should receive five key documents:

- an annual written report on the progress of their child
- performance tables providing information on all secondary schools (and in time primary schools) in the area
- a short summary of a recent inspection report of the school from the independent inspectors, organised by the Office for Standards in Education (OFSTED), who have to inspect state schools once every four to five years
- an action plan from governors on how they propose to tackle problem areas in the light of the inspectors' reports
- an annual report from the school's governors, prepared for discussion at their annual meeting with parents.

The main provisions of the Parent's Charter in Scotland similarly give parents the right to detailed information about their child's school and about other schools. For example, they can get a single booklet comparing the examination results of every secondary school in Scotland. The Charter also guarantees information on job and college destinations of leavers, absence rates, how each school provides for special education needs, and on each school's policy on developing pupils' spiritual, moral, social and cultural values.

Scottish schools must also provide parents with an annual written report on the progress of their child, with a comparison against national standards.

How children are grouped within schools

Some schools group children according to ability, others do not, and the different approaches have given rise to some terminology with very specific meaning, as described below.

Mixed ability Most state primary schools and many state secondary schools have mixed ability classes, which, as the term suggests, include children of all abilities in the same class.

Setting Under this system, pupils are put into higher or lower groups according to ability in different subjects. They might find themselves in a higher set for, say, English and a lower set for, say, history. Setting takes place mainly at secondary school level, though many primary schools have sets for particular subjects, such as maths.

Streaming Pupils are grouped into classes by their overall ability and they remain in these classes, regardless of subject. Primary schools are unlikely to stream.

These three methods of organising children into groups are not mutually exclusive and some schools may practise a mixture of all three. For example, they might have a high ability or 'express' stream, together with other mixed ability classes, with some setting taking place in particular subjects.

Differentiation This crucial concept can be applied in both primary and secondary schools, but especially secondary schools. It implies a certain flexibility of approach and is extremely important in mixed ability classes where schools and individual subject teachers must be able to show that different strategies are being used to teach the subject to the different levels of ability. But it is still important in classes that are streamed or set, for even here there will always be children who do better than other children, and others who fall behind: as a parent: you need to be assured that teachers are differentiating their teaching methods to take account of this. (See also page 86 under 'What to look for and ask when visiting a school'.)

Schemes of work These subject policy documents explain how and when the school intends to teach each individual subject, and although they are not publicised or volunteered they should be freely available to parents on request. If your child were for some reason to miss several weeks of work, the subject policy document should be able to tell you exactly what he or she has missed in each particular subject.

For up-to-date advice on the National Curriculum, write to the School Curriculum and Assessment Authority (SCAA).★ The Parent's Charter and a list of other Department for Education and Employment publications for parents are available from DfEE Publications Centre,★ or, in Scotland, the Education and Industry Department of the Scottish Office.★

How to choose a school

Choosing a school for your child can be complicated: there is a lot to consider and it helps if you know what your rights are and how to find all the information you need. Although this section starts with nursery education, it should be noted that as we go to press there is no right to a school place until a child is five. However, changes are on the way under the proposed voucher system, explained below.

Nursery schools

For some children entry into the education system happens at as young an age as two, at some independent nursery schools. Opinions differ as to the benefits or otherwise of starting any sort of schooling that young. Nursery education on offer from the state system does not start until the age of three, and as local authorities have not been under an obligation to provide it, its provision has varied widely.

In some areas parents will have very little choice on offer. In others there will be a range of options from state-funded nursery education in nursery schools or classes to pre-school playgroups, often run by groups of parents, and independent nurseries. The number of sessions provided varies too, from (say) three to five half-days a week to a full school day. Playgroups usually have one or two fully trained supervisors, who may be supported by volunteer parent-helpers. There is also some overlap with day-care nurseries, where the main aim is to provide care while parents are at work. The hours of the latter are much longer than the school day and they may be open from, say, 8.30 a.m. to 6.00 p.m.

According to government figures, just over three-quarters of all 4-year-olds were attending state schools in 1994 in the year before compulsory school age, and half of these were in primary school reception classes, not in specially designed nursery schools or classes.

But in July 1995 the government announced that it planned to provide, over time, a nursery education place of good quality for all 4-year-olds whose parents wished to take it up. In order to put this into practice a new scheme was announced, the nursery voucher scheme, under which parents will be able to exchange vouchers for up to three terms of nursery education for their child. These vouchers can be used in participating nurseries in the state, voluntary and private sectors.

The first nursery voucher places in England were available for the first phase of the scheme from April 1996 in four areas, three in London (Kensington and Chelsea, Wandsworth and Westminster) and one in Norfolk. Pre-school vouchers were available in Scotland from May 1996 in four pilot areas in parts of Highland, Argyll and Bute, East Renfrewshire and North Ayrshire.

For the second phase it is planned that places will be available throughout England from April 1997 and throughout Scotland from August 1997.

Separate schemes will operate for Wales and Northern Ireland and information about these schemes can be obtained from the education departments in those regions.

Vouchers are a relatively new concept in the UK education system. For the scheme's first phase they were worth £1,100 per child and could be exchanged for three terms of education at participating schools, nurseries, pre-schools and playgroups.

In the pilot areas for phase 1, vouchers were issued by the voucher agency which wrote to eligible parents via the Child Benefit Centre (CBC) enclosing a voucher application form. Parents wanting to take up a voucher were asked to complete the form and return it promptly to the agency, and vouchers were distributed to parents before the start of term.

Places in the local authority- and grant-maintained sectors will continue to be free: parents will receive a place in exchange for the voucher. In the private and voluntary sectors, parents will be able to top up the vouchers from their own resources if higher fees are charged.

The scheme aims to provide 'good-quality education'. To this end, providers will have to:

- confirm that they will work towards 'desirable learning outcomes': essentially, levels of attainment for the child, such as being able to write his or her own name, that should have reached at the end of the period spent at the nursery
- agree to be inspected
- agree to publish information for parents
- give details of their policy and arrangements for children with special educational needs.

Extending choice for parents is one of the principal objectives of the nursery voucher scheme. The information contained in the prospectus of any provider participating in the scheme should include:

- staffing policy, including staff numbers, qualifications, training
- educational programmes and activity
- methods of record-keeping, progress-recording, reporting to parents
- premises and equipment
- admissions policy
- term dates and timetable
- discipline policy
- complaints procedure.

Information about the nursery voucher scheme is available from leaflets, published in several languages and in Braille, and on audio-cassette. In addition, parents in all areas can ring the Nursery Voucher Scheme's information line.★ For information about what is available to you locally, contact your local authority; your Social Services department will be able to advise about other provision for the under–5s.

It is expected that, as for the first phase of the scheme, there will be a publicity campaign prior to the second phase, due to start in April 1997.

If the nursery voucher system is introduced across the whole of the UK, it is predicted that the number of nursery places available will increase, subject to the policy of the government of the day.

Primary and secondary schools

It is advisable to start thinking about what type of school you want for your child long before he or she reaches school age: some primary schools, for example, take names of children from the age of two. Local playgroups and nurseries often have established links with schools and can help to enrol your child.

You should also start thinking about secondary schools one or two years in advance: stories abound of people moving house to get within a school's priority catchment area, but it is not something most of us would be prepared, or able, to do at short notice.

Practical steps you can take to ensure your eventual preference is well founded include:

- getting hold of written information: state schools in England and Wales must publish two important documents to help you choose, a school prospectus and an annual report from the school governors. The prospectus should explain the aims and values of the school as well as examination results, including results of and National Curriculum tests, which are taken at the ages of 7, 11 and 14. Neither type of information is available in Scotland, where few state schools have a board of governors and few if any produce a prospectus. However, local education authorities are required to produce a handbook which describes all the schools in their area and gives similar information to that found in prospectuses in England and Wales
- reading reports of inspections: OFSTED reports should be available in public libraries or obtained from the school (a charge may be made), and summarised in the school's annual report. Some schools may not yet have had their first inspection
- for secondary schools, looking out the performance tables: these compare the examination results for all your local secondary schools, including grant-maintained schools, technology colleges and independent schools. Parents are entitled to a free copy of the tables for their area and neighbouring area from the education department of the local

authority. Summaries of results are usually presented as league tables in the press, but it is as well to be aware of the limitations of these tables: it is particularly difficult to compare the results of schools which select pupils by their ability with schools that take children from across the ability range.

Allocation of places in state schools

Parents have a right to a free place in a state school for their children aged 5–16 and a place in a school or college from age 16 to 18. As a parent (or guardian), you have the right to say which school you want your child to go to but that does not mean you can insist on a place at a particular school. Every year each LEA publishes a leaflet about the admissions arrangements for all its schools. The 'admissions criteria' – rules for deciding who will be offered a place – must be explained in each school's prospectus. Your choice must be honoured unless there is a legitimate reason for turning your child down: the school is full, for example, or your child does not meet the school's entry requirements. You have the right to appeal if you are unhappy with a decision.

Admissions criteria in state schools

Admissions authorities must state clearly how the decision is made to offer a place if there are more applicants for a school than places available. This prevents places being allocated at random (by lot, for example). A school may, however, give priority to children who live nearest, or who have a brother or sister at the school.

For selective secondary schools, try to find out about the sort of competition your child may face, and think about how you might feel if there were, say, 700 children competing for 90 places in any one year. Ask whether sample papers for the tests given to applicants are available. Even non-selective secondary schools may offer up to 10 per cent of their places on the basis of ability or aptitude in certain subjects, such as music, art, sport and technology.

A school may keep places empty, even if there is a demand for them, although it still has to explain in the prospectus how the decision is made. For example, church schools may limit the number of pupils from other faiths with the agreement of the local authority or the Secretary of State for Education; and selective schools can withhold places if not enough children pass the selection test.

Before you make any decision about which schools to apply for you should arrange to visit some schools. Schools make special arrangements for such visits:

- open evenings: many schools hold a series of these over the school year for prospective pupils, offering the chance to talk to the head teacher, staff and pupils. At secondary schools these would usually take place in the autumn term. Dates should be available from the schools; otherwise, some might advertise in the local newspaper (church schools would advertise in the local or national church newspapers)
- open days: some schools offer open days which provide the chance to see the school in action and lessons being taught. Some even offer visits to parents on a 'drop-in' basis, making a virtue of the fact that their school is open to inspection at any time
- personal appointment: if for whatever reason you cannot attend fixed times for open evenings or open days it should be possible to arrange to visit the school at some other time.

What to look for and ask when visiting a school

Looking around any school can be very revealing. As you walk round, ask yourself these questions:

- are you being made welcome?
- do the pupils appear to be well behaved?
- is the children's work on display? If so, is it up to date? What is the standard of the written work? Are the displays bright, colourful and well presented or does the work comprise only fair copies of exercises done in class?
- does the school appear to be well equipped and cared for?
- at secondary schools, how well equipped are the rooms for practical subjects such as science, art, and design and technology?
- how many computers are available and what is the pupil/computer ratio? Are the machines reasonably new? Do

they have colour monitors and CD-ROMs? Is the school on the Internet? What percentage of the school's teachers are computer-literate themselves?

- what sports does the school offer and what are its facilities like? If pupils have to travel to sports facilities, how long does it take? How large is the school gym and is it well equipped? What importance does the school attach overall to P.E and sport? How much time would the pupils spend doing sport each week? How is sport organised within the school? Is there, for example, a house system under which houses can compete with each other? Is there an annual sports day?

Some· of the information you might need will be in the prospectus or local education authority handbook, but if not you should ask questions on your visit. For example:

- if the school does not select by ability, what is its policy on teaching children of different ability? Does the school have setting, streaming or mixed ability?
- what are the average class sizes?
- if the school has mixed-ability classes, does it have a policy on differentiation?

At secondary level there will be many other questions you might want to ask about the subjects taught and the choices on offer. Most schools run an options system for choosing what subjects pupils will study at GCSE (Standard grades in Scotland) and you may wish to know what subjects, if any, are mutually exclusive.

- what happens if a child is keen on, say, both music and drama? Is he or she likely to made to choose between them by year 10?
- what languages are taught?
- what are the school's policies on matters such as homework, uniforms, sport and out-of-school activities, and on social issues such as bullying and equal opportunities? (In each of these cases current good practice for schools is that there should be written policy statements that parents are entitled to see, and for certain matters, such as special educational needs and sex education, written policies are a legal requirement.)

87

If possible, talk to parents of children who are already at the schools you visit. Although everyone has different ideas of what makes a 'good' school, there might be common agreement on some questions. Would they call it a happy school? Is there any problem with bullying, violent behaviour or truancy?

Having done this, made some school visits, asked questions and discussed with staff the issues of most importance to you, you will probably have formed an opinion of which school you would like your child to attend. The following section explains how to apply to a non-independent school. For independent schools, see page 92 under 'Choosing an independent school'.

How to apply for a (non-independent) school place

As a parent, you will probably need to fill in an application form, although procedures vary from area to area and from school to school. If, having read the prospectus, you are still not clear about what to do, contact the local authority or the school's governing body for advice.

- Remember that you can apply to more than one school, and it may be advisable to do so, although priority may be given to parents who make the school their first choice.
- Make a careful note of deadlines for applications and of subsequent examinations for selective schools.
- For church schools you may need to obtain a supporting reference from a minister of religion.
- The application form is likely to ask you to give your reasons for applying. It is worth giving this some thought: for example, consider the sort of thing you would say if you had to argue your case at an appeal (see below). If space is not provided on the application form, consider writing a covering letter to go with it.

It will help you to know about the number of applicants to the school in previous years and the numbers admitted under each relevant criterion. According to the Department for Education and Employment, this information should be readily available to all parents and schools are encouraged to provide it in their school prospectuses. If it is not provided, ask for it. This is particularly important if you are asked about your first choice of school. It may be the case that all first preferences are considered before any others, and places allocated on that basis. If you make a first-choice application to a very popular school, this preference may in effect be wasted unless you are reasonably confident of meeting the other criteria. The next and subsequent schools on your list may also fill up with first-choice applicants, so you risk not getting a place at any of your preferred schools.

What happens if your child is refused a place

Although the government has publicised an objective of giving parents greater choice in the selection of their child's school, the reality is that parents often find the school of their choice to be over-subscribed, with a substantial waiting list, and it is not uncommon for children to be offered places in schools that are inconvenient to get to and were not even on the parents' list of preferred schools.

If the school you have chosen for your child is a popular one, and has been inundated with applications, inevitably not all applicants will be offered a place. Disappointed applicants may be assigned a place on a waiting list according to the admissions criteria, but these lists can be very long. You should be told your child's position on the list, if you ask, unless the admissions authority has published in its prospectus a policy of not revealing this information.

The placing of a child's name on a waiting list does not remove your right of appeal. The letter informing you of the decision to refuse your application should tell you how to appeal and by what date. Whether the school is maintained by the local authority, voluntary-aided or grant-maintained, the appeals process must be entirely separate from the allocation of places under the admission arrangements. Places given on appeal are intended to be *in addition* to places offered up to the published admissions limit. Appeals bodies must consider each case individually and on its merits. Appeal hearings are supposed be conducted in as informal atmosphere as possible – unlike the formal atmosphere and procedures in a court of law, for example – and are usually in private. Decisions are binding on the authority or governors who set them up.

School places can be very emotive issues and it is easy for parents to become upset and angry. If you are considering an appeal, try to avoid this: have your arguments well-ordered and get support from doctors or social workers as appropriate. The Advisory Centre for Education (ACE) advises parents to be very specific about what their child needs and why a particular school either will or will not meet those needs in the way you would like. In its publication *School Choice and Appeals* it suggests some reasons parents might reasonably put forward for wanting their child to go to a specific school:

- brother or sister at the school
- strong family associations
- medical, social or psychological reasons: ACE suggests that parents should concentrate primarily on matters relating to the child's welfare, e.g. a long journey to school, special reasons relating to fear of bullying, need to stay in a particular locality
- a strong preference for a single-sex school or, alternatively, co-educational school
- a strong preference for a school with a particular religious tradition
- a strong preference for a particular curriculum or specialisation such as music or foreign language which is not available at other schools
- teaching of the Welsh language.

In addition, ACE suggests that whatever the basis of their appeal, parents should produce evidence to support what they say: for example, a letter from the doctor or from the child's previous school. If the child has failed the test for admission to a selective school, parents might wish to show that the test was not fairly administered, or that their child was unwell on the day.

Secondary school appeals should be heard and a final decision made before the summer holidays, but if not you should complain and ask for an earlier date. Primary school appeals should be dealt with either before the school year begins or in the term before the child is due to start. If you want to transfer your child to another school in the middle of the school year and are refused a place, you may appeal straight away even though this is not the usual time for making an appeal.

You will be given a date by which you should appeal and ACE advises that you should meet it, although there is nothing in law to prevent you making a late appeal.

The appeals committee will consider a number of factors: for example, the legal rules on admissions to state schools mean that a child must be admitted to the school for which his or her parents have expressed a preference unless the admission of the child would 'prejudice the provision of efficient education or the efficient use of resources'. This might be the case if the school is already full, for example. ACE suggests that when you are told that the school is full and you want to appeal for a place in spite of this you could try to persuade the appeals committee that the admission of your child would not affect the provision of efficient education or the efficient use of resources, and cite the numbers in the school in previous years. However, if the class sizes in the school are already large you need to consider carefully whether you want your child to be the 31st or 32nd pupil to be admitted into a class.

If there are many other appeals for places at the same school the appeals committee will have to judge who has the strongest claim for a place. It is unlikely that any appeals committee will be able to make a practical intervention on behalf of more than three or four children where a school has, say, a waiting list of a hundred.

If your appeal is unsuccessful and you are not satisfied with the way the appeal was held, you complain to your local ombudsman. The ombudsman will deal only with maladministration, not with the appeal decision itself. Your LEA should help you make contact. Otherwise, you can complain to the Secretary of State, who cannot review the decisions of individual appeal committees but can consider whether the admissions authority acted unreasonably or in default of its statutory duties.

As a last resort, you also have the right to apply for leave to for a judicial review to be held. This means making an application to the Divisional Court to order a fresh hearing of the appeal. The court may consider that the decision was so unreasonable that no appeals committee should have reached it, or that there was a failure to comply with the procedural rules, or that other irregularities took place in the way in which the appeal was handled.

Further information, including the leaflets *Your Child's Next School, a Guide to Secondary Schools Admissions, Admissions to Maintained Schools* (Circular 6/93), *Implementation of More Open Enrolment in Primary Schools* (Circular 6/91), are available free from the Department of Education Publications Centre.★ A handbook entitled *School Choice and Appeals* is available, price £4.50, from the Advisory Centre for Education (ACE).★

Note that many public libraries have a school governors section, from which you may be able to borrow some of the above publications.

Choosing an independent school

All schools which charge fees and offer full-time education to five children or more of primary school age or older must register with the Department for Education and Employment (DfEE), but it does not supply lists of independent schools to parents. About 80 per cent of these schools (1,350) belong to the Independent Schools Information Service (ISIS), which aims to answer parents' questions about independent schools and help them with educational problems. There are eight ISIS regional offices, six of which serve English and Welsh regions and one each for Scotland and Ireland. Each publishes its own handbook giving details of independent schools in the region, although they do not recommend individual schools. National ISIS publishes an annual guide to all member schools (£7.95 at present) and also offers a fee-paid placement and consultancy service.

Independent schools are not obliged to follow the National Curriculum, but many claim to fulfil, or even exceed, its requirements. Nor are they obliged to participate in the testing arrangements for the National Curriculum key stages, but they may do so.

Independent schools are organised by age group: pre-prep schools take children aged 3–7 and may be linked to a prep (preparatory) school, usually taking children from 8–13, but sometimes 5–11, and either single-sex or mixed; for senior schools (again, either single-sex or mixed) entry may be at 11 or 13, or either.

As for state schools, the prospectuses produced by the individual schools should be the best starting point for finding out about the choice available. The prospectus should state the school's aims and objectives, how it organises the curriculum and 'pastoral' care, how it allocates places and whether or not it is selective. If pupils are selected, the prospectus should tell you whether entrance examinations and interviews are held, when they take place and the closing dates for applications.

One vital piece of information is what it will cost to send your child to the school. There will be a basic termly fee but it is very important to find out what the fee covers. If items such as books and stationery, medical supplies and insurance are not included you will want to know how much these are likely to cost.

Help with school fees

Not all the children at independent schools are paying the full fees. About one in four pupils receives financial help – and most of this help comes from the schools themselves. Some pupils are given scholarships because of their academic ability or outstanding talent in art or music, for example. Scholarships vary but may, for example, cover half the annual fees.

Other pupils may have assisted places. This government-funded scheme helps with the cost of tuition at certain independent schools for parents who could not otherwise afford them. The scheme was set up in 1981 for academically able boys and girls of secondary-school age but it has recently been extended and some schools have been given additional places for pre–11 and sixth-formers.

The actual amount available depends on family income. The scheme does not help with boarding fees. For the school year 1995–6 parents did not have to pay anything if their relevant income (i.e. total earned and unearned income before tax) was £9,572 or less after subtracting the allowance (of £1,165) for each additional dependent child. With an income of £25,000 parents would be expected to contribute £3,867 to fees for the 1995–6 school year for one assisted place. The amounts differ if you have two or more assisted places in one family. The schools in the scheme have complete scales of contributions and should be able to advise on the amount you would have to pay. There is only a limited number of assisted places at each school and the individual schools will tell you how places are allocated.

In 1996 5,700 new assisted places were available at independent schools. A list of schools offering assisted places is available from the DfEE or the Welsh Office. The assisted places scheme in Scotland is different in some respects. There have been 3,500 assisted places in Scotland since August 1996, and the government plans to increase this to 6,000 in the next few years. The scheme has recently been extended to include children from the age of six who are receiving primary education in participating schools with an integrated primary department. In 1996 there are 55 Scottish independent schools in the assisted places scheme. More information about the scheme is available from the Scottish Office Education and Industry Department.*

Although the assisted places scheme could be affected by a change of government, any existing assisted places would be honoured.

Scholarships and bursaries

Individual schools may offer scholarships. It is worth getting the relevant information as much in advance as you can, in case, for example, your child needs to be able to produce a portfolio of drawings and paintings for an art scholarship, or show other evidence of a particular accomplishment. For academic scholarships you should make sure your child is well prepared for the examination.

Many independent schools have grants available in the form of bursaries for children of parents who would not otherwise be able to afford the fees. These usually require parents to declare all sources of income and are given at the discretion of individual schools, which should be able to provide you with details.

Entrance examinations

Many independent schools set their own entrance examinations at both primary level and secondary level, when entry may be at age 11 or age 13 (and separate entry at 16+). There is usually a registration fee for taking the examinations. Those who are successful in the examinations are usually interviewed as well before being offered a place.

Try to get hold of an examination paper from a previous year from the school so that you can make sure that your child has covered the likely topics.

Bookshops also stock (or can order) a wide range of publications which contain practice test papers to prepare children for entrance examinations in, for example, verbal and non-verbal reasoning as well as English and mathematics. The papers usually state recommended times for completion so that children can get accustomed to working to a set time-limit as well as becoming familiar with the sorts of questions they may face.

Common Entrance

Children transferring from independent prep schools at 13 usually sit the Common Entrance examinations, for which there is a specific syllabus, including Latin and French. It is used predominantly by boarding schools but also by some independent day schools. A child transferring from the state sector at 13 would not usually be expected to have passed Common Entrance, but would have to take the 12+ entrance examinations set by the individual schools.

The procedure for making applications to independent schools will be detailed in the prospectus for each school: many co-ordinate their closing dates for application and their examination dates so that they do not clash. ISIS offers a fee-based placement service through the National ISIS Consultancy Service (NICS) to UK and overseas parents. NICS will co-ordinate visits, advise on guardians and oversee administrative arrangements until a school is finally chosen, or through its consultancy service provide detailed personal advice on suitable schools. They also run a clearing house which will provide parents with a short-list of schools appropriate to their child's needs. ISIS also publishes leaflets on a range of subjects, including school fees planning, scholarships and grants and questions to ask when you visit a school.

Boarding schools

The popularity of boarding has been on the wane for some years. Many parents do not like the idea of sending their children away and it is a costly option: about £12,000 a year in 1995 per child (except for the 40 or so state boarding schools where parents pay boarding fees only, at about £3,000–£5,000 a year in 1995). For further information contact the Independent Schools Information Service (ISIS)★ or the Boarding Schools Association;★ the *Gabbitas Guide to Independent Schools* (£9.99) contains information on over 2,000 schools and can be obtained from the Gabbitas Educational Trust;★

For information on assisted places in England contact the Department for Education and Employment Assisted Places Team,★ or, for Wales, the Welsh Office.★ Information about the assisted places scheme in Scotland can be obtained from the Scottish Office Education and Industry Department.★

Special educational needs

If your child finds it much harder to learn than most children of the same age, or has a disability which makes it difficult to use the educational facilities in the area, he or she has special educational needs and has a right to help known as special educational provision. This can start even before your child starts school. ('Gifted' children, on the other hand, who find learning much easier than their peers, present a different set of problems: advice can be found on page 98.)

The procedures surrounding the provision of education for children with special educational needs are complex. The DfEE has published a guide for parents which outlines the legal requirements imposed on schools and local authorities in dealing with children who have special educational needs and also explains what the parents' rights are. It gives the following examples of problems:

- a physical disability
- a problem with sight, hearing or speech
- a mental disability
- emotional or behavioural problems
- medical or health problem
- difficulties with reading, writing, speaking or mathematics.

The guide stresses that these are just examples and a child may have more general difficulties with school work. Many children experience problems at some stage in their schooling, but these may be transient and require special support only for a limited duration: for example, while adjusting to their parents' divorce or prior to an operation. Other children need continual support. The local education authority will assess the needs of a child under the age of two. For an older child the LEA must decide whether or not to make a statutory assessment, which is a detailed report by a specialist analysing the child's needs and advising on the type of help required. The LEA may then draw up a 'statement of special educational needs' in accordance with the assessment.

If your child is already at school and you are concerned that he or she has a learning difficulty you should discuss your concerns with the school. All ordinary schools must provide help for children with special educational needs. In particular, state schools must:

- have regard to the Code of Practice on the Identification and Assessment of Special Educational Needs, and
- publish information about their policies for children with special educational needs, which parents have a right to see.

The Code of Practice is a guide for schools and LEAs about the practical help they can give to children with special educational needs. It recommends that schools should deal with children's needs in stages, matching the level of help to the needs of the child. The Code suggests that schools might use three stages, but some use two, others four. The school's published policy should tell you:

- what its arrangements are for deciding which children need special help and their plans for giving that help, stage by stage
- how it plans to work closely with parents, who have the right to be involved at all stages
- the name of the teacher who is responsible for children with special educational needs.

As far as choice of school for a child with special educational needs is concerned, parents have a right to express a preference for which state school they want their child to attend. This preference, however, is subject to the LEA's agreement that the school is suitable, the efficient education of other children already at the school and the efficient use of the LEA's resources. If you want your child to attend an independent special school the LEA will consider your wishes carefully, but has no legal duty to place your child at a non-maintained or independent school if there is a suitable state school. The Special Educational Needs Tribunal, an independent body, hears parents' appeals against LEA decisions on statutory assessments and statements.

The Department for Education and Employment Publications Centre★ has several free publications that provide further information: *Special Educational Needs: a guide for parents*, listing over 60 voluntary organisations which offer help and general advice to parents of children with disabilities or learning difficulties; *Code of Practice on the Identification and Assessment of Special Educational Needs*; *Pupils with Problems* (Department of Education circular); *Guide to the Special Educational Needs Tribunal*. In Scotland, *A Parents' Guide to Special Educational Needs* is available from the Scottish Office Education and Industry Department.★ ACE,★ which offers confidential advice to parents, has published a *Special Education Handbook* (£7.50) explaining the intricacies of assessment and 'statementing', appeals, reviews and assessments and including model letters for parents.

The Council for the Registration of Schools Teaching Dyslexic Pupils★ has information on independent schools that specialise in this type of learning difficulty (send a stamped addressed envelope). The Centre for Studies on Inclusive Education (CSIE)★ may be another useful source of information.

'Gifted' children

Children who are particularly able do not usually come into the definition of special educational needs, though it is argued by some that the 1944 Education Act (which is still in force) provides for children's education according to age, ability and aptitude, which should include providing for children of high ability. However, no guidance is given to schools on this issue, and no recommended system is in place in the state or independent sectors for dealing with children of high ability.

If very bright children are not sufficiently motivated and stretched they can become bored and disruptive. The National

Association for Gifted Children (NAGC) provides information, advice and counselling to gifted children and their parents and in some areas of Britain it runs Explorers' Clubs on Saturdays offering activities such as chess, computing, drama and creative writing. For further information contact the NAGC.★

Home-based education

Some parents beat the education system – or at least the school system – by educating their children at home. As ACE explains in its information sheet on this subject, although there is a legal duty on parents to make sure that their child is educated, i.e. receives 'efficient full-time education, suitable to his age ability and aptitude', and to attend to any special educational needs he may have, this 'does not mean that the child has to attend school'.

If it appears to an education authority that a child is not receiving a suitable education, the authority has a legal duty to take certain steps which are set out in the Education Act 1993. How the LEAs fulfil this duty is at their discretion. Parents who decide to educate their offspring at home are under no obligation to follow the National Curriculum, provide a timetable, work during school hours or for any particular number of hours a week. ACE does advise however that parents should plan carefully how they intend to educate their child, and that it is in their interests to provide the LEA with clear information about these arrangements (which might include tuition in sports or music, visits to the library, museums and the theatre, computer programmes, video and television, craft work and so on).

For anyone seriously contemplating home education for a child who is a registered pupil at a school, ACE warns that it is very important to make sure that the child's name is removed from the admissions register. Parents may be prosecuted if their child is a *registered pupil* who is not attending school regularly and the fact that a suitable education is being provided at home is no defence to this charge. In order to remove a child's name from a register, parents must provide written notification.

For children with special needs, ACE notes that when a child has a 'statement' (see page 97, under 'Special educational needs') which names a special school, the child's name may not be removed from the register without the consent of the education authority. If the authority refuses to give consent, parents can apply to the Secretary of State for a direction that the child's name be removed from the register.

As far as formal examinations are concerned, if parents want their child to follow GCSE and A-level courses, or Standard grades and Highers in Scotland, they can be taken privately at home and the child entered as an external candidate – although the examinations will have to be taken at an approved centre. Some colleges of further education may provide open or distance-learning courses which enable students to study mostly at home but also have the support of a college tutor. Although fees may be payable for attending a course at a further education college, ACE notes that it is worthwhile approaching the LEA to discuss the possibility of college fees being paid for a student who is being home-educated. The LEA is not bound to do this, as it fulfils its duty by providing school places.

The above-mentioned information sheet from ACE★ is entitled *Home Education* (£1); it also lists a number of useful organisations to contact including Education Otherwise,★ a self-help group that supports home-based education.

Your child at school

Once a child has been accepted by a school and begun formal education, most parents will want to keep a close eye on his or her progress through the various school stages. According to the Parent's Charter, you have a right to a good education for your child, which means a right to expect that the school will do its best to make sure your child does as well as he or she possibly can.

You also have the right to influence how your child's state school is run. This may in practice be fairly limited but you do have the right:

- to vote for parent governors at your school and to stand for election as a parent governor yourself, so that parents have a strong voice in school policy. Nearly all secondary school and most primary school governing bodies now appoint teachers and decide how the school spends its budget

- to go to the annual parents' meeting, which allows parents to give their views on how the school is run (do consider exercising this right: all too often, governors out-number parents)
- to vote, if the governors hold a ballot, on whether the school should apply for self-governing (grant-maintained) status. All governing bodies of schools run by local authorities must now consider each year whether to hold such a ballot. Even if the governors decide against doing so, parents can force their hand if at least 20 per cent of parents of pupils registered at the school sign a petition supporting a ballot.

School reports and records

All schools have to provide parents with a range of information to enable them to see exactly how their child is doing. Schools must provide parents with a written report on their child's progress at least once a year. As well as giving feedback on your child, the report should tell you how you can discuss the issues it raises with teachers. If, as a parent, you are not happy about any lesson-related matter, approach first the subject teacher, then the head of department, then the head teacher, and lastly, if the problem has still not been resolved, the school governors.

Schools keep a record for every child. Parents of pupils under 18 and pupils aged 16 or over have a right to see their records.

Parents' meetings

In addition to the governors' annual meeting which usually follows the publication of the Annual Report to parents, many school have regular information meetings, which are a good way of finding out what is going on at the school. Information meetings are particularly important at those stages in a child's education when vital decisions are taken:

- at age 10 or 11 when the child is transferring from primary to secondary school

- at age 13 or 14 when the pupil must choose which subjects to study for GCSE (Standard Grade in Scotland) and GNVQ (or GSVQ in Scotland) examinations two years later
- at age 15 or 16 when subjects are chosen for A-levels, GNVQ Advanced and, in Scotland, H-grades
- at age 17 or l8, when applications are prepared for college or university entry.

Pupils' options at 14

The National Curriculum is not compulsory after year 9 in state schools, and, as mentioned earlier, not at all in independent schools. Most schools nevertheless guide pupils towards a broad set of subjects in order to keep options open for later courses and careers. Most run an options system, whereby after key stage 3 pupils must decide which subjects they follow for the GCSE examinations. Whereas some subjects such as English and maths are compulsory, many subjects are optional and are pursued only by pupils who have shown a particular aptitude or interest in that subject. Schools usually have an options evening some time during year 9 (age 13 or 14: see above) which parents are invited to attend so that they can hear about courses and talk to teachers.

The main awarding bodies for courses taken at age14–16 are:

- the General Certificate of Secondary Examination boards, for an examination generally taken at 16. GCSE is the examination target for 70–80 per cent of this age group. In Scotland, 90 per cent take the Scottish equivalent, Standard grade
- the Business and Technology Education Council (BTEC), which validates awards for the General National Vocational Qualification (GNVQ) and National Vocational Qualification (NVQ) and their Scottish equivalents. These courses are more appropriate for 16-plus students, but some schools incorporate them in their curriculum
- the Royal Society of Arts (RSA) and City and Guilds of London Institute (CGLI): these too are more closely linked to further education but some schools offer these vocational courses.

The objectives of any course for 14- to 16-year-olds are to give pupils a general education suitable for a job, a training scheme, a further education course, A-levels or any other alternative at 16-plus. What is important about GCSE is that pupils who pass one or more subjects can go directly on to one of these courses or into a job, knowing that they have received good grounding in that subject during the two-year course. In addition, the assessment of their work is likely to be helpful for employers and for colleges. The GCSE examination is still developing. If parents are not fully aware of a school's policies on GCSE they should ask the school for information about this and other courses offered.

Pupils' options at 16

The updated Parent's Charter explains that young people are entitled to continue their education and training beyond 16. Tuition is free for full-time students aged 16–18 in state schools, CTCs and colleges in the further education sector.

A 16- or 17-year-old who wants to add to his or her qualifications has a number of choices. Depending on the area and the institutions within it, one of these school-based options may be available:

- staying on in the sixth form of the present school, which could be a comprehensive for an 11- to 18-year-old, a school for a 14- to 18-year-old, an independent school or a school of some other type
- joining the sixth form of another school: e.g. some boys' schools have places for girls for sixth-form entry. Some independent schools offer entry into the sixth form and the government's assisted places scheme (see above, pages 93–4) is available in some schools for the sixth form
- leaving school and going to a sixth-form college. There are now over 160 sixth-form colleges in England and Wales, with more opening each year.

Most students who stay on at school after the age of 16 or 17 are aiming for higher qualifications, especially A-levels (H-grades in Scotland). These are needed for entry to university and other courses that start at age 18 or 19, as well as for jobs that require

A pupil aged 16 or 17 can take any of the paths shown in this diagram

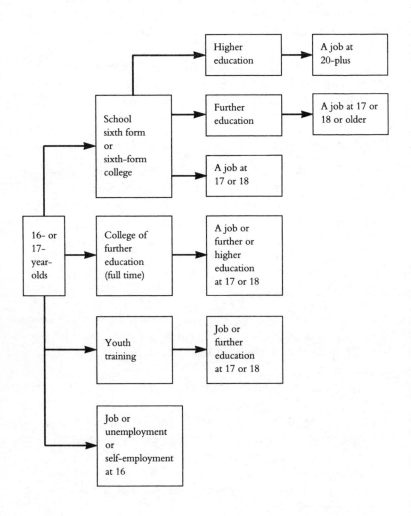

better qualifications than GCSEs. A student's choice of A-levels (H-grades) is vitally important. Although they do not give special training in anything they add to one's resources when applying for a course or job. They also show an employer that a student has the ability to learn at a higher level. Choosing A-level subjects is discussed in greater detail in the book *Which Subject? Which Career?*. ★

Homework and private coaching

Homework plays an increasingly important part in education as children move through the system. Apart from demonstrating that education is not confined to school, it can help children to work on their own and it should reinforce the work that they have been doing at school. Schools should have a clear policy on homework, and on examination revision. It is worth parents' while to discuss with the school how best to give support and encouragement.

There are mixed views about using private coaching to boost children's school work, but it is used by increasing numbers of parents who do not want to leave education entirely to the school. Lessons may take place at weekends or after school and cost about £12-£15 an hour at secondary level. The cost will vary and be lower for children of primary-school age and more for subjects such as A-level science. It may be that you want help with maths, or learning a language, or specialised tuition for a child with a learning difficulty such as dyslexia.

A recommendation from another parent is often a good way of finding a tutor, although you should always check credentials. Tutors and classes are also widely available for learning to play a musical instrument, dance, drama and a range of sports.

National networks exist of tutors and specialist teachers (see *Yellow Pages*). For language tuition, contact the Centre for Information on Language Teaching★ (send a stamped addressed envelope).

Music teachers should be graduates of one of the major music colleges such as the Royal Academy of Music, with a teaching qualification, or university graduates with a teaching qualification.

The Council for Dance Education and Training* can supply information about approved dance schools (send a stamped addressed envelope).

Behaviour and discipline

Education is of course much more than simply following a curriculum. According to the Department for Education, head teachers should ensure that school staff, parents and, above all, pupils, are in no doubt about the standards of behaviour expected, the consequences of not achieving these standards (distinguishing clearly between minor and serious misbehaviour) and the types of wrong-doing which are likely to lead to exclusion. 'Exclusion', which used to be called expulsion, is a very serious step for a school to take. Under the 1993 Education Act two kinds of exclusion are allowed: either permanent, or for a fixed number of school days, not exceeding fifteen.

If your child is excluded, or suspended, the head teacher must tell you why, and that you have a right to put your case to the governing body; and, in the case of a permanent exclusion, to appeal against the decision.

ACE* publishes an information sheet, *Exclusion from School*, on this subject.

If, as a parent, you have any problems with behaviour and discipline or other non-lesson-related issues (sometimes called pastoral matters), approach first the child's form teacher, then the head of year, then the head teachers and, if the problem is still not resolved, the school governors.

Playground problems

As a parent you will be want your child to be happy at school and get on well with the other children. But problems in the playground, in particular bullying, are very common. A recent study by the DfEE showed that one in four primary-school children had been bullied during a single term and one in ten during a single week.

Every school should have a policy on bullying, involving everyone from dinner ladies to governors, while for their part children need to know that bullying includes being teased or isolated as well as physical threats, and what action will be taken if they report it.

For help with this problem, contact the Anti-Bullying Campaign★ or ring the Parents' Bullying Line run by Kidscape.★ The latter publishes a leaflet entitled *Stop Bullying*.

Further education

Further education provides opportunities not only for 16- and 17-year olds who leave school and want to continue with a full-time or part-time course but also for people of any age group who want to study for vocational qualifications or take a non-certificate course in a leisure subject. A huge and overlapping group of institutions make up the further education sector. Further education colleges, which in England and Wales were removed from the control of the LEAs in 1992, include:

- further education colleges, providing GCSE, GNVQ, A-level, BTEC, City and Guilds and other vocational and non-vocational courses
- colleges of further and higher education offering a similar range of further education (FE) courses and degree and HND courses franchised from a local university
- colleges of arts and technology
- colleges of art and design, specialising in these and related subjects
- tertiary colleges, combining elements of sixth-form and FE colleges
- specialist colleges of horticulture, agriculture, building, printing, etc.
- adult education centres, offering courses for adults returning to work or special skills or leisure courses
- independent further education colleges, which are fee-paying and often attract overseas students.

Special needs at 16+

Local education authorities and the Further Education Funding Council have duties towards young people with learning difficulties who on leaving school want to continue their education either full-time or part-time in a college of further education, or in a sixth-form college or another special kind of institution. For further information see the ACE★ information sheet *Further Education for Young People with Learning Difficulties* (£1).

For more about college courses and the opportunities available in your area, students should contact their careers teacher, or local careers office. For information about apprenticeships and other opportunities contact the Training and Enterprise Councils (TECs) throughout England and Wales and from Local Enterprise Companies (LECs) in Scotland. Addresses are in the telephone book.

Higher education

Higher education, at age 18 or older, usually means post A-level courses that lead to degrees, diplomas of higher education (DipHE), HNDs, HNCs and similar awards. The courses are run by universities, institutes and colleges of higher education, and specialist colleges, such as colleges of art and design, building, agriculture or printing, and in some colleges of further education whose degree courses are 'franchised' from an associated, and often local, university.

In recent years, dramatic changes have affected the structure of higher education The Further and Higher Education Act 1992 brought about the following important changes:

- the end of the separation between polytechnics and the older universities. All polytechnics were renamed universities and some higher education institutions also became universities
- further education colleges became independent institutions, separate from LEAs and funded directly from central government. Scottish colleges also achieved independent status
- the Higher Education Funding Council and the Further Education Funding Council were given the responsibility for allocating money to these institutions. Separate funding arrangements were made for Wales, Scotland and Northern Ireland

- the Council for National Academic Awards (CNAA) was abolished and 'new' universities, like the old ones, became responsible for validating and awarding their own degrees.

Those unfamiliar with the procedures may find the procedure for university and college applications rather a minefield. There are hundreds of different courses and subject combinations at degree level in higher education institutions. It can be difficult for an A-level or H-grade student contemplating the complex procedures of the Universities and Colleges Admissions Service (UCAS)★ or other application forms to know where to start. The following section outlines the main types of qualification and courses available in higher education.

Degrees

These include Bachelor of Arts (BA), Bachelor of Science (BSc), Bachelor of Engineering (BEng), Bachelor of Commerce (BComm) and Bachelor of Education (BEd).

Degree courses come in various forms and with different requirements:

- in England and Wales they usually last three years, or four years if they are sandwich courses, mixing work experience in industry or a year abroad with full-time study at college. In Scotland most honours degrees take four years, while ordinary or general degrees take three years
- in England and Wales they normally require a minimum of two A-levels and another three subjects at GCSE. Most Scottish universities specify a minimum of three Highers and S-grade English. Realistic entry requirements are usually much higher than the minimum. Scottish students wishing to study in England or Wales, or *vice versa*, should be aware that three Highers are generally considered to be equivalent to two A-levels
- courses can be vocational, such as engineering, or non-vocational, such as English literature, philosophy or history
- they can be in single subjects (geography, say) or two subjects of roughly equal weight (such as French and Spanish), or combined studies, which might comprise a group of subjects (such as English, history, archaeology and media studies)

- courses can be modular: modules are units of study and students build up a package of modules equal to three- or four-year courses
- in Scotland some universities accept students to a faculty (such as science or arts) rather than to a specialist course. Others admit students to the university as a whole or to a department or course. Students do not usually specialise until their second or third year.

The costs of taking a degree course can be broken down into two parts: tuition fees and maintenance or living costs. Degree courses qualify for LEA awards. The maintenance part of the grant depends on the income of the student's parents. The tuition fees are generally paid by the student's own LEA, even if the student does not qualify for a maintenance grant. Students therefore need to discuss with their parents at an early stage what, if any, contribution they can make to their son's or daughter's maintenance.

For details of individual degree courses, the differences between them, entry requirements and special aspects, consult *Degree Course Guides* (published by CRAC*), which are available for all degree subjects.

Diploma of Higher Education (DipHE)

The course leading to this qualification is generally of shorter duration than those for degree courses: two years is the norm, although many DipHE courses allow students to continue for a further one or two years for a degree. The DipHE:

- requires a minimum of two A-levels and appropriate GCSE passes at grades A–C
- is sometimes non-vocational
- usually involves the study of more than one subject. Students may be able to develop an individual course of study from the options or 'modules' available
- can include both previously studied and new subjects
- is available in some of the 'new' universities and colleges and institutes of further and higher education
- qualifies for a mandatory award from the LEA.

Scottish Vocational Education Council Higher National Diplomas (SCOTVEC HND)

The course for this vocational qualification is usually of two years' duration, full-time, for business and administrative subjects, or, for technical and scientific courses, a three-year sandwich course.

Entry requirements are set by the individual colleges. Generally they accept three Highers and two Standard grades for business and administrative courses and two Highers and three Standard grades for technical or scientific courses. SCOTVEC National Certificate modules are also accepted for entry to HND courses.

A wide range of subjects is available, in courses angled to the needs of industry and commerce.

Business and Technology Education Council Higher National Diploma (BTEC HND)

This vocational qualification is usually of two years' duration when full-time, three years if a work placement is included as part of a sandwich course. The BTEC HND:

- requires a minimum of one A-level pass with, usually, one other A-level subject to have been studied
- is usually offered as a single subject (for example, applied physics) but can involve study of several elements under a single-subject heading (for example, business studies, which can incorporate law, accounts, economics, marketing, sociology, statistics, psychology and a foreign language)
- teaches traditional school subjects (for example, maths), if selected, in a manner relevant to the needs of employers
- is available in the 'new' universities and colleges and institutes of further and higher education
- qualifies for a mandatory award from the LEA.

Applying for a place

Applying for a place in higher education can be both time-consuming and confusing. Before getting involved in the detail of the various procedures it may be helpful to note these general points:

- applications are usually required nine months before the course begins. Nothing is gained by delaying an application
- it is wise to make some decisions about the choice of possible courses while still in the first year of A-levels
- applications for most courses are made through centralised application procedures. These include applications for first degree, DipHE and HND courses at university, made through UCAS; and for art and design courses and Higher National Diplomas, made through the Art and Design Admissions Registry (ADAR)
- offers of places are usually conditional upon a specified level of performance at A-level. The grades required vary from course to course and institution to institution
- as a (very) general rule, some of the 'new' universities and the colleges demand lower grades than the 'older' universities for comparable courses
- while academic achievement is usually the major criterion used by admissions tutors, other factors such as motivation, interests and any relevant work experience are taken into account
- it is possible to make applications after A-level results have been published, but there are fewer vacancies and the grades required will be generally higher.

For further information consult the following publications: the *UCAS Handbook,* available free from UCAS,★ contains the titles of every first degree and HND course in over 240 institutions; *University and College Entrance - The Official Guide,* available from Sheed & Ward Ltd,★ is the essential starting-point for general and course entry requirements for UK universities; a lot more detailed information on higher education courses and a list of numerous other publications appears in *Which Subject? Which Career?* published by Which? Ltd.★

For information on fees, grants and loans see *Student Grants and Loans, A Brief Guide,* available from the Department for Education and Employment's Publications Department;★ or *Student Grants in Scotland* from the Scottish Office Education and Industry Department,★ or *Grants and Loans to Students; A Brief Guide,* from the Department of Education for Northern Ireland.★

Mature students

There are more mature students than ever before and the number of mature students starting full-time and part-time courses available increased by more than three-quarters between 1980 and 1990. About a third of the population goes on to higher education nowadays, compared with one in seven in the 1960s to the 1980s. About 70 per cent of mature students are women.

Profound changes in the job market, the communications revolution and the ever-increasing importance of information technology, and social changes, including the trend for women to pursue careers rather than staying at home to raise their children, have contributed to the expansion of and changes of emphasis in higher education, and to an emerging culture of 'life-long learning'. Quite apart from this, many people whose schooldays are behind them feel that they did not fulfil their academic potential first time around and decide either to go back to college or to go to college for the first time as a mature student. Fortunately, the opportunities available for those who feel that the education system beat them in their early youth make it possible for them to 'start over' and rectify the situation, or, on the other hand, to increase the knowledge and skills required for survival in an intensely competitive employment arena.

The term 'mature' for first-degree students means 21 years old or over, and for postgraduates indicates those who are 25 or over on the first day of their course. Entrance requirements vary and a lack of formal qualifications need not be a deterrent. For example, an access course may be the ideal entrée to the qualifications required.

Access courses

Access courses, such as those on offer at further education colleges or adult education institutes, require no entry qualifications and provide study skills and a more rapid route to higher education courses than A-levels. They may last one or two years, be full-time or part-time, and may specialise in vocational areas such as design, media, engineering and catering as well as communications and numeracy. Mature students can apply direct to a university or college for entry to a degree or HND course.

The success rate of both entry to degree courses (usually by students who do not normally have A-level passes) and of completion of a degree or HND is remarkable, showing the dedication and determination of the people who have been motivated to apply for them.

To qualify for a grant, you have to have been a resident in the UK for the past three years. You are not eligible if you have already attended a full-time course of advanced further education for more than a year, or successfully completed a similar part-time course. A mandatory grant (which local authorities must pay) is awarded for designated courses. If you are 25 or over, or have been married for at least two years, or have been self-supporting for at least three years before taking up a college place, you qualify as 'independent' and no parental contribution is expected towards a grant.

For further information see *Second Chance: a guide to education and training courses at all levels for adults,* published by Careers and Occupational Information Centre (COIC) at £25; or *Returning to Work: a directory of education and training for women* by the Women Returners Network (MJ Publishers, £15.50); or, for information on fees, grants and loans, *Student Grants and Loans* from Department for Education and Employment's Publications Department; *Student Grants in Scotland* is available from the Scottish Office Education and Industry Department; *Grants and Loans to Students* is the equivalent for Northern Ireland, available from the Department of Education for Northern Ireland.

Distance learning

Distance learning has shaken off its old image of low-status correspondence courses. No fewer than 150,000 degree students have 'beaten' the education system by registering with the Open University. Established in 1969, the Open University is still expanding and its open entry policy and flexible study methods have made it possible for many people to take the opportunity of a second chance in education.

The tuition fee for 1997 will be £320 for one undergraduate full course; summer school is likely to be £210. Students need six credits (course passes) for a BA or BSc. For honours, two must be at a higher level. The likely cost of a degree will be something over £2,500. Although no grants are available, some students may be able to get help in the form of a discretionary award from their local authority or financial help from their employers. For a copy of the general prospectus, contact the Open University's Central Enquiry Service.★

A wide range of other courses is offered by other institutions for distance learning, many of which advertise in the education pages in the national press. Contact the Open and Distance Learning Quality Council★ for further information.

Questions and answers

Q *My child is dyslexic, but I can't get the school to recognise that there is a problem. What can I do?*

A Unfortunately no school or local education authority is likely to recognise the term 'dyslexia' *per se*. It is usually used to mean difficulty with words, and is not associated with intelligence, but educational psychologists are likely to refer to the child's problem as a 'specific learning difficulty', and as such it would come under the heading of special educational needs (see page 96).

If you have already talked to your school's special educational needs teacher and to the head teacher and are not happy with the response there are a number of ways of pursuing your problem, which are explained in the DfEE's guide for parents to special educational needs. For example, if you are still not satisfied after complaining to the school, you should contact the LEA, or the governing body if it is a grant-maintained school. The guide explains that if the school cannot provide the extra help he or she needs, you can ask the LEA to make a statutory assessment of your child. The LEA has six weeks in which to decide whether to make a statutory assessment. It will ask your views about your child's needs, and should provide you with the names of people and organisations who can help and advise you, and information about the special help available in state schools. If after six weeks the LEA decides that an assessment is not needed it will write to you and your child's school giving the reasons for its decision.

If you ask for a statutory assessment and the LEA decides not to make one, you have a right to appeal to the Special Educational Needs Tribunal, an independent body that hears parents' appeals against LEA decisions on statutory assessments and statements.

For further information on dyslexia, contact the British Dyslexia Association★ or the Dyslexia Institute.★

Q *My child is in his third year at secondary school and I don't think he is making much progress in maths. I am worried that the class teacher is part of the problem. How can I find out whether or not my fears are justified?*

A Any concern you have about your child's subject teacher would best be taken up with the head of the department concerned. Telephone for an appointment. You could ask to see the schemes of work for that particular term and perhaps also some of the lesson plans for how these schemes of work are put into practice. If you are not satisfied after this, ask for an appointment to see the head teacher. If you are still not satisfied, write to the chairperson of the governors.

Q *My child, who has just transferred to secondary school, is being bullied. What can I do about it?*

A Make an appointment to see the form teacher. If this does not resolve the problem arrange to see the head of year. If this fails, see the head teacher. The school should have an anti-bullying policy, which teachers will discuss with you, and should take the matter seriously. If you are still not satisfied that the problem is being dealt with after you have seen the head, get in touch with the chairperson of the governors.

Q *I would rather my child did not attend our local school. What are the drawbacks to sending my child to a school outside the area?*

A The most obvious problems are likely to be distance and perhaps difficulty of travelling between home and school, and cost of transport. LEAs are unlikely to fund your child's transport to a school outside their area if what they deem to be an appropriate school is available within it. Also, bear in mind that your child's schoolfriends are always going to be a journey away and that this will make it difficult for younger children to see their friends after school. If the child is a little older, consider whether or not he or she will easily be able to stay on after school for clubs and societies.

Before making any decisions, it is also worth finding out if there are a lot of children who travel quite a long way to school or whether your child would be one of a small minority who do so. You may be able to find out from the school whether there are any other pupils who might share part or all of the journey and whether or not the school would be able to help in putting the children in touch with each other.

Q *My child hasn't yet started school. Do I have to send her or can I teach her myself at home?*

A You can teach her at home: although there is a legal duty on parents to make sure that their children are educated, this does not mean that their children have to attend school. See pages 99–100.

Q *Can my son study at home for re-sits of GCSEs? He doesn't want to go back to school to do this.*

A Yes, provided he enters himself as an external candidate. But do remember that periodically syllabuses change. Pupils intending to study at home for re-sits of GCSEs or A-levels should check to make sure that they know about any changes that might have taken place.

Q *I missed out on education when I was younger. I'm nearly thirty now and I regret not having any academic qualifications. Is it too late to get some?*

A No. There are more mature students today than ever in the past, and the options open to them for obtaining qualifications are wider than ever before. See pages 113–14.

Q *I'd like to improve my career prospects, but I can't afford to give up my job to go back to college. What can I study in my spare time?*

A There is a great deal on offer, whether you opt for an Open University course or one run by one of the many correspondence colleges that advertise in the national press. See pages 114–15.

CHAPTER 3

LOCAL GOVERNMENT

WE ALL live under some form of local government structure and rely on local councils for basic services which should serve us from cradle to grave. How we gain access to those councils, and the rights of the citizen to easy access, has become a major political issue in recent local elections. Every year election manifestos contain promises about consultation, partnership and power-sharing. How much each political party delivers on these issues, as well as on service delivery, is taken into account by voters at election time.

If you want to sort out an issue that falls within the remit of your local authority, you will have to get in touch with the local council, and in order to use the system effectively you need to be sure that you know whom to contact on which matter.

Local government structure

Local government is in a state of structural change. London government was last completely re-organised, into London boroughs and the Greater London Council (GLC), in 1963. The rest of Britain was re-organised in 1972 into a two-tier structure which placed most strategic roles and some service delivery in the hands of county councils (regions in Scotland), with the remaining services delivered by district councils. However, the government was opposed to the spending policies of the GLC and the metropolitan counties which ran the urban conurbations, councils which were usually run by the Labour Party, and so abolished them in 1986.

After the 1992 general election the government again decided to restructure the whole of local government but local opinion and the cost of change have led to a less wholesale approach. Some councillors felt an opportunity was missed in the 1992 consultation process to reduce the number of councils, especially county councils, and thereby simplify the system. Now, the local government map is beginning to take on the complexity it had before the re-organisation of 1972, a complexity that the 1972 changes were designed to eliminate.

London

There are 32 London boroughs, responsible for all the services within their area. These include education and youth employment, personal social services, housing, refuse collection and street cleansing, town planning, local roads and parking, recreation facilities and parks, environmental health and trading standards, cemeteries and crematoria and electoral registration. Elections to the boroughs take place every four years, at which time all councillors are elected.

The Corporation of the City of London remains an historical anachronism, owing more to the concept of government in the Middle Ages rather than twentieth-century democracy. The Corporation has all the powers of a London borough but over the years has also been made responsible for other areas of London such as Epping Forest and Coulsdon Common, which are miles away from the City's square mile. The population of the city is a mere 4,000.

The metropolitan districts (Mets)

The 36 Mets, created in 1972, make up the urban conurbations of the West Midlands, Merseyside, Greater Manchester, South Yorkshire, West Yorkshire, and Tyne and Wear. They carry out the same functions as the London boroughs. One-third of councillors stand for election in three years out of a four-year cycle, the year without elections being free because it was the year in which elections to the abolished metropolitan counties took place.

County councils

County councils cover most of England outside London and the conurbations. Since 1994 some county councils created in 1972 have been abolished and others have lost responsibility for some big towns or cities but retain responsibilities for the rest of their country areas.

As part of the mid–1990s re-organisation the counties of Avon, Cleveland, Hereford and Worcester, Humberside and the Isle of Wight have been abolished, although Herefordshire and Worcestershire are being re-created.

County councils are responsible for education, social services, strategic planning, national park and countryside functions, traffic and transportation issues, highways, caravan sites, trading standards, libraries and museums, refuse disposal, fire services and police.

County councillors are elected every four years, at which time all seats are up for election.

District councils

There are nearly 300 district councils in England, forming a second tier below the county councils. District councils are responsible for housing, swimming-pools and parks, car parks, town planning, cemeteries and crematoria, environmental health, refuse collection, and licensing of pubs and entertainments.

District councils have a choice as to the electoral cycle they follow. Most districts elect all their councillors once every four years, but some have opted to elect a third of their councillors in each year when they do not have county council elections.

Unitary authorities (England)

Unitary authorities are new creations. Those already in existence are the Isle of Wight, South Gloucestershire, Bristol, North West Somerset, Bath and North East Somerset, North East Lincolnshire, North Lincolnshire, Kingston-upon-Hull, East Riding of Yorkshire, City of York, Redcar and Cleveland, Middlesborough, Stockton-on-Tees and Hartlepool. In 1997 Bournemouth, Brighton and Hove, Darlington, Derby, Leicester, Luton, Milton

Keynes, Poole, Portsmouth, Rutland, Southampton, Stoke-on-Trent and Thamesdown will become functional. More are likely to be established in the future.

The unitary authorities have the same range of functions as the Mets.

The election cycle is variable, as for district councils.

Unitary authorities (Scotland and Wales)

The government chose to re-organise local government by a different process in Scotland and Wales and passed legislation to abolish the two-tier system of Scottish regions and districts and Welsh counties and districts and replace them with a single-tier unitary authority system.

The areas of responsibility are roughly the same as for the unitaries in England, with allowances made for different powers under the Scottish legal system.

Elections to all councils take place on a four-year cycle.

Town and parish councils

Some areas have town and parish councils (community councils in Wales), which are a third tier of local government. All parishes and communities must hold an annual meeting open to all voters. But if the parish has more than 200 electors, the district council must establish a formal parish council. (Smaller parishes may also opt to have a parish council.)

Parish, town and community councils are responsible for local footpaths, recreation grounds, cemeteries, street furniture (such as seats and bins), provision of allotments and suppression of public health nuisances. They also have the right to consider all local planning applications and to make recommendations to the planning authority. Other powers, such as licensing of pubs and taxis, can be delegated to parish, town and community councils, and there are proposals in a government white paper to delegate more functions to these councils.

Elections are held every four years, usually coinciding with district council elections, and generally the whole parish, town or community council is elected.

Town and parish councils do not exist in London of the metropolitan areas and do not cover the rest of Britain consistently as they are brought into existence by local petition and the agreement of the Secretary of State. Before you contact your council, check whether you have a parish or town council and, if so, what its powers are.

Councillors and politics

When you have worked out which council structure you have you must decide whether to talk to elected councillors or employed officers.

Party politics has gradually extended its grip over most of the local government map. In the 1970s the impact of independents was significant but now they are common only in rural Scotland and Wales, in the English rural areas on the borders of those countries, and in some parts of Cornwall and the counties of Lincolnshire and East Anglia.

Now most councillors will have stood with a party label and will be part of a political group on the council in much the same way as we see in the House of Commons. They will have stood on a local manifesto which will set out the way in which they view their relationship with their electorate. For example, voters need to know whether candidates view their election as giving them *carte blanche* for four years to do what they like or whether they have a commitment to ongoing consultation; whether they have a commitment to developing ways of devolving power to local people; whether they plan to develop local opinion polling and surveys, and if so whether this would extend to such issues as priorities for the annual budget.

Membership of a party does not itself affect the attitude of the councillor to his or her responsibility to constituents, but individual local councillors have different subject areas or activities on which they will concentrate. At the two extremes of activity, there are those who are interested only in doing casework on behalf of their local community and there are those who are interested only in the strategic direction of the council. Most councillors have a position somewhere between these two ends of the spectrum. If you are a constituent trying to get things done you may have to push some of your local representatives harder than others.

One point worth remembering is that councillors probably have a job and personal commitments. Many members of the public believe that they are elected in the same way as MPs and are paid as full-time employees. That is not the case. Indeed, many councillors make a decision to become active in politics knowing that it will limit their career prospects and earning power. Councillors are paid allowances for attendance at formal meetings and may get a responsibility allowance if they chair a committee. They are not paid anything for the many hours they spend on individual casework. Town, parish and community councillors do not even receive an allowance. The system is therefore very demanding of the individuals who take on the responsibility and it cannot work properly without a high degree of commitment from them (and which most give); however, it means that they are not always readily available to take calls or meet people and that they have to fit casework in amongst work and personal commitments.

All councils have a structure of committees on which councillors sit to develop and implement policy and to make decisions. The committee structure varies enormously from council to council, depending on the powers of the council and on the way in which councillors choose to organise themselves. There will probably be a powerful Policy and Resources Committee and there may be a number of resource committees or sub-committees, such as the Finance Committee, Personnel Committee and Property Committee, which look at the way council resources are used. There will also be a number of service committees, which are mainly responsible for spending the money, such as the Education Committee, Social Services Committee, Highways Committee, Leisure and Recreation Committee, and so on. Planning committees do not spend much money but their decisions on town planning in some places probably affect more people than almost any other committee.

Some local authorities are now developing neighbourhood committees, instead of some service committees, which make decisions on a range of services as they affect a defined geographical area.

The other activity of the ordinary councillor is to do casework on behalf of local people. The amount and type of casework will depend on the electoral ward which they represent. Some councillors will wait for constituents to contact them while others will go out and look for casework and may become the leader of local campaigns on issues such as traffic-calming or the installation of traffic lights. A councillor for a ward with large run-down council estates and pressing social needs will do personal housing and social service work on behalf of individuals or families. The councillor for an affluent ward may have more casework with groups on town planning and traffic issues.

In addition councillors in the political group running the council may have jobs as committee chairs with responsibility for the activities within the sphere of their committee. There will also be a Leader and Deputy Leader who are responsible for the strategic direction of the council as a whole.

Councillors in opposition parties may have jobs as spokespersons on particular committees or topics and be responsible for co-ordinating activity on a given subject, such as housing. There will also be a Leader and Deputy Leader responsible for the strategic direction of the group.

Councillors may also be involved with local trusts, charities and other groups, either because the council gives a grant to the organisation or because the organisation itself wishes to develop a partnership (not necessarily financial) with the council.

Council officers

Most people who contact the council deal with the paid officers who are responsible for the day-to-day business of the council. The smaller district councils employ only a few hundred staff whilst the larger counties employ over 10,000. Their jobs range from typists or technicians through social workers and planners to directors and chief executives. A small town, parish or community council may simply have a single clerk, though larger town councils may have more employees.

Most council staff see themselves as being there to help the public, but that is often not the way that they are seen by those they serve. Council housing tenants often regard their housing officer as the person who can evict them rather than the person who can help put a stop to a noise nuisance. A social worker may be perceived as the person who can take a child away from its family rather than as someone who provides support to people in need. Local government officers may be considered rather frightening people.

By being seen as too concerned with rules and regulations rather than community need, officers have not helped themselves. There has often been too little explanation as to why a course of action has been taken and so decisions are seen as arbitrary. But bear in mind that officers are there to carry out the policy of the council, so the officers may not have much discretion to waive or bend the rules.

Also, residents have often felt that they are not consulted enough, or are consulted only after a decision has been taken and it is too late to make any difference: however, this is not the fault of the officers, but of the councillors.

Partly, the poor reputation of council officers has come about because people are unaware of the mass of legislation that has to be enforced, and of the conflicting priorities that officers have to contend with, and do not appreciate the very real shortage of money and other resources with which local government has to cope. However, it has also evolved through conflict between cautious officers, who are protecting the council and identifying priorities (no easy task considering their over-stretched budgets) according to their professional judgement, and residents who see priorities in terms of the reality of their daily needs.

Since the mid–1980s many councils have attempted to tackle their image problem, through investment in customer care training, Citizen's Charter initiatives and comprehensive complaints procedures. Some of these strategies have been very effective in changing the culture of local authorities to one that is more customer-aware, but many have been seen as just another gimmick.

Many authorities are taking customer-conscious initiatives. One in Somerset has been to bring county, district and local councils together under one roof, so that a one-stop centre can serve a single area. This has made the system easier for the public to understand. In the end, it is up to local people to decide whether the cost of such an initiative is justified by the benefits.

Whom to contact at the council

Most officers prefer to be contacted first about a problem rather than after the issue has been raised with councillors. This may reflect a degree of defensiveness amongst officers and may be the result of a tendency amongst councillors to blame officers before they have the full details on which to take a view. Whatever the reason, there is no hard and fast rule and people should do whatever they consider to be most suitable for their personal circumstances. Large bureaucracies can be very daunting to ordinary people; a councillor may appear to be more user-friendly. The councillor may advise the constituent on whom to contact rather than deal with the case himself (or herself) in the first instance, but that will be a reflection of experience and knowledge of the best way to handle the problem.

Before you phone or write to the council, think about exactly what you need. It is better to tell the switchboard operator that you want to talk to someone about road crossings than to ask for the Highways Department and find that you are talking to someone who deals with road maintenance, or street trees, or street-sweeping or traffic-calming, and so on.

If you are writing to the council there are two alternatives. You could address the letter to the director of whichever department you need, such as the Director of Highways, or you could phone the council first and ask for the name of the officer who would actually be dealing with your query. Writing to the director will get your letter to the right person in the end but not necessarily as quickly as you would prefer, and it is more difficult to follow up if you do not receive a reply. If you have the name of the responsible officer then you can develop direct access and follow-up will be easier. Always ask for the name of the person you have dealt with even if he or she has just taken a message for someone else. You can get a feel for the council's customer care standards through the willingness staff show in giving out their names. All too often, officers prefer to remain anonymous.

What to do if you are not satisfied with the response

If you are not satisfied with the service which you are getting, ask whether there is a Citizen's Charter for that department and ask for it to be sent to you. In itself this may produce a more co-operative attitude as some officers prioritise their work on the basis of which customer may give them the most difficulty.

Not all councils have a Charter. This is not because they do not care about service but may reflect the councillors' view that the Charter was a government gimmick without substance. If they do have a Charter, it should give an indication of the standard of service constituents can expect so that you can judge your situation against their standard. But watch for the council that has set a low standard.

If you are still not getting the service you require, ask the officer for a copy of the complaints procedure (especially if you did not like the way that you were personally treated) or ask for the phone number of your local councillor. Staff should be willing to provide you with either of these. If they are not then make sure that your councillor knows that too.

Finally, if you are still not getting anywhere, contact your local government ombudsman.

When, and on what issues, to contact a councillor

There is nothing that a local council does that should not be open to scrutiny and question. People have the right to talk to their councillor about any council service with which they are dissatisfied or where they need help. A councillor may not support the constituent's position but should at least explain why.

Gone are the days when it was difficult to get access to a councillor's address and phone number. You will be be able to get that information from the council offices if it is not made available by the councillors themselves through local newsletters.

Councillors can make direct representations to officers on an individual basis and most individual casework is done in this way. Typically, if a resident contacts a councillor about, say, a housing case the councillor will then speak to the housing officer in charge of the case. In some cases the councillor may arrange a meeting between the officer and the resident. Often that will be enough, especially where the complaint is about the speed at which something is happening (or not). It is a sad truth that residents often accomplish things more quickly if they have a councillor speaking on their behalf.

Of course, it can be argued with some justification that it is unfair that a resident will be dealt with more quickly if a councillor is involved. One day, perhaps, councils will be sufficiently open and responsive, and resourced, for residents not to feel that they have to have a councillor on their side in order to get a prompt reply and an effective service. For the time being, however, it is as well to realise that life is not always fair.

Where residents have a more complex case which deals with a number of people or where the problem to be resolved requires money to be spent (for example, on a traffic-calming measure), the councillor will probably need to get the issue put on the agenda of a council committee. In such cases councillors may need to lobby both their own council group and others.

For this type of issue (traffic-calming) a town or parish council can also be a very effective ally. Constituents can place a public question or send a letter to the town or parish council, or ask a councillor to place the item on the agenda. That council can then lobby the district or county council, and because the town or parish council is the more expert on local needs and conditions its lobby can carry some weight.

Public attendance at council meetings

The public has the right to attend most committees and all full council meetings and the agenda have to be published and made available. Some items remain confidential where they affect contracts, individual staff or legal issues. Many councils allow for the presentation of petitions to committees, either directly or through a councillor. Many also allow deputations to talk to committees, and in a small number of cases committees will allow members of the public to take part in debates, although in a limited way.

On planning committees there is often a perception that individual planning applications are not political issues, so there is a much greater degree of cross-party voting. This is very useful when a planning application, perhaps for a block of flats in a road of semi-detached houses, is unpopular. In planning cases the normal method is for officers to make a recommendation to the committee based on the planning policies of the council. Planners are naturally cautious people, likely to recommend permission rather than refusal on planning applications that are borderline, because they are worried about the costs of a public enquiry, which could be called for if they refuse planning permission. Councillors are usually less cautious and are more likely to refuse applications in borderline cases where there is public opposition to an application.

On highways committees, too, councillors will often take a more populist line than council officers, especially when it comes to traffic-calming measures and pedestrian crossings. Many people find council engineers to be amongst the least public-friendly officers employed by the council. This is because they take a professional engineering view of need rather than a resident's view.

Of course, in the battle for scarce resources and money the engineers may have a valid point about technical priority between one crossing and another and councillors have to take this into account when making responsible decisions. However, it is the councillor who is directly responsible to the residents though the electoral process, not the engineer.

Taking more direct action

If you are getting directly involved in an issue and are intending to organise a campaign, ask yourself the following questions:

- have you got enough support to set up a campaign group?
- will you have the support of your councillor and, if so, to what extent?
- if your own councillor will not support you, would his or her political opponents?
- is it worth raising a petition?
- will you be able to take a deputation to a council committee?
- will the press be interested?

Some issues involve more than one person. If you object to a planning application it is always worth seeing if other people in your road feel the same way. If you are interested in getting a pedestrian crossing you will be far more successful if other people agree with you. No council is going to spend £80,000 on a toucan crossing if only one person wants it and there has never been an accident at that location. The proximity of an election can also have an effect on council decisions.

You could begin your campaign by asking for the support of your councillor. Councillors may have more experience in developing a public campaign and they may have the time to head one up for you. If yours does not have the time to deal with this within the timescale you have in mind, at least find out if he or she is prepared to back you. Of course, your councillor may disagree with your campaign. If so, find out whether he or she will at least present a petition on your behalf through the council's petitions process. Most councillors are prepared do this.

Raising a petition is not as daunting as it may sound. Collecting signatures is fairly easy if the petition is about something that people feel strongly about, for or against. If it is a petition to achieve something positive, like a pedestrian crossing, many people will sign even if they do not feel strongly about it. People are always prepared to support something that is positive even if it does not directly affect them.

When writing the text of the petition try to be dispassionate, especially if you are opposing something, like a planning application. Using words like 'disgusting', 'outrageous' and so on may make the petitioner feel good but could have a negative effect on councillors or officers whom you want on your side. If it is a planning issue, and the application is going to the Planning Committee, the officers will have to tell the councillors about the petition and the objections. They are required to do so by law.

Deputations to committees are useful for getting your point across without fear of officers re-interpreting your concerns or putting more emphasis on the opposite view. You would have a limited amount of time to present your own case, usually about five minutes, and councillors will usually then ask questions. The experience is not as bad as it sounds. Councillors are usually pretty polite and attentive, even if they disagree with you. It is always useful to have a deputation of more than one person, and to have your supporters in the public gallery. After all, you are trying to persuade councillors and officers that you have public support and that you should be listened to. The more support you have, the more politicians will start thinking about your voting strength at election time.

Try to involve the press. A good local interest story that involves ordinary people taking on the council or big developers can make the front page, especially in free papers, and creates a lot of awareness amongst councillors. Phone your local newspapers; issue a press release (setting out precisely what you are trying to achieve and why, under a clearly worded heading, and with your contact name and telephone number); and write letters to the editor for publication.

Even if your campaign eventually fails, press coverage will have spread information to a much wider audience and may prove to be the snowball that turns into an avalanche at a later date.

On highly emotional issues people often try to highlight a situation through direct action: for example, by climbing trees that are due to be cut down, or blocking roads that are dangerous. This will certainly get press interest because it is very visual and will make a good front-page photo. It may also be illegal. Some issues may be worth getting arrested for, but do think about the implications. You may also alienate more people than you impress.

Questions and answers

Q *Something is being built next door without planning permission. What should I do?*

A Whenever someone applies for planning permission the Planning Department is required to notify all affected properties. Officers' interpretation of this requirement can vary widely, from notifying the next-door neighbours to contacting the entire street. Make sure that your objections are registered. Sometimes householders start building work before getting permission. As soon as you notice building going on to which you object, contact the enforcement officer in the local council's Planning

Department to find out whether the householder has permission, and, if so, for what. It is not unusual for people to get planning permission for something that no one objects to and then build something taller or larger.

Planning departments usually do not have the staff to check on all developments, especially the smaller ones. They rely on neighbours to be vigilant for them. This also means that they do not give priority to infringements of planning permission that no one makes a fuss about. Make sure that you get the name of the enforcement officer and arrange a time when someone will come and inspect the site. Confirm it in writing so that there is no misunderstanding about how serious you take the situation to be.

If you are not satisfied with the result, contact your councillor. Enforcement cases that have attracted the interest of a councillor are likely to rise in the list of priorities.

Note that it is not easy to get an unauthorised development 'reversed': if it would have received consent, then it will stand; enforcement of a reversal decision is a lengthy procedure.

Household extensions may appear to affect only one neighbour but their presence can cause more widespread concern, so it is worth finding out what other neighbours think. A petition to the council will help you to get priority.

In this sort of situation you may wish the objections to be anonymous so that the householder (probably a neighbour) does not know exactly who is complaining: councillors and officers should respect that. Neighbour violence has been known in some cases. Under these circumstances it is not usually helpful to involve the press.

Keep making a nuisance of yourself to the officers and the councillors until you get a result. Be polite if you can, though, because you need their support. But do not let them think that the matter has gone away when it has not.

Q *I want to have a pedestrian crossing set up on a busy road. How do I go about it?*

A Crossings are expensive. The least expensive is the old-fashioned zebra crossing. The toucan crossing, with pedestrian-directed traffic lights, is very costly. Pedestrian refuges in the middle of a busy road are often a reasonable compromise. A good case has to be made in order to get a crossing and it is worth approaching the councillors before the officers. You need their support for having money put into very tight capital programmes.

It is worth doing some research first and finding out what the accident rate is on that road. Fear of possible accidents may not be a powerful enough argument. The police are often helpful, at least in giving anecdotal evidence, and they will have details of all reported accidents. The more accidents there have been, the greater the chance of getting a crossing.

This is certainly the sort of issue that is helped by a petition, especially if the crossing is to be sited near a school or shopping parade. Petitions of parents and teachers or shopkeepers are effective because they represent a recognised sectional interest group. Collecting a petition outside the school gates is always helpful because you may find like-minded people who are prepared to help.

Deputations to the Highways Committee will also help, especially if you can get a lot of people along to the meeting to show the strength of feeling. It would be a very brave councillor who refused to hear a petition on a road safety issue.

The council's engineer will come to the committee meeting armed with statistics about numbers of vehicles using the road, the speed of traffic and the number of accidents. Residents will talk about how they feel and the fears they have for the children and the elderly. The safety of a road is often about perception rather than about engineering problems and solutions. A councillor will often be more in tune with the depth of public feeling and will care less about the issues that concern the engineers. After all, a councillor is elected to represent the residents, not to represent the engineers.

The press will also enjoy this sort of campaign, especially if there is an accident black-spot to focus on and provide a photograph.

As with all matters raised with the council, persistence pays. Examples abound of projects that have been turned down, even by the Department for Transport, as being too costly; but if a council is really convinced by the force of the argument and is prepared to get behind the project, it is not unknown for councillors to arrange to have the data (for example, on traffic volumes) collected that could get the decision reversed.

Q *I want to have a traffic-calming scheme introduced in my area. What do I do?*

A Traffic-calming is another expensive exercise for a council: one ordinary road hump costs about £2,000. Comprehensive traffic-calming schemes can easily cost hundreds of thousands of pounds.

One of the problems with these schemes is that you are unlikely to get unanimous support. Certainly you should try to get councillors involved early and should work out what sort of scheme you would like, though without committing to a solution. Your initial aim is to get the Highways Committee to instruct officers to work up some options which can be put forward for public consultation. A certain amount of work can be done even if no money is immediately available, because the work can be used as the basis of a bid for a government grant.

Petitions and deputations are again helpful. It is not so easy for newspapers to focus on as a crossing unless there has been a serious accident, so you may consider organising an open meeting for local people or some sort of demonstration at the spot that causes most concern.

Campaigns on traffic-calming can be very frustrating. Typically, a scheme will take up to two years to plan and implement and, if money is tight, a scheme may be put off for a higher priority. But if new development is taking place and contributing to the problem (for example, by increasing pedestrian usage of a busy road), it may be possible to get a contribution to the calming scheme from the developer through a planning obligation (a tactic which stands a better chance of succeeding since the cost to the public is reduced).

It is very important to keep up the pressure for implementation after the decision to proceed is made, by writing to or phoning the responsible highways officer or councillors. Never be put off.

If traffic schemes have some political support but the officers are not so supportive you would be surprised how many obstacles can be put in the way of implementation. Do not end the campaign until the scheme has been built.

Q *My neighbours are noisy. Who is responsible for making them be quiet?*

A Councillors tend not to like cases involving noisy neighbours, which are very difficult to resolve where the residents are owner-occupiers. The police are responsible for disorder and nuisance. The council is responsible for noise pollution. One of the difficulties is that prosecutions require evidence, which is not always easy to get when the noise occurs irregularly.

A few councils have established noise patrols which can be called out, but most have not. It is not seen as a priority for most councils, because they are likely to have other calls on their budgets, in (say) social services or education, that they consider more important.

Councillors will take on an advocate role to get officers to investigate, but this role may be limited if there are no officers specifically employed to carry out call-out duties. At officer level you will usually find a great deal of sympathy. You may be asked to make a note of incidents, but bear in mind that officers' powers are limited to dealing with very loud noise.

The situation is easier where the parties are council tenants. Most council rent agreements will contain a good neighbour clause and the council has the power to evict persistent offenders. Housing officers will ask you to keep records. Officers do not really like having to evict people and the legal processes take some months, even when pursued vigorously. You need to keep up the pressure on the officers, perhaps using your councillor, to make sure that action is taken as quickly as possible. It is one of those areas where housing departments can blame the legal departments for delay and *vice versa*.

As this book went to press, a new Noise Act was passed that provides authorities with additional powers to deal with the problem of excessive noise from domestic premises at night. The

Act creates a new night-time noise offence and clarifies the powers available to local authorities to confiscate noise-making equipment. An objective standard will be used to measure noise where appropriate.

Q *I can't get my child into the school of my choice. What do I do?*

A See Chapter 2 (pages 89–92). The powers of the councillor to intervene are strictly limited. There is an appeals procedure and the Education Department should readily provide you with information and advice on how to proceed with the appeal. The appeal hearing itself involves councillors and lay people and they will consider mainly social and health issues when reaching their decisions.

Briefing your local councillor and getting support may be helpful but councillors are reticent about getting involved in what is a quasi-legal process in which so many people are caught.

Q *The old people's home where my mother lives is being sold off. How do I stop it?*

A A decision to sell an elderly person's home, whether to a private provider or to the voluntary non-profit sector, will usually have been a political decision rather than a professional officer recommendation. The campaign of which you might become part is bound to have a political, and party political element.

A council has to demonstrate a duty of care and consult the residents of a home, their relatives and advocates. Council officers are likely to be extremely sympathetic and to allow people to express their views. To affect the decision, however, you would need to get access to the politicians who are key to the process. This will involve councillors who sit on the Social Services Committee and certainly the chair and vice-chair of the committee.

It is important that, as a responsible relative, you become part of a group. All of the residents and their relatives are likely to be worried. Press the council to call a meeting of all those involved at the home and make sure that you are able to get access at that meeting to the relatives' names and addresses. Establish a link group responsible for putting pressure on the council and keeping everyone in touch, particularly about the dates and times of the Social Services committee meetings where decisions are to be taken.

Use all the devices at your command. Raise petitions, organise deputations, and make sure that the committees are well attended by your supporters. If there are political parties and councillors who will support you, by all means use them but avoid their being labelled as political tools. Use the media. This is the sort of issue that the press will love: for those who are trying to close the home, it will be a political nightmare.

CHAPTER 4

PARLIAMENT

THE UNITED Kingdom is currently divided up into 651 constituencies, due to increase to 659 in the 1996/7 general election. Each constituency is represented by a Member of Parliament, elected by a relative majority according to a system known as 'first past the post'. This voting system almost invariably means that the party allegiances of those elected as MPs are not in the same proportions as the votes cast throughout the country for their various parties, and that the overall majority of the electorate in any given constituency may not have voted for its sitting MP. However, this has no bearing on your MP's duty to represent you, regardless of how you voted.

General elections must be held at least every five years. In the run-up to a general election each of the main political parties in the constituencies selects a candidate, in respect of which local constituency parties hold considerable sway over their MPs. Each MP is answerable to his/her constituency organisation as well as to the central headquarters of the party represented, which can be important if an MP takes a stance against official party policy (perhaps at a constituent's behest). In addition to the main party candidates there are 'independent' candidates who are not affiliated to a particular national political party but may be campaigning on a single issue, such as the environment or demands for a referendum on Europe, or a local issue. At the time of writing, nine parties are represented in the House of Commons: Conservative, Labour, Liberal Democrat, Scottish National Party, Plaid Cymru, Social Democratic and Labour Party, Ulster Unionist, Ulster Democratic Unionist and United Kingdom Unionist. One MP is an Independent.

What MPs do

There is no formal job description setting out what MPs must do, and nothing to say they have to fulfil their election promises. No 'MPs' Charter' specifies the amount of time they must spend on constituency business, how quickly they should reply to letters, and so forth. But they are in Parliament because the voters elected them, so they need you as much as you need them. It is your vote that decides their future, and provides them with their legitimacy in Parliament. They will have fought a general election not only on the policies of a wider political party, but on local issues ranging from new roads (for or against) to local employment opportunities. If they need to bend a minister's ear to make this change, a groundswell of support in the constituency will prove invaluable in gaining a sympathetic hearing.

Like any individual, each MP will have particular interests and opinions, and how much your MP can achieve for you will depend very much on the individual case and the MP in question. It will also depend on the research assistance the MP has available, and the contribution the local party agent and other helpers make to constituency work. All MPs receive an 'office allowance' to put towards these costs, but this is set (currently at £46,634 per annum) regardless of the electoral size and geographical distribution of the constituency represented.

Getting an MP to champion your cause

If you want to get an MP to back an issue, consider it first from the MP's point of view. What is it that makes your case special? Why should your MP give more than a cursory glance to your request for time when there are 70,000 other voters in his or her constituency potentially clamouring for attention?

If your cause falls into a subject area that you know to be a particular interest of the MP, you are likely to get a sympathetic hearing. Check local press reports, *Hansard* and so forth to see what issues he or she has acted upon in the past and what 'spin' would work to your advantage.

Try to get the press, the chamber of commerce or the local branch of a trade union involved on your side. MPs are responsive to local press pressure: the anticipation of a popular cause, and publicity, may swing the decision to expend some effort on your behalf.

Contact the MP's researcher or secretary. If you can get him or her to back you, your battle may be as good as won, because such people will know how to enlist the MP's support. Most are hard-pressed for time, but many act as the MP's main adviser on what is worth taking up.

You may also be able to get some local councillors behind your campaign. If the MP's party is running the council, and you have councillors supporting you, the chances are that he or she will pay attention to what is being said. Even if a different party is in charge of the council, it is worth getting some of the minority councillors on board and bringing their influence to bear.

If you can get an MP to champion your cause, you may be well on your way to beating a blockage in another part of the 'system'. House of Commons notepaper can be a valuable weapon in getting a problem acknowledged or solved, and it may be that your MP has already found a way of overcoming official obstruction when dealing with similar constituency casework. However, while they may work wonders on individual problems, do not over-estimate an MP's ability to change the course of government policy – whatever his or her political allegiance.

MPs and local councillors: how they differ

Local and general elections are completely separate affairs, and your MP may be of a different political hue to your local council. Your MP is elected to represent you in the national Parliament, the seat of central democratic decision-making. Your local council is elected to ensure that local responsibilities such as housing, education, planning and social services are handled in the most efficient manner. The relationship between local and central government is inherently a financial one: Parliament allocates funds to local authorities and it is up to them to spend them wisely. There are certainly areas of cross-over, but it is important to be clear in your mind as to whether your problem is first and foremost one for your local councillor or for your MP.

Action that can be taken by MPs

Contacting an MP is often seen as a last resort when all else has failed. It should not be. Although any MP will soon tire of you if you deluge him with every problem encountered, you need not wait until you are at your wits' end before asking whether he or she can help. If a travel company has already gone into liquidation, taking your money with it, or your local railway station has already seen the last train depart, it is a bit late to expect your MP to work miracles.

When and how to contact your MP largely depends on why you are asking for help. Are you looking for a solution to a personal problem, such as a complaint against a company which seems to be going nowhere? Are you asking your MP to take on a local cause, such as the closure of a school, hospital or local youth club, or do you want to bring about a change in public policy – on, say, pensions regulation, the council tax or the right to buy the freehold of your house or flat?

If you are looking for help on a personal matter, do check that you have tried the best route to getting your problem solved before you contact your MP. For example, if there is a problem with refuse collection or local road re-surfacing work, you should take it up first with your local council and the contractors in question before involving your MP. The problem might be something the local government ombudsman should review, or, if the complaint is about failings in the health services, referred to the local health authority, and perhaps subsequently the Health Service Commissioner (ombudsman). Various types of ombudsmen are listed in the address section of this book as appropriate.

If you are campaigning on a local matter, alert your MP at an early stage: he or she may have ideas on how to attract support, and will help you to interest the local press. For example, the threatened closure of the Settle–Carlisle railway was halted after a well publicised campaign in Parliament and the constituencies.

If you wish to register an objection to public policy, the sooner you alert your MP to your concerns, the better. Once a law has been made, it can take years to amend it, but if it is still sitting on a civil servant's desk or being debated by Parliament, there is still the chance that MPs can change a minister's mind, especially if it can be demonstrated that the policy change will have an adverse effect on constituents.

Making contact with MPs

There are various ways of getting in touch with your MP. If you do not know who your MP is, ask at your local library or town hall, or contact the local political party headquarters, to find out who it is and when and where he/she holds surgeries.

MPs' surgeries

These are sessions at which you can raise all manner of issues directly with your MP; they are usually held on a Friday, sometimes Saturday, once a week or once a fortnight. You do not normally need to make an appointment, but if you have a complicated matter to discuss ring the local constituency party or the MP's office in the House of Commons★ to arrange a time in advance.

Surgeries are generally taken up with more personal matters than issues of policy (such as housing or social security) and your MP can be a powerful ally not only in Parliament but in contacting local authorities or private companies: if you have a problem, for example, with a car manufacturer who is refusing to recognise what is probably a design fault, or a travel company that is ignoring your request for compensation, a negligent surveyor, or similar matter, a letter on House of Commons paper can be a prod to action. It alerts companies to the fact that you are not going to let the matter drop and will use all the means available to pursue your case.

There are no set rules for MPs' constituency work, so the frequency, length and effectiveness of surgeries depends very much on the MP. An MP who is also a minister is not necessarily more or less involved in constituency matters than an Opposition backbencher and may be much more effective than a back-bench MP in raising issues with a government department, since he will be writing to ministerial colleagues on your behalf.

Letters, e-mail and phone calls

MPs receive huge amounts of mail from a wide range of people and organisations every week. If you want to get your letter noticed, it will help if the envelope is handwritten and the postmark and address are from within the constituency. This alerts the MP to the fact that it is a constituency matter rather than a briefing paper or a company's mail-out. Letters to MPs should be concise and clear and copies of any relevant documents – previous correspondence, etc. – should be enclosed with them.

If you are writing on a personal matter and you know of others in the constituency with the same problem (for example, road works disrupting water or gas supplies on a regular basis), ask them to write in similar terms and cross-refer. If the matter is one of policy, or a local campaign, again get as many others as possible to write to the MP, but avoid using standard letters – they tend to get standard responses.

Alternatively, many MPs now have e-mail addresses, so if you have access to an electronic mail system this may be quicker. However, some MPs still deal with all correspondence in the same manner regardless of the means of communication. Also, e-mail may not be the best method of contact if you want your request to be forwarded on to a minister for his answer, or to a company for its response. If you are providing supporting documents, again, you should use the ordinary mail system. If you *do* use e-mail, keep a hard copy of your message so that it can be referred to in later correspondence.

The main political parties are also making increasing use of the Internet. Political parties now have Web sites detailing their policies and some MPs encourage interactive debate on-line.

The address for all MPs is the House of Commons★ and if you telephone an MP there the main switchboard will find a way to leave messages for MPs who are unavailable.

Meetings

If you want to have a face-to-face discussion with your MP, other than in the limited time available for surgeries, always write first requesting a private meeting. Although every constituent is entitled to go to the Central Lobby of the House of Commons and ask to see his or her MP, an unannounced meeting would be risky, because the odds on your MP being available, willing to see you and able to remember the details of your case are not good.

If you have arranged a meeting with your MP, go well prepared with documentation to back up what you are saying. Think about what you are going to say beforehand, to ensure that you cover everything relevant and keep the meeting on track. Depending on the nature of your problem, it may be worth having copies of papers you can leave behind as an aide-memoire: if you do this, bear in mind that reams of paper will not be well received.

After the meeting, it would be polite to write thanking your MP for his/her time.

Mass lobbies

If you are taking part in a mass lobby of Parliament, perhaps one organised by a pressure group or union (see 'Campaigning groups', page 151) in protest about some failing of government policy or impending changes in the law, it is worth writing to your MP in advance to say that you are intending to take part, thereby registering your support for the cause and increasing the chance of your MP being there to listen to your concerns.

Getting information

Information is power. If your information is not as complete, authoritative and up-to-date as possible you could waste a lot of time and effort – both yours and other people's. Do not assume that your MP will already have all the facts on any given issue. The more clearly you are able to set out the facts, the better-off you will be; and the more your MP is convinced that you know what you are talking about, the more confidence he/she will have in what you say. If you are raising a national issue, it is important to know before you approach an MP what his position is on the issue, and to know what the government's position is; and whether there are important recommendations, from a select committee or other body, which help your case. Use a local library to help you: librarians themselves can be invaluable at such times. Collect local or national press cuttings as appropriate.

You should also look at the information put out by Parliament itself. Parliament is continually publishing committee reports and recommendations, as well as *Hansard*, the daily record of proceedings in both Houses. These publications are available from HMSO bookshops and other bookshops will order them for you.

If the topic in question is coming up in a debate in the House of Commons and you wish to attend, you can either go there and queue (probably for some time, especially in summer) or write to your MP asking for tickets. Each MP is allocated daily tickets, but if you want to go to Prime Minister's Question Time or listen to a particular minister you will probably have to request tickets well in advance as demand is high.

The House of Commons also has a Public Information Office,* as have all of the government departments and the main political parties; staff may be able to point you in the right direction for obtaining more information to build up your case. If you think information exists that is being withheld from you, you may be able to request it through the Code of Practice on Access to Government Information (see 'Referral to the Parliamentary Commissioner', page 149).

Action an MP can take on your behalf

What your MP can do to help you will depend on the nature of the case. MPs can help by getting more information for you, or by ensuring that some body or organisation looks at your case more seriously than it did when you pursued the matter in the past. In seeking information, the MP can table a parliamentary question (for example, to establish how many dentists in your area still treat patients under the NHS) or may write on your behalf to the relevant minister (asking, for example, why no dentist in your area is prepared to treat you under the NHS).

If it is a matter of getting a company or other organisation to take note of your previous representations, a letter from your MP on House of Commons notepaper may do the job in itself. If not, the MP may suggest referring the matter to an ombudsman, or have a word with some of his/her colleagues to see whether they have been contacted by constituents with similar complaints, and co-ordinate the action to be taken.

If you have suffered a major injustice, or you have demonstrated that the issue is important, whether locally (and affecting a considerable number of constituents) or nationally, your MP may decide to take further action; if the matter illustrates a failing of government policy and your MP is a member of the Opposition, he/she may be keen to highlight it. The MP may raise the matter in a short adjournment debate, to which the relevant minister will have to give an answer, or he/she may publicise it through a Private Member's bill.

Be aware, however, that the chances of such bills succeeding are very remote: this option is normally used more for gaining publicity for a cause than in the expectation that legislation will result. But if the bill attracts sufficient support from the government, it could succeed.

For example, in 1995 David Jamieson MP used a Private Member's bill to ensure that all children's activity centres were registered following the death of some of his constituents in a canoeing accident at Lyme Bay. Other MPs have succeeded by this means in changing the law to ensure that patients have the right to see their medical records, to improve consumers' rights to a refund on faulty goods, and a host of other issues.

Approaching relevant authorities

A typical personal complaint about an authority or firm, such as one concerning bad treatment from a public utility, will seldom be investigated personally by an MP: if MPs did so, all their time would be taken up on people's personal complaints. The first step taken by your MP may be to forward your letter to the minister responsible and ask for comments. You could write directly to the minister, but the intervention of your MP is likely to mean that the problem is dealt with at a more senior level, achieving a response signed by the minister, and more promptly.

Until quite recently, MPs could expect a personal reply from ministers, but there is a trend now towards dealing with executive agencies, where relevant (for instance, the Benefits Agency for a benefits issue) or officials with hands-on experience.

Letters have several advantages over other parliamentary means at your MP's disposal: they can be sent at any time, rather than just during the parliamentary session, and they can enclose material of a more confidential or private nature.

If there is more than one person with the same problem, your MP may arrange a delegation to put the case personally to the minister or the officials in charge.

Tabling parliamentary questions and adjournment debates

If your MP is not happy with the response to the letter, he or she may decide to 'go public' (though not with any personal information you have provided, except with your explicit permission). This means utilising some of the other standard procedures. MPs can table parliamentary questions to the minister to try to obtain a fuller answer (which will then be on the record for all to see); this tactic has been used in connection with Gulf War Syndrome and also, frequently, in cases clearly referring to an individual constituent where there has been substantial delay in dealing with the matter. Other possibilities are to table an 'Early Day Motion' (which will not be debated but to which other MPs can put their signatures, thus indicating support) or request an adjournment debate.

An adjournment debate is one conducted 'on the adjournment' of the House of Commons, i.e. at the close of business, whereby a back-bench MP speaks for around 15 minutes on the subject of his or her choice and a minister then responds. One example of such a debate, in June 1991, concerned an incident in Canada in which three young guardsmen had their legs blown off in a training accident. Their lawyers faced official obstruction in getting hold of the necessary information to pursue a negligence claim. Jonathan Sayeed, the constituency MP of one of the guardsmen, succeeded in calling an adjournment debate to highlight the problem, and secured a commitment from the minister that further information would be released. After some 200 MPs had signed an Early Day Motion calling for further action, the Ministry of Defence agreed to meet the injured grenadiers' solicitors.

For matters of wider concern, a back-bench MP can request a Wednesday-morning debate: these are longer and more speakers take part. MPs who are ministers do not have this means at their disposal but can arrange for a parliamentary colleague to raise the matter – perhaps a neighbouring MP. These types of debates are an effective means of alerting ministers to strong feelings on particular subjects.

Adjournment debates and questions may not get you the answers you want – MPs have no power to force an answer – but they can be useful in generating publicity. Furthermore, when speaking in Parliament MPs are protected by parliamentary privilege, which means they can risk making allegations (about child abusers or miscarriages of justice, for example) when no one outside feels they have the necessary evidence to support a public campaign.

Referral to the Parliamentary Commissioner for Administration (Ombudsman)

If the nature of your complaint is one of maladministration by government departments or their agencies (for example, the Child Support Agency) or certain public bodies, your MP can take the case to the Parliamentary Commissioner for Administration★ (Ombudsman) for investigation. However, you must have exhausted the internal complaint mechanism of the particular department or agency first, so be sure to tell your MP you have done so. Whilst the Ombudsman's recommendations are normally taken by the department under scrutiny, there have been exceptions.

The Ombudsman also rules on official secrecy: if you are being denied access to information to which you think are entitled, you can ask your MP to ask the Ombudsman to investigate. In April 1996 Consumers' Association, working alongside the research group Social Audit, had a case concerning data on prescriptions referred to the Ombudsman following many attempts by Social Audit to get information from the Department of Health – and being continually denied for reasons that did not seem to hold water. The MP Hugh Bayley referred the case to the Ombudsman under the Code of Practice on Access to Government Information, which is a government commitment to supplying information to the public on request. The Department of Health has now released the information it had refused to make available for several years, and the Ombudsman's decision is awaited at the time of going to press.

Almost all central government departments and their agencies are covered by the Code. If you would like information on a particular subject, write to the relevant department or agency setting out as clearly and precisely as possible exactly what information you require. Provided that this is not commercially sensitive or on sensitive matters of defence, national security or law enforcement, the information should in theory be sent to you. The Code specifies that a response should be given within 20 days, although in practice often all that arrives is an acknowledgement. You may be charged for the information provided. The cost and charging framework varies from department to department, so ask about charges when you request the information.

If you feel that you have been unfairly denied information, ask the relevant department to review its decision; if this does not result in the information being provided, you can then ask an MP to take the case to the Ombudsman.

In addition to the parliamentary Ombudsman, various other ombudsmen have been appointed by particular professional or trade bodies to investigate complaints and to gain redress for consumers; this they typically do more effectively, quickly and cheaply than the courts. Most ombudsmen belong to the British and Irish Ombudsman Association, which sets out the standards to which they must adhere, such as maintaining independence from the industry over which they preside. Several ombudsmen are listed in the address section at the back of this book.

Exerting pressure through publicity

Your MP is likely to have access to more information than you and should be a useful tool in obtaining publicity, locally if not nationally. He or she will have established contacts with the local press and will always be happy to be reported as working for constituents. He/she will also be aware of the political climate and the potential for change and will be able to advise you on the likelihood of success. The local press, at least, will take much more notice of your campaign if you have your MP on your side.

Another useful weapon is a petition. A 'photo opportunity' with the MP and constituents handing a mammoth petition in to 10 Downing Street, or constituents handing one to an MP outside Parliament, is fairly sure to draw the attention of some media. Afterwards, your MP can present the petition to Parliament. It may be that the other people you persuade to sign it do not care as deeply about the matter as you, but you will have provided your MP with proof that you are not the only one who may make a nuisance of him or herself if someone in authority does not take note.

Campaigning groups

Various pressure groups, or special-interest groups, devote their time and effort to speaking on behalf of particular groups of people, then target particular MPs who they believe will be sympathetic to their cause, rather than their local MP alone. A wide variety of all-party parliamentary subject or country groups exists, comprising MPs and peers with interests in a range of subjects from asthma to water. The secretariat of all-party groups is often provided by an interest group or section from industry (such as the Cable Communications Association, which provides the secretariat to the all-party Cable and Satellite TV group). They meet at regular intervals to debate and discuss their subject. However, these are ad-hoc groups: some may meet regularly and hold debates, others are a group in name only.

Your being a member of a pressure group, and having a problem/complaint that it is prepared to take up on your behalf, may increase the likelihood of MPs becoming involved, and the number who do so.

MPs will pass any direct constituency matters on to the relevant MP but may speak on a subject relating to another member's constituency.

Typical campaigning groups include CAMRA (the Campaign for Real Ale), the Campaign for Freedom of Information and the Campaign Against Residential Landlord Abuse; Age Concern and Help the Aged campaign on behalf of the elderly, on a range of issues from long-term care insurance to housing; Friends of the Earth champion the environment; Transport 2000 works towards a better, integrated transport system. Consumers' Association (CA) campaigns on behalf of consumers on a range of issues, many of which are initiated by consumer complaints and problems drawn to its attention by subscribers to the magazine *Which?*. Its activities have on several occasions resulted, ultimately, in changes in the law. One of its greatest successes was the Unfair Contract Terms Act of 1977, which Lord Denning described as 'one of the most important [civil] reforms in our time'. CA was also responsible for the Unsolicited Goods and Services Act of 1971, the Consumer Credit Act of 1974, the Cheques Act 1992, the Property Misdescriptions Act 1991, revisions to legislation that brought about an improved Sale and Supply of Goods Act in 1994, and for breaking the solicitors' monopoly on conveyancing.

The House of Lords

Members of the House of Lords, comprising hereditary and life peers, are not elected and have no constituents to represent. Although the Lords are under no obligation to help with personal problems, they may be able to help if you are seeking publicity for a local issue, or want to draw attention to a concern relating to public policy. Sometimes they act as party spokesmen on a particular subject, and they can make useful allies if you want to get certain local or national problems acknowledged.

Peers have much the same weapons in their publicity armoury as an MP: tabling questions, speaking in debates, writing to ministers, etc. Some sustain long-running campaigns to get information or acknowledgement of fault from departments. For example, one peeress has long battled to make the government acknowledge the occupational hazards of sheep-dip. The House of Lords also has a role in scrutinising legislation, other than financial matters, and can bring about revisions to legislation or even change the course of government policy.

Unless you know that a member of the House of Lords is interested in a certain matter, perhaps through mentions in the local or national press, you may get help from a library with reference books such as Dod's *Parliamentary Companion*, which lists peers' areas of interest. Relevant debates can be checked in libraries which keep back copies of *Hansard*, and before long parliamentary documents will be available on the Internet. Alternatively, you could try phoning the House of Lords library* to ask whether a peer has raised a particular matter in the past.

Questions and answers

Q *Is my MP obliged to help me, even if I didn't vote for him? How can I influence his views?*

A MPs are elected to represent all their constituents. The majority of the electorate in the constituency is quite likely to have voted for other candidates, but all constituents have equal rights to approach the MP for help. How much notice your MP takes, and how far he is prepared to go on your behalf, is another matter.

Your MP is more likely to help if he or she knows that others share your concern. If you are asking him to do more than help with a simple complaint and want him to take up a cause, you will stand a much better chance of success if you can demonstrate local support. The local constituency organisation could be crucial. As the MP is answerable to it for his selection as a candidate at the next election, he will be more likely to champion a cause if he knows it will support his stance. If, for example, he has the full backing of his local party in opposing local hospital closures, he is much more likely to chance his neck, even if not to the extreme of threatening to resign the government Whip. The support of the local party organisation will be similarly important if you are trying to persuade your MP to oppose a plank of party policy. Several Conservative MPs, for example, were able to oppose the community charge (poll tax) in this manner. If they have the backing of their constituency, MPs tend to be less fearful of incurring the wrath of their party Whips. If they are not happy to go the whole hog and oppose party policy, they may at least be moved to press for improvements to it.

If an election is looming, other ploys may be at your disposal. If your MP will not listen to your concerns, one of the other prospective parliamentary candidates might. In addition to the main political parties, independent candidates may be standing; they often put themselves forward on a single-issue ticket, such as opposition to a local bypass, or a national matter such as a referendum on Europe. If you can get any of the prospective candidates to support you in advance of the election, your MP may decide that it is in his or her interest to listen to you now, ahead of polling day.

Q *I'm about to lose my MP as a result of boundary changes. Who keeps changing them, and why?*

A To ensure that changes in population distribution do not result in areas being over- (or under-) represented by MPs, an independent commission conducts a periodic review of constituency boundaries. Reviews result in MPs losing and/or changing seats as constituencies are amalgamated and redrawn: this could mean that your MP has now found him/herself in competition with a neighbouring MP of the same party in the process of selection for the seat he or she currently holds. The most recent review has resulted in an extra five seats in England, two in Wales and one in Northern Ireland.

Q *My MP can't or won't help me. Should I try another?*

A Although MPs are elected to represent their constituent's interests in Parliament, there is nothing to stop them taking on a cause which may emanate from another's constituency. However, they need to let each other know if they are going to do this, so it is important to let the MP you approach know what contact you have made, or tried to make, with your constituency MP.

It may be that your MP is unwilling to take up an issue for political reasons, because it involves challenging a policy he supports, or that another MP is already involved in running a campaign which addresses your problem. In the latter case, your MP may suggest you contact his colleague, or pass on your details (with your approval) himself.

One MP may be better placed than another to help if he is serving on a relevant committee. For example, your constituency MP may have no interest in a certain piece of legislation which you think needs to be amended, and is not serving on the committee that scrutinises it. If you want to raise concerns about, say, ferry safety, and a select committee is already enquiring into general transport safety, a letter to a committee member may result in the enquiry being broadened to consider your concerns. Information about what the select and standing committees are considering, and their membership, is available from the House of Commons Public Information Office.*

On the other hand, it may be worth persevering with your own MP. It may be that you have not made him realise the strength of feeling in the constituency for the cause. Remember that MPs do not work in a vacuum: they have to be aware of what the local press, employers, council etc. think of a matter, so check that you have brought all available sources of influence to bear. Have you persuaded others who share your concerns to approach the MP in his surgery? Have you got local party officials on-side? Do any local councillors belonging to the same political party share your views? Is the local press interested in the issue? Has the local Chamber of Commerce or trade union branch got a view?

If your MP is not interested, it may be worth spending a bit of time finding out why. Does he have any conflicting interests? All MPs now have to register any interests for which they receive payment in the Register of Members' Interests; if your local library does not have a copy, the House of Commons Public Information Office should be able to help. Another useful publication in this respect is Roth's *Parliamentary Profiles*, which contains background information on all MPs.

Finally, remember that even if your MP has not been interested in the past, he may take note of what you are saying when a general election is in the offing, particularly if the constituency is a marginal. If you still have no luck, look to the longer term and try the opposition candidate.

Q *How can I register a protest against government legislation?*

A After a general election, the first few sessions of Parliament will see the government giving priority to implementing its manifesto commitments. If you see something you do not like in a manifesto, make sure your MP is aware of your opposition at an early stage.

Most legislation will go through some consultative stages – green papers and white papers – before a bill is drafted, and occasionally a draft bill will be issued for consultation before the legislation starts on its way through Parliament. The key to influencing legislation is to strike early: it is much easier to change things by lobbying civil servants before a bill is printed than it is to force the government to backtrack when the bill is going through Parliament.

Do what you can to persuade your MP about the seriousness of your objections: for example, by getting others in the constituency to join with you or by collecting signatures on a petition. If your objection is based on local grounds, make sure your MP is aware of any similar objections from neighbouring constituencies. If it is a national issue, keep an eye on the press to see if any pressure group has mounted a campaign with which you could involve yourself. If your MP is of the same party as the government, you will get much further if you can present a constructive solution to the problem, and provide him with evidence to show his Whips (who are responsible for getting the legislation through and maintaining party discipline) that the matter will not quietly disappear: for example, local press commentary, local councillors' letters/speeches and so on.

Once persuaded, your MP may lead a delegation to the relevant minister, or may suggest a meeting with the civil servants. This may be in conjunction with other MPs or in isolation. Make sure he has all the necessary supporting evidence to argue your case.

If you fail to win at this pre-legislative stage, all is not lost. Parliament is there to scrutinise legislation, and MPs can force amendments on an unwilling government if they can muster a sufficiently strong lobby against it. One way to demonstrate the force of objections is to organise a mass lobby, whereby you muster as many willing souls as possible to lobby their MPs in Parliament. This could comprise either constituents from one area, if it is a local matter such as the closure of a rail link, or from across the country on a matter such as disabled people's rights. Your MP will know the procedure for organising this: most crucially, the office of the Serjeant at Arms in the House of

Commons must be alerted. You should also try for as much press coverage as possible.

MPs can amend legislation when the bill is in Standing Committee: that is, when some twenty MPs are selected to scrutinise the detail of the Bill. Quite often, press reports of what is going on tend to die down at this stage, so anything you can do to keep the pressure up will be extremely useful. If your MP is not serving on the committee, he can still table amendments but one of his colleagues on the committee will have to move them for him. Remember, if he is a member of the government party, he will be having to defy the Whip if the government decides to object, in which case, if he has any ministerial ambitions, he may back down. Public pressure and media attention will be needed to steel his resolve. (If he does face down the Whips, be sure to thank him very warmly indeed.)

If you have failed at committee stage, the whole House of Commons has another chance to comment on the Bill, and table amendments, at report stage. Failing that, there is still the House of Lords. Peers have the same opportunities as MPs to amend legislation: the only difference in procedure is that the committee stage normally takes place in the main chamber of the Lords, so any peer can take part. (See this chapter's section on the House of Lords.)

During each session of Parliament, some bills start off in the House of Lords before going to the House of Commons. Ask your MP which peers he recommends you to contact.

CHAPTER 5

THE FINANCIAL SYSTEM

NO ONE escapes the financial system. It pervades everyone's life in one way or another from running a bank account to planning for retirement, from paying tax to claiming social security benefits, from taking out car insurance to buying a home. Yet for the most part we are turned out into the financial world badly prepared and ill-equipped to question the rules and regulations imposed upon us by 'the system'. And there are so many rules. That is understandable, perhaps, when dealing with the bureaucracies of the state – the tax authorities and the Department of Social Security, for example, which have grown out of detailed legislation and a history of bureaucracy. But why do banks, insurance companies and other operators within the free market seem to embrace a similar culture? All too often, the customer's reasonable requests are met with replies such as 'We can't offer that', 'The computer does it that way', or 'You'll have to deal with another department'. But there are ways to beat even the financial system.

Banks

There is no doubt about it: while individual banks might provide an excellent service, banks as a whole have a bad image. They are frequently perceived as arrogant and high-handed. Of all financial institutions, they are the ones which seem most often to hide behind the skirts of their computer systems, washing their hands of blame for errors or inappropriate application of their rules, or apparently 'trying it on' by imposing large and unexpected charges. Take, for example, the case of Mr X, who wrote out a cheque for £195 which was bounced. The cash to cover the cheque had been paid into the account but was not cleared until a day later. As a result of this one-day discrepancy, Mr X was fined £25. That sent the account overdrawn, resulting in a further £17 fine. The account went into the black the next day and the cheque was re-presented. But because of the fines, there was now too little in the account to cover the cheque, so there was a yet another £17 fine, together with 76 pence interest on the unauthorised overdraft! Similar nonsenses occur every day. Who invented this crazy system?

Consumer fury is commonly aroused in other ways, too: by banks making unauthorised withdrawals from one account to set against an overdraft in another which the account-holder has at the same branch; failure to pay standing orders as instructed; imposing charges for writing straightforward letters of information (just imagine how your bank would react if you reciprocated by charging it for your letters and time); and staggeringly high charges, despite very slow service, for administering the estates of deceased relatives.

But perhaps the most acrimonious disputes have been those concerning unauthorised cash machine withdrawals. At their peak, such disputes accounted for over a third of the complaints being dealt with by the Banking Ombudsman* (see page 161). Typically, the customer claimed that both card and personal identification number (PIN) were in safe keeping at the time when a disputed withdrawal was made from his (or her) account through a cash machine, so presumably the bank's security systems had been breached in some way. But the banks strongly defended their systems and alleged, in most cases, that the customer must have lent his (or her) card or let slip his (or her) PIN to someone else. Such disputes have not gone away, but there are signs that they have become less acrimonious as banks have become more willing to come to some form of settlement rather than pursue each case to the bitter end – and the probable loss of the customer.

Standards of practice

In 1992, banks, building societies and card issuers together implemented a voluntary code of practice to guide their relationships with personal customers. Optimistically called 'Good Banking', it received a sceptical welcome. The revised code of March 1994, which is still in effect, was received with hardly more enthusiasm. Rather than being an attempt to identify and promote best practice, the code pitches standards at a very basic level and seems merely to enshrine the mediocre way in which many banks carry out business normally. For example, if a bank alters the terms and conditions of a service, the code imposes only the vague obligation to *'tell customers how any variation . . . will be notified'* and to *'give customers reasonable notice before any variation takes effect'*. How much tougher the code would be if it required notification in writing to the customer's address at least x weeks before the change came into effect. Similarly, too much latitude is given to banks when it comes to informing customers about changed rates on their accounts: *'Banks and building societies will make information about the rates on interest-bearing accounts . . . freely available and accessible to customers by one or more effective means, for example (a) notices in branches (b) press advertisements (c) personal notice (d) a branch/central telephone service.'* Surely, only *'(c) personal notice'* can really be described as accessible and effective, particularly when many banking customers these days seldom visit their branch and many high street branches have been closed.

Some parts of the code are simply amusing, such as the paragraph stating: *'To help customers manage their accounts and check entries, banks and building societies will provide them with regular statements . . . this should be at no less than 12-monthly intervals.'* A statement once a year would be of very little help to anyone trying to manage an account efficiently.

All in all, the code imposes such undemanding, bland, loosely defined requirements on banks that it is unlikely to be breached, even if a bank is acting in a way that seems totally unreasonable and unacceptable to the customer.

How to complain

Often, given the terms of your contract with the bank, it is *legally* entitled to act as described above, but it is questionable whether such treatment of customers is either just or even good business sense. It seems that the banks also have misgivings on this score, because if you complain loudly enough and persistently enough, staff will often have second thoughts and try to mend the situation. If your complaints fall on deaf ears, you should invoke the formal complaints procedure.

The code of practice requires that each bank and building society will have its own internal procedures for handling complaints and that you should be notified (how is not specified) of its existence. The code also spells out that bank staff who deal with customers should be aware of the procedure and able to give customers correct information about it. All the main clearing banks belong to the Banking Ombudsman Scheme,★ details of which should be available from your bank.

Before taking a dispute to the Ombudsman, you must have exhausted the bank's internal complaints procedure and to have reached deadlock. This is a weak link in the system: the bank with which you are in dispute is required to issue a letter of deadlock, and in some cases it proves reluctant to do this. However, if there seems to be an unreasonable delay, you can ask the Ombudsman to put pressure on the bank to co-operate. Sometimes, this alone will be enough to prompt the bank to resolve the dispute. In other cases, the letter is produced and your case can go forward with the Ombudsman.

The Banking Ombudsman can deal with most complaints you might have about banking services, but not complaints about a bank's policies (for example, on what types of customer qualify for loans). However, disputes concerning insurance or investments offered by a bank will normally fall within the scope of the Insurance Ombudsman★ (see page 166) or PIA Ombudsman★ (see page 165).

It is not obligatory for banks to belong to the Banking Ombudsman Scheme, but most of the main ones do. Decisions by the Ombudsman are binding on the bank, but you still have the right to pursue your complaint through the courts if you do not agree with the Ombudsman's verdict. The Ombudsman can make awards of up to £100,000.

Financial advisers

Until the late 1980s financial advice was something of a Cinderella industry. Unless you had large sums to invest, any financial advice tended to be part and parcel of the process of selling you insurance, investments or other financial products, rather than a separate service to be valued in its own right. The main system of paying for advice reinforces this twilight existence: in general, the adviser receives commission from the provider whose products you buy. This has led to the mistaken impression that advice is free but, of course, the reality is that you do pay for the advice through the charges built into the product.

However, change is being thrust upon the world of financial advisers. Since January 1995 the commission the adviser receives for selling you an insurance or pension product has had to be disclosed in writing. Before then, the adviser had to disclose the commission only if you specifically asked about it. Although the impact of commission disclosure is taking time to have an effect, it is gradually achieving the following:

- there is a growing understanding among clients that advice is not free
- independent financial advice is becoming more widely recognised and valued as a service in its own right
- there is some shift away from paying for advice through commissions and product charges towards direct payment for advice by fees. This is most marked where advisers are catering for wealthy clients, but even if your means are more modest you might now be offered a choice of paying by commission or fees.

Commission disclosure is one development in the evolution of the regulatory system introduced by the Financial Services Act 1986. There has been another important change: the regulators, initially concerned mainly with the honesty and solvency of advisers, have been swung round to the view that competence is also a fundamental prerequisite for good advice. Once a transitional phase has worked through, all advisers – whether 'tied' and able to sell the products of just one company or 'independent' and able to recommend from the full range of companies in the market – will have to have passed exams showing a basic level of competence. The level is not very demanding at present, but it is a start on the road to introducing acceptable standards across the whole financial advice industry. The challenge for you, the consumer, is how to avoid the pitfalls of this still formative system and to get the best deal out of it.

Standards of practice

Under the Financial Services Act, the Treasury is ultimately responsible for regulating the investment industry, but day-to-day regulation has been delegated to a self-regulating body, the Securities and Investments Board (SIB).★ The SIB, in turn, delegates large parts of the job to self-regulating organisations (SROs) which specialise in particular areas of investment business. Most financial advisers come within the scope of the Personal Investment Authority (PIA).★

It is a criminal offence for an investment business to operate unless it belongs either to SIB, an SRO or one of a handful of recognised professional bodies (RPBs). RPBs cover solicitors, accountants, actuaries and registered insurance brokers and can regulate their members' investment business provided it accounts for only a minority of a member's activities. The regulators have three main functions: authorising (i.e. licensing) members to carry on investment business; setting and enforcing rules to ensure good standards within the investment industry – these cover, for example, training and competence, advertising, the information to be given to customers, safeguards for clients' money and investments and complaints handling; and dealing with problems through formal complaints procedures and disciplinary action. The PIA rules include the following measures to protect customers when dealing with salespersons or advisers:

- at the start of your dealings, they must make clear whether they are independent or tied to one company and what types of business they are authorised to carry on
- in most cases, they comply with the 'know your customer' rule. This means they must find out enough about you to put themselves in a position to be able to recommend suitable products. Usually, this will be done by carrying out a written fact-find
- they must give you 'best advice'. This means recommending only products which are suitable for you, given the details from

the fact-find. If there are no suitable products in their range, they should say so and can, if you agree, pass you on to another adviser or salesperson who can help

- with some products, there is a cancellation period during which you have the right to change your mind and pull out of the deal
- with insurance and pension products, you must be sent a 'reason why' letter setting out in writing the justification for the advice given.

The Financial Services Act is limited to regulating *investment* business. Investments are defined within the Act and exclude many financial products, most notably deposits (such as bank and building society accounts), non-investment insurance (such as term insurance and some types of disability insurance – though companies can now volunteer to have these treated under the Financial Services Act régime) and mortgages.

Banks and building societies are regulated by the Bank of England★ and the Building Societies Commission★ respectively, each of which is responsible for ensuring solvency and sound practice. However, there are no formal controls on the way in which their non-investment products are marketed to the public.

Term insurance and some types of disability insurance count as general insurance. If you go to a registered insurance broker (the only insurance intermediary legally allowed to use the title 'broker'), the sale of these policies is covered by a code of conduct established and monitored by the Insurance Brokers Registration Council (IBRC).★ *Inter alia*, the code requires brokers to give independent advice and to place the interests of clients above all other considerations.

In the case of non-broker intermediaries selling general insurance, there is no formal regulation, but the Association of British Insurers (ABI)★ operates a voluntary code whereby its members – which are insurance companies – are responsible for ensuring that intermediaries selling their products abide by the code. Such intermediaries do not have to give independent advice – they can be representing one or a handful of companies. But the code incorporates a requirement that intermediaries make their status clear and ensure as far as possible that recommendations are suitable.

With mortgages, there is again no formal code, but the Council of Mortgage Lenders (CML), part of the Building Societies Association,★ is in the process of introducing a code of selling practice for mortgage advisers, and the British Bankers Association★ has recently published guidelines, concerned mainly with giving clear information and explanations to customers, for banks to follow when giving mortgage advice. It is too early to say whether these voluntary approaches will be effective in raising standards of advice.

How to complain

Whatever the type of adviser you are dealing with, if something goes wrong you should first take your complaint back to the adviser, if necessary going to the senior management of the firm. If this does not produce satisfactory results, your next step depends on the type of adviser.

If your complaint concerns investment business falling within the scope of the Financial Services Act, complain to the SRO or other regulatory body to which the adviser belongs. The adviser's letterheads, business cards and other literature will tell you which body this is; usually it will be the PIA. You can take the complaint either to the PIA itself or to the PIA Ombudsman★ – either way, it will be the Ombudsman who handles your enquiry. As a first step, he (or she) will probably encourage the adviser to come to a settlement with you, but if this is not forthcoming, the Ombudsman can make a formal investigation and make a decision which is binding on the adviser. You still have the option of pursuing your complaint through the courts if you are not happy with the Ombudsman's decision. In most cases, the Ombudsman can make awards of up to £50,000 (or £20,000 a year in cases concerning investment-type disability insurance). Where companies have voluntarily agreed to the PIA Ombudsman handling complaints about their non-investment business, the limit on lump sum awards is £100,000. (The Ombudsman is at the time of going to press urging the PIA to increase the maximum award for all cases to £100,000.)

If a bank or building society has failed to meet your complaint about its non-investment business or is taking an unreasonable time to do so (i.e. more than, say, six or eight weeks), you can take your case to the Banking Ombudsman★ (see page 161) or the Building Societies Ombudsman★, as appropriate. Unlike most of the other ombudsman schemes, the Building Societies Ombudsman Scheme is a statutory one and all building societies are required to belong to it. The Ombudsman's decisions are binding on neither you nor the society, unless you have agreed to the Ombudsman acting as an arbitrator, in which case his decision is binding on both of you. The Building Societies Ombudsman can direct that awards of up to £100,000 be made.

A complaint about non-investment insurance which has not been resolved by the firm involved can be referred to the Insurance Ombudsman,★ provided the insurance company involved is a member. Decisions by the Insurance Ombudsman, which can include awards of up to £100,000, are binding on the company concerned, but you still have the option to take your case to court. A few insurance companies are not members of the ombudsman scheme but instead belong to the Personal Insurance Arbitration Service (PIAS),★ which can decide a dispute through arbitration. Such decisions are binding on both you and the company concerned.

If you are dealing with an insurance broker, you can take your complaint to the Insurance Brokers Registration Council,★ which can investigate and, if appropriate, discipline the broker. However, the IBRC does not itself make awards, so, if you were seeking compensation, you would have to take your complaint to the appropriate ombudsman or pursue it in court.

A complaint concerning mortgage advice would fall under the aegis of the Banking or Building Societies Ombudsman if it concerned a bank or building society. In other cases, there is no formal complaints mechanism and you would have to pursue compensation through the courts, if the firm involved refused to settle the matter satisfactorily.

If this all seems complicated, it is. A serious problem with the financial system is the multiplicity of bodies involved in handling disputes. In general, if you direct your complaint to the wrong scheme, they will pass it on to the appropriate body. But, even so, the system is unacceptably confusing for the average consumer.

Pension providers

The transfer and opt-out scandal of the early 1990s, whereby people were persuaded to take out personal pension plans in preference to superior employer pension schemes, has badly tarnished the reputation of plan providers, mainly insurance companies and 'bancassurers' (insurance subsidiaries of banks and building societies selling through the branch network). Employer pension schemes have also been cast in a doubtful light by the Maxwell fraud and other cases.

However, these frauds need to be put in perspective. The risk of losing part or all of your pension savings because of fraud, malpractice or negligence is much, much smaller than the risk of an impoverished old age as a result of not saving at all.

Standards of practice

Personal pension plan providers come within the scope of the Financial Services Act. The standards applying to selling practices described on pages 163–5 apply as much to a pension provider's salespeople as to independent financial advisers.

Although there is no lack of legislation applying to employer pension schemes, until recently very little of it was concerned directly with protecting the members of pension schemes. This changed with the passing of the Pensions Act 1995, most of which comes into force in April 1997. The Act sets up a three-pillared system of regulation made up of a new Occupational Pensions Regulatory Authority (OPRA),★ scheme advisers (for example, actuaries, lawyers, auditors) who will be under a duty to 'blow the whistle' if they suspect that anything is amiss with a scheme, and scheme trustees who will act as the regulators at the coal-face. There is also a basic requirement that schemes should have a minimum number of trustees who are nominated by the scheme members, although the requirement is flawed in several respects, particularly since employers can opt out of it, and can veto member-nominated trustees who are not actually members of the scheme: for example, trade union officials chosen to act as trustees. Trustees will have a key role to play in the new system, but unfortunately there are no requirements for trustees to receive even the most basic training, so standards are likely to vary widely from scheme to scheme.

How to complain

Problems with the marketing and selling of personal pension plans are dealt with under the Financial Services Act system (see page 165). If your complaint involves the running of the underlying pension fund, you might take your case to the Investment Ombudsman,* set up by the Investment Managers Regulatory Organisation* (another SRO). However, you will have to have exhausted the pension provider's own internal complaints procedure first.

If you are in dispute with your employer pension scheme, you should first contact the pension administrator or the trustees of the scheme: literature from the scheme should tell you who they are; alternatively, ask your personnel department at work. Under the Pensions Act 1995, all scheme providers are being required to set up their own internal complaints procedures and they must tell you how to use them.

If the internal procedure does not produce a satisfactory outcome, you may need to invoke the help of the Pensions Ombudsman.* But first you are required to take your case to the Occupational Pensions Advisory Service (OPAS).* Often, pension problems arise out of misunderstanding or lack of communication. OPAS tries to resolve such disputes through mediation and communication. If this does not work or if the case is more complex, OPAS will – with your consent – refer it to the Ombudsman.

OPAS can also consider problems with personal pension plans. If unresolved, they are generally passed to the PIA Ombudsman.

Mortgage lenders

After your pension, your home is likely to be the most valuable financial asset you own. Few people can afford to buy their home outright for cash; instead, they rely on a mortgage to finance the deal.

Standards of practice

Banks and building societies are regulated by the Bank of England★ and the Building Societies Commission★ respectively, as far as their solvency and prudent running are concerned. But the sale of mortgages has so far been totally unregulated. The Office of Fair Trading★ has expressed its concern over this lack and called for a 'best advice' requirement to apply to mortgages. The Council of Mortgage Lenders (contactable via the Buildings Societies Association★) is about to introduce a voluntary code of practice but it is too early to say whether this will be effective. The British Bankers Association★ has set out guidelines concerning the information to be given by banks to their mortgage customers.

How to complain

Complaints must first be taken up with the mortgage lender concerned, going to the senior management is necessary. If this fails, take your case to the Banking Ombudsman★ (see page 161) or Building Societies Ombudsman★ (see page 166), if the lender is a bank or building society.

Insurance companies

Insurance companies have long suffered an unpopular image, often being seen as eager to take ever-increasing premiums but reluctant to pay out when you have a claim. Some companies, particularly the newer insurers running direct telephone operations, are challenging this image and offering much more customer-focused services. But in other parts of the industry there is still an unhappy tension between consumer and company.

You, the customer, want peace of mind. When you take out insurance, you want a simple promise that your policy will pay out quickly and without fuss if you suffer a loss. But insurance companies are in the business of predicting risks and making some level of profit from these predictions. From the company's point of view, it is essential that the risks covered by a policy are not open-ended, so a barrage of small print and caveats aims to define precisely what is covered and what is not. The result is that insurance often fails to live up to the consumer's expectations, seeming to be unnecessarily complicated and delivering far less cover than it had appeared to promise.

Standards of practice

Insurance companies are regulated by the Department of Trade and Industry,★ which is responsible for ensuring that they are solvent and run in a prudent way.

When you buy non-investment-type insurance products, the insurance company employee or the intermediary you deal with is bound by the ABI Code of Practice (see page 164), assuming the insurance company is an ABI member. If you use an insurance broker, the IBRC code of conduct applies (see page 166).

How to complain

Complaints, in the first place, should be taken up with the insurer concerned, going to the top management of the organisation if necessary. If this does not produce a satisfactory result and the complaint concerns a non-investment insurance product, you can take your case to the Insurance Ombudsman★ (see page 166) if the insurer is a member of the scheme.

The Inland Revenue

The Inland Revenue deals with income tax and capital gains tax. This is part of the financial system which virtually everyone has to deal with. If you work for an employer or receive a pension from a former employer, all or most of your income tax will be paid through the Pay-As-You-Earn (PAYE) system. If you are self-employed, have income or gains from investments or your tax affairs are complicated in some other way, you will usually have to fill out a tax return each year and pay some or all of your tax in lump sums following an 'assessment' of the amount due.

Your tax affairs are handled by a tax office which is not necessarily close to where you live or work. If you get a salary or pension from an employer, your tax office will usually be close to your employer's main office. If you are unemployed, you usually remain with your last tax office. If you are self-employed, your tax office will be close to your business address. You should take queries specific to your particular tax affairs to your own tax office. But, if you have more general queries, you can contact any Tax Enquiry Centre.★

The Inland Revenue publishes a wide range of explanatory leaflets which are available from tax offices and Tax Enquiry Centres. Public libraries, post offices and Citizens Advice Bureaux★ also often have copies of some leaflets.

Standards of practice

The Inland Revenue administers the tax system as set out in Acts of Parliament and related regulations. Its interpretation of the tax laws is given in guidance manuals which you can ask to see at any Tax Enquiry Centre.★

A Taxpayer's Charter sets out the principles governing the Revenue's dealings with you. It commits the Revenue to being fair, helpful and courteous and to treating your affairs confidentially. For your part, you are committed to providing the Revenue with the necessary information about your income and gains.

Codes of Practice expand on the Charter's principles, setting target times for dealing with queries and explaining the circumstances in which tax or interest on it might be waived.

How to complain

If you have a problem with the way the Inland Revenue is handling your tax affairs (rather than a dispute over the amount of tax due), first take up the matter with your tax office. If you are not satisfied with the response, write to the District Inspector whose name is on tax office letters. If this fails, you can refer the matter to the Regional Inspector. Your tax office must tell you how to go about this. If, having exhausted these routes, you are still not happy, either take the complaint to the Independent Adjudicator★ or, alternatively, ask your MP★ to make a complaint on your behalf to the Parliamentary Ombudsman. (You cannot approach the Ombudsman direct: you must go through your MP.)

The Department of Social Security

There are two public faces of the Department of Social Security (DSS) which you are most likely to be dealing with: the Contributions Agency, which is concerned with National Insurance payments, and the Benefits Agency, which is concerned with claims for state retirement pensions, income support, incapacity benefit and so on. Both agencies work through local DSS offices★ although you will need to deal with your local JobCentre★ if you are claiming jobseekers' allowance for the unemployed. Local DSS offices can give you a freephone number for benefits queries. Both agencies publish a wide range of leaflets covering particular aspects of the contribution system and specific benefits. Leaflets often contain the forms you will need to carry forward an enquiry or claim, and are available from DSS offices. Public libraries, post offices, Citizens Advice Bureaux and local authority offices also often have a selection of these leaflets.

Standards of practice

The DSS administers the National Insurance and benefits systems as set out in Acts of Parliament and related regulations. The benefit laws are drawn together and published in loose-leaf books known as the 'blue volumes'. The way in which the benefit and contribution laws are interpreted by DSS staff is set out in manuals. Both the blue volumes and the manuals are kept in each DSS office and you can ask to see them. Some public libraries also have copies of these manuals.

A charter sets out standards for, *inter alia*, responding to queries within a specified period of time and your right to a private interview if you request one.

How to complain

If you have a complaint or problem concerning a DSS matter, you should first take your complaint to the office with which you have been dealing. If the staff cannot deal with the issue satisfactorily, ask to see a manager. Complaints can be in writing or by phone and the manager is required to investigate and provide you with an explanation, apologising if appropriate and taking steps to put right any mistakes. If you are still unhappy, you should take your complaint to the Chief Executive of the Contributions Agency★ or Benefits Agency★ as appropriate.

If a complaint taken to the chief executive of the Contributions Agency is still not resolved satisfactorily, you can within six months take it to the Independent Adjudicator★ (who also deals with complaints against the Inland Revenue). You cannot go direct to the Adjudicator: the chief executive must have considered your case first. If the dispute is still unresolved, you have the right to pursue your complaint through the courts.

The procedure for benefits disputes is more complex and varies slightly according to the benefit in question. In general, most claims are initially dealt with by the local Benefits Agency. If you are unhappy about the decision, you can ask for it to be reviewed by the local office and, if you are still not satisfied, your case can be referred to an independent tribunal service which operates a system of tribunals across the country. You can challenge the decision of a tribunal, but only on a point of law, by referring it to the Social Security Commissioners. Your local DSS can tell you how to do this.

If you are claiming housing benefit or Council Tax benefit, decisions and appeals are dealt with by your local authority.

Questions and answers

Banks

Q *I am furious. My business account regularly has tens of thousands of £££s passing through it on which no doubt my bank makes a fortune. But my wife was overdrawn by 50 pence for a few days and they had the cheek to charge her £20. Is this customer care?*

A The days of the friendly bank manager to whom all customers were personally known and individually valued are largely gone, and he has been replaced by elaborate computer software which triggers charges at the drop of an overdraft without any thought about the damage which might be done to customer relations or the potential loss to the bank if the customer moves elsewhere.

But you can, and should, challenge this approach. In many cases, if you complain to your branch, pointing out how ridiculously inappropriately the rules have been applied, you will find that the rules are waived and the charges refunded. If your first attempt is not successful, do not be daunted; take your complaint higher within the bank. Persistency can pay off.

Q *I strongly resent being charged for making cash withdrawals through a cash machine. I live in a remote area and it's some miles to the nearest bank, so I have no choice but to use these machines. Cash machine networks must save the banks money, because they can reach lots more customers without having to keep open expensive branches. Why should the customers be penalised?*

A When banks and building societies first started to link up their cash machines, there was usually no charge for using any machine within the linked network. Unfortunately, some members of networks started to grumble about the cost of processing the withdrawals of other banks and societies and introduced charges for some members' customers. This smacks of petty in-fighting and it is you, the consumer, who loses. There are several possible solutions:

- check with your card issuer which banks' and building societies' machines you can use without charge and avoid other machines
- if you have a limited choice of machines, check with the bank or building society which operates them which cards can be used free of charge and consider switching to those cards (which may mean switching your current account)
- arm yourself with several cards so that, in each machine, you can use the appropriate one, giving you free use.

Q *I applied to one of the major banks for a credit card and was turned down. I can't imagine why – I've already got another credit card and I always pay it off in full each month, I've never had problems with other types of loan, so why should I be blacklisted?*

A There is no stigma to being turned down for credit or a loan. Different lenders look for different types of borrowers: for example, some lenders do not want young borrowers, others specialise in home-owners, some do not make small loans, and so on. From a credit card issuer's point of view, a customer who has a consistent record of paying off his or her balance in full each month might not look as attractive as a customer who borrows and so pays interest. Most lenders operate according to guidelines drawn up by the credit industry's main trade bodies. These guidelines say that lenders must tell you why you have been turned down if you are refused credit. There are three types of reason:

- **credit scoring** was used and you have failed to score enough. You will be given a general explanation only. Lenders treat the score cards they use to assess your loan application as top secret. They believe that revealing too much about the way they rate different characteristics makes them vulnerable to fraud
- **a credit reference agency** was used and there was some specific information on your file – e.g. unpaid debts – which make you look a bad risk. You will be told how you can check your file and amend it if it is incorrect (see below)
- **a policy reason** Here, the lender must be more specific and tell you which of its policies you do not match up to; e.g. you do not own your own home, your income is too low, etc.

Lenders subscribing to the industry code must have an appeals procedure. Usually, you will be told about this automatically at the time your credit application is refused. It would be worth making an appeal if, say, you have extra information that is relevant. Lenders do not have to tell you about the appeals procedure, but even if they do not, you still have the right to appeal, so make a point of asking about it.

Q *I applied to my parents' bank to open my own account. The bank has turned me down on the basis, it claims, of a credit reference search. I don't know why I should have had a bad reference and I'm worried that, if I apply to another bank, I'll be turned down there as well. What can I do?*

A If you are turned down for credit, you have the right to ask within 28 days if a credit reference agency had been consulted and, if so, the name and address of the agency or agencies involved. By paying a small fee and writing to the agency, you can get a copy of the entry relating to you. Check this carefully: it might contain incorrect information about you or erroneously contain information about someone else. If the entry is incorrect, ask the agency to amend or remove the erroneous entry. If it does not agree to do this, you can send it a 'notice of correction' setting out your case and this must be appended to your entry at the agency. The amended entry or entry with notice of correction must be sent by the agency to everyone who has consulted your entry within the last six months. If, for any reason, the agency will not accept your notice of correction, complain to the Office of Fair Trading.★

Q *A year ago, I took out a £5,000 bank loan to help me buy a car. The loan was due to run for five years, but I've come into some money and decided to pay it off early. Despite my having paid £120 a month for the last year, the bank has told me that I'll have to pay £5,250 to clear the loan! How can I owe more than I started with? Surely the bank can't do this?*

A If you pay off a fixed-term loan earlier than originally intended, the lender 'loses' some of the interest you would have paid had the loan run its full term. It is allowed to recoup some of this loss by levying an early repayment charge. Generally, the longer the loan and the earlier you repay, the higher this charge will be. There are two possible ways round this charge:

- try negotiating with the lender. The law sets out the maximum early repayment charge, but there is nothing to stop a lender charging less
- check the loan agreement. Some allow you to make capital repayments and calculate any early repayment charge on the outstanding balance. If this applies, you could pay off all but £1 of the loan in the first instance. Then when you repay the last £1, the early repayment charge will be calculated with reference to that amount only.

Financial advisers

Q *I am self-employed and have recently started to think that I should sort out a pension plan. I received all the details for putting £200 a month into a plan for the next 30 years or so and I was staggered to see that the adviser would immediately get over £1,700 for signing me up! That seems a lot. Do all plans pay the same commission? Should I shop around?*

A Most advisers receive commission from the company whose products you buy. They generally either keep this as payment for their work or offset it against what you pay if the adviser charges fees. As you have discovered, the amount can be substantial. To answer your specific queries:

- the commission is not the same on all plans. Each provider sets its own commission structure and rates on the basis of commercial factors. The commission needs to attract advisers to place business with the company, yet not be so large that the resulting charges for the company's products would be unacceptably high
- if the commission on a product you are recommended looks high, it should trigger questions in your mind, but is not necessarily a reason to reject the product – see the next question.

You may be able to turn the commission payment to your own advantage. Many advisers are willing to rebate part of the commission in order to attract your custom: this could be as a cash sum or used to enhance the terms of the investment or product you are buying. The market for financial advice is very competitive, so don't be shy about asking for a rebate – be prepared to haggle.

Q *If companies set their commissions in order to persuade advisers to place business with them, how can the adviser be concerned primarily with giving me best advice?*

A This is a good question. It is the paradox which the financial services industry has for years been trying to explain away. There can be no doubt that the commission system poses a potential conflict of interest for advisers. The adviser should be concerned solely with your best interests, but the prospect of receiving commission could sway the advice in three different ways:

- the adviser might overlook investments which do not pay commission (for example, building society accounts and National Savings) even where they would be the most suitable for you
- the adviser might recommend those providers which pay the higher commissions and exclude totally providers which do not pay commission at all, such as Equitable Life
- since commissions are usually a percentage of what you pay into a product, the adviser might recommend you invest more or pay larger premiums than you had intended or perhaps can afford.

A good adviser will not succumb to the temptation of commission bias: not only is it unethical, but it makes better sense to put the customer's interests first, because a contented customer is more likely to return to do further business in future. The problem is that it is very hard for you to know whether the advice you are being given has been influenced by commission. Now commissions are disclosed, you can compare the amount the adviser stands to earn on competing products and/or providers. If you suspect that the commission on the recommended product is relatively high, raise the following issues with the adviser:

- doesn't the high level of commission feed through into high charges for the product?
- if charges are high, your money will have to work harder to overcome this drawback. So what are the advantages of this product which outweigh the drawback of high charges?
- would the adviser be prepared to rebate part of the commission?

If you are not happy with the responses given, go to another adviser. To avoid the risk of commission bias altogether, choose a fee-based adviser: contact Money Management National Register of Independent Fee-Based Advisers.★

Q *A chap telephoned me out of the blue and, having made an appointment to meet, he is saying I should invest in a personal equity plan. He explained all the tax breaks and left me lots of paperwork, which I've read. It seems a sensible enough idea. Is there anything I should check out before I take the plunge?*

A Whether or not a personal equity plan (PEP) is suitable for you depends on your circumstances. The adviser you met should have asked you for details about, for example, your age, family situation, tax position, attitude towards risk, other financial arrangements, and so on, before making his recommendation. Assuming he did all this, investing through a PEP may well be a good idea. However, before you take the plunge, you should consider which PEP provider you want to invest with. Under the Financial Services Act, there are just two types of investment adviser: those who are tied to one company and those who are independent (see page 162). An adviser who 'cold calls' you is most likely to be tied. By all means listen to what a tied adviser has to offer, but do not make any decision until you have considered what competing providers have to offer. It would be pure coincidence if the provider this adviser represents is the best one for you. You need to look at the range of providers in the PEP market by, for example, consulting published surveys or enlisting the help of an independent adviser.

Q *Reading through the stack of paperwork I've been given in connection with a 25-year endowment policy, I'm shocked to see how little of the premiums paid I would get back if I stopped the policy early. These penally low surrender values go on for years. How can insurance companies get away with this?*

A Low surrender values in the early years of an investment-type insurance policy are a direct result of the commission system (see page 177). Traditionally, advisers have received the bulk of their commission as a lump sum at the time you first took out the policy. The provider plans to recover the cost of the commission from you through the charges levied against the policy over its lifetime. But, if you stop the policy early, the charges are in effect brought forward in the form of surrender penalties.

There are ways round this problem. The first is to take out policies from companies which do not pay commission, which includes insurers who sell direct to the public, often through telephone-based services, thus cutting out any middlemen. The second is to opt for providers which pay commission largely over a period of years rather than as an up-front lump sum. More and more insurers are moving to this sort of commission structure, following the introduction in January 1995 of tough new rules about disclosing commissions and the effect of charges. In both cases, surrender penalties for stopping or cashing in the policy in the early years are generally much lower.

However, if you anticipate that you might want to stop the policy early, you should seriously question whether an endowment insurance is an appropriate investment for you.

Q *Stocks and shares have invariably been a good bet over the long term, so isn't a unit-linked insurance policy always going to be a better buy than a with-profits one?*

A There are two points you should consider: first, what is your attitude towards risk? As you say, a unit-linked investment might reasonably be expected to out-perform a with-profits policy over the long-term. But the unit-linked policy exposes you to greater risk of loss because the value of the policy can fall as well as rise. In contrast, a traditional with-profits policy cannot fall in value.

The second point to bear in mind is that an insurance policy might not be the best way to link into stocks and shares. Unless you are a higher-rate taxpayer, unit trusts are usually a more tax-efficient investment than unit-linked life insurance, especially if you invest through a PEP. Unit trusts also tend to have lower charges and are much more flexible than life insurance.

Q *I'm no financial expert and I really do need help sorting out my investments. But there seem to be so many frauds and scandals these days – who can I trust?*

A There are plenty of good, honest advisers – the problem is how to identify them and steer clear of the bad ones. Ultimately, the only certain way of doing this is to equip yourself with at least a basic knowledge of personal finance. It is unlikely that you would buy a car, say, or a TV or even a pair of jeans without (a) being clear about whether you needed the item (b) what type or features you wanted and (c) whether what was on offer met your needs. The same basic rules of shopping apply equally to financial products and services.

Q *If I've got to swot up on personal finance to protect myself from bad advisers, surely I might as well do without an adviser altogether and simply handle my own finances – though goodness knows where I'd find the time for all this.*

A Running your own finances involves a lot more than just knowing the basics of personal finance. To do the job properly, you would need to develop a good understanding of, for example, the tax and benefit systems, of how insurance works, and of investment theory. And the most daunting task would be keeping abreast of new products in these highly competitive and fast-moving markets. Many people do not have the time or inclination to develop this level of financial expertise and it is more practical for them to turn to a professional adviser who has access to detailed sources and up-to-date product databases.

However, there is a core of people who do feel confident about making their own investment decisions, and they are the target of the 'direct companies' which sell their products on a no-advice basis direct to the public by phone, mailshots or direct response advertisements. But a word of warning: if you make investments or take out insurance or pensions without taking advice (i.e. on an 'execution-only' basis), you lose some of the protection of the Financial Services Act. There is no 'cooling-off period' during which you can alter your decision and, if things do go wrong, you are less likely to be able to bring a complaint against the provider or to be entitled to any compensation.

Pension providers

Q *An acquaintance who works as an investment adviser for one of the high street banks has recommended that I take out a pension plan through the bank. I work part-time as a nursing auxiliary, so I don't have a huge amount to invest. Is it worth taking out a plan?*

A The first point to consider is: what options are open to you? You have not said whom you work for, but if it is the National Health Service you might well be eligible to join the NHS Superannuation Scheme, which would almost certainly be more appropriate for you than a personal plan. If the bank adviser did not question you about your other pension options, or recommended the personal plan despite your being eligible for the NHS scheme, he (or she) is probably guilty of mis-selling and you should complain to the bank's regulator under the Financial Services Act (most likely the Personal Investment Authority:* check the bank's literature).

If, however, your only option is a personal pension plan, you are right to consider whether your contributions are large enough. Charges for these plans can be high and any flat fees eat disproportionately into a small investment. Ask for an illustration which will show you the impact of charges.

Q *I've been in discussion with a pension company recently. The salesman is very insistent that I should take out a regular premium plan. But I'm not sure I'll be able to keep up the payments year in, year out – it depends how well my business goes.*

A Do not commit yourself to regular payments if you are unsure that you can keep them up: there may be hefty penalties for missing payments or stopping them altogether. Instead, either choose a plan which gives you complete flexibility to make payments as and when you decide, or take out a separate single premium plan each year for the amount you can afford. It is possible that the higher commission payable on a regular premium plan is influencing the advice you have been given.

Q *I know pensions are important, but I'm not comfortable with tying up my money so permanently. Is there a more flexible alternative?*

A At present, there is no compulsory requirement to save privately towards retirement. (This could change in future.) That said, it is clearly important that you do make some pension provision, and pension plans and schemes are a tax-efficient way of doing this, because:

- you get tax relief on your contributions
- your savings build up tax-free
- you can take part of the proceeds as a tax-free lump sum. The rest must be taken as taxable income.

Apart from the lump sum, it is important to realise that these plans and schemes do not give you *tax-free* savings. Instead, they give you *tax-deferred* savings: i.e. you are shifting the tax burden from now until the time at which you start to take your pension. And, as you point out, these plans and schemes are inflexible in the sense that, once your contributions are paid in, your savings are tied up until at least the minimum age for starting your pension, which would typically be 50 or so.

If you really cannot cope with that inflexibility, an alternative to consider would be saving through a personal equity plan (PEP). There is no tax relief on what you pay into a PEP, but your investment builds up tax-free and you can take the proceeds completely free of tax, which makes them only a little less tax-efficient than a formal pension scheme or plan. Moreover, they are extremely flexible: you pay in what you like (subject to the legal maximum) and when you like and you can make withdrawals at any time. However, if the investment in the PEP is to survive to fund your retirement, you must be a disciplined investor.

Q *How can I be sure that my company pension scheme is safe?*

A You can never be absolutely sure, but you can minimise the likelihood of something going wrong if you and other members get involved in your scheme, by, for example:

- becoming a trustee. Trustees take care of the pension fund and ensure that it is used properly
- reading the information you are given about your scheme
- asking questions about aspects you do not understand. Put your queries to the pensions administrator or trustees, or ask your trade union to follow them up
- taking your concerns to the new Occupational Pensions Regulatory Authority★ if you suspect that something is going wrong with the scheme.

Mortgage lenders

Q *I'm about to buy my first home. There are so many mortgage deals around that I decided to get a mortgage broker to sort out something for*

How repayment and low-cost endowment mortgages compare

	Repayment	Low-cost with-profit endowment
Guarantees to pay off loan	YES	NO
May give you extra lump sum at maturity	NO	YES
Tax advantages	NO	NO[1]
Life insurance built in	NO	YES
Monthly payments can easily be reduced	NO	NO
Monthly payments can easily be increased	YES	NO
Mortgage can be completely paid off whenever you choose without penalty	YES[2]	NO
If you move in early years, some capital paid off or contribution towards it has built up	NO	YES[3]

[1]Unless you are a higher-rate taxpayer.
[2]With some loans, there is an early redemption charge if you pay off in the early years.
[3]But essential to keep the policy going, otherwise the capital sum built up could be wiped out by surrender penalties.

me. He has recommended that I take out a 25-year low-cost endowment mortgage with one of the smaller building societies. It seems a reasonable deal, but I'm sure I read somewhere that repayment mortgages were better. The broker didn't mention that type of mortgage at all.

A Endowment mortgages used to benefit from significant tax advantages, but despite the removal or erosion of these they have continued to be popular. It is hard not to suspect that the continuing popularity of endowment mortgages is linked to the substantial commissions which building societies and others arranging mortgages receive as a result of selling the associated insurance policies (see page 178). But which type of mortgage is right for you depends on a whole variety of factors, such as tax treatments and your attitude towards risk. Endowments may not be the best choice for everyone. The Table on page 184 summarises the key features of repayment and endowment mortgages: you should weigh up these for your own particular situation before you make your choice.

Q *I've been paying off my mortgage now for nine years. It makes me hopping mad to see my building society offering cut-price mortgages and huge cash-backs to attract new customers when I'm stuck on the standard interest rate. Why can't existing customers benefit from these deals?*

A Maybe you can. You are correct that most lenders offer special deals, such as discounted rates and cash-backs, only to new customers who are either moving home or just switching their mortgage. The reason for this is simple: the lender in most cases simply could not afford to offer the deal to everyone. It is the existence of a large base of customers paying at the standard rate which gives the lender the resources to make attractive offers to lure in new customers.

One way you could benefit from the special deals is to switch your mortgage to another lender. But you might be able to get a better deal even if you stay put. Lenders do not want to lose their existing customers: they are hoping that most will not make the effort to switch. But, if you are shopping around for a better deal, make sure you talk first to your existing lender. It may well be willing to offer you improved mortgage terms, either from its standard product range or on a one-off basis, rather than lose you to a rival.

Q *I am buying a new house and had planned to take out the mortgage with my current building society, but the society says I must also take out my buildings insurance and contents insurance through it. That will work out a lot more expensive than using other insurance companies. Can the society insist on this?*

A It depends. Often lenders offer a mortgage package, which attaches various benefits and conditions to the loan, one of which might be that you take out buildings insurance, and sometimes other types of insurance too, through that lender. You cannot normally opt out of part of the package because, for example, the commission the lender receives by arranging the insurance might be helping to subsidise a particularly competitive interest rate on the loan. You need to weigh up the value to you of the package as a whole. If the drawback of expensive insurance outweighs the advantages of the mortgage terms and any other perks, you should look elsewhere for a mortgage.

In other cases, the lender might *prefer* you to take out insurance through it, but will not insist on it, so ask what its policy is on this. But, as far as buildings insurance goes, the lender will want to make sure that the property is adequately covered, so it will vet the policy you choose and will usually charge a fee for doing this, generally in the region of £25.

Q *When I took out my mortgage, I had to pay a one-off £1,400 premium for mortgage indemnity guarantee (MIG) insurance. The mortgage was meant to last for 25 years, but I've decided to switch to another lender after just 18 months. I asked the original building society to refund the bulk of the MIG premium but it has refused. Do I have a right to a refund?*

A This is a grey area. MIG insurance is usually a requirement if the loan you are taking out represents a high value of the property you are buying (e.g. more than 75–80 per cent). The premium goes by various names, such as MIG, MIP or high loan-to-value fee. MIG insurance is a contract between the lender and an insurance company which protects the lender against loss if your home is sold for less than the outstanding mortgage. However, it is standard practice that, even though you are not a party to this insurance, you pay the premium for it.

Until a few years ago, many lenders did refund part of the MIG premium – and a few still do – if the loan is repaid well before the end of its term. But most do not and, unless your agreement with the lender entitles you to a refund, you have no legal right to one. However, it is still worth asking if your lender would reconsider and you could point out that the Banking Ombudsman★ has stated that he finds it unsatisfactory where there is no refund.

Q *My mortgage is just coming to an end, so I have been talking to my building society about arrangements for transferring the deeds. I'm appalled that they say they will release the deeds only to a solicitor and not direct to me. Why on earth should I have to pay a solicitor's bill?*

A There is no legal reason why the deeds should not be handed over direct to you and many lenders are happy to do this. You should challenge your building society's policy and, if it persists in its attitude, complain to the Building Societies Ombudsman★ (see page 166). However, you might want to reconsider taking over the deeds at all. They are valuable documents which must be kept safely. An obvious place would be a safe deposit box at a bank, but you would have to pay a regular fee for this. If, instead, you pay off all but a token amount of your mortgage, the building society will continue to hold the deeds for you at no cost, and you will avoid any deeds fee or sealing fee which would become due if the mortgage were paid off completely.

Insurance companies

Q *Our flat was burgled and all our hi-fi equipment and CDs stolen. The insurance company has agreed to pay in full for the hi-fi but argues that our CDs (some 60 or so worth over £650) constitute a 'collection'* *and are subject to a limit under our policy of £500. I thought 'collection' meant things like stamps. Does it really apply to CDs? And what about books?*

A Confusion over policy terms and wording is a major cause of insurance disputes. When you first consider taking out a policy, it is vital that you read it carefully to check that it does give the precise cover you require. You should query anything that seems ambiguous, ideally getting the insurance company's interpretation in writing. If you are not confident that the policy does meet your needs, try another company.

If you have already taken out the insurance and the problem arises when you come to make a claim, you should challenge an unreasonable interpretation of the policy wording by the insurance company. In your case, your policy refers to *'stamps, coins and other collections'* and precisely what is included is open to interpretation. Some other companies have more precise wording: for example, *'collections of stamps, coins and metals'*, which clearly does not extend to CDs, tapes, books and the like. You should certainly challenge your insurer's refusal to meet the claim in full. First make your complaint to whoever is dealing with your claim and, if necessary, to the company's management and/or head office. If this does produce satisfactory results, take your case to the Insurance Ombudsman★ (see page 166).

Q *I live in an area where the ground is mainly clay and there have been problems with subsidence because of recent dry summers. As a result my house buildings insurance premium has rocketed. This is totally unfair, given that my own house is built on chalk and not affected by the dry weather. But my insurance company refuses to lower the premium and says that it looks at the area as a whole, not at the individual houses. What can I do to make them see sense?*

A A key factor which insurance companies take into account when deciding what premium to charge for buildings insurance is the area in which you live. To sort the nation into areas they use the standard postcode classifications. As you might expect, postcode areas do not naturally coincide with geological features, such as clay soil. This means that homes which are very unlikely to suffer from subsidence are sometimes lumped together with others which are at high risk. This is a particular problem in the south-east of England.

It sounds as if your present insurer is adamant that it will not look at your case individually, but it would be worth getting quotes from other companies. Although it is standard practice for insurers to use the postcode system for rating risks, many (possibly including yours) still use a relatively crude method based on the first three characters of the code. However, about half of the companies offering buildings insurance now use a more refined system based on the first *four* characters of the postcode. This divides up the nation into much smaller areas and makes it less likely that your home will be grouped with an adjacent higher-risk area.

Q *I bought my house several years ago. At that time, the building society which arranged my buildings insurance recommended that I insure the house for the same amount I paid. The policy is index-linked and the sum insured has now risen to £70,000, but working through a leaflet sent to me by the society, I reckon that I should only be insured for £40,000. I don't want to pay for more cover than I need, so can I get the sum insured reduced?*

A The amount of cover you have under a buildings insurance policy should be enough to pay the cost of clearing the site and totally rebuilding your home using similar materials in the event that the home is completely destroyed. This will not necessarily be the same as the market price you pay for your home, though in practice the amounts are sometimes similar. Once you have bought your home, it is important to keep the cover up to date and, assuming you have an index-linked policy, this is done by automatically increasing the sum insured in line with an index of rebuilding costs which is prepared by the Royal Institution of Chartered Surveyors.* However, the use of this index has been questioned. A newspaper investigation in 1995 argued that the index was flawed: it over-estimated increases in rebuilding costs, leaving policyholders paying as much as £300 million a year too much for their buildings insurance. A further problem *Which?* magazine has highlighted is that, when occasionally rebuilding costs have fallen, insurance premiums have not been reduced. So it is possible that your home is over-insured and that you are paying too much.

To remedy the situation, you should contact your insurance company to present the facts of your case. The insurer might want your home to be professionally valued before it accepts your argument: if so, insist that the insurer pays for this. Provided there is good evidence that the sum assured should indeed be lower, your insurer should agree to the reduction in cover and premiums. You should also press for a refund, if the over-payment has been going on for some time. If your insurer does not co-operate, consider going to the Insurance Ombudsman★ (see page 166).

Q *We had a pipe burst this winter and water cascaded through the ceiling into the living room. The settee was ruined and we have claimed for it on our insurance, but the insurance company refuses to replace the two matching chairs which were undamaged. Surely we are entitled to replace the whole three-piece suite?*

A This is one area where you cannot beat the system. For years, the treatment of matching items has been a bone of contention between policyholders and insurance companies. Now, it is standard for house insurance policies specifically to exclude cover for undamaged parts of three-piece suites, bathroom suites, and so on.

Q *Our house was broken into and various things stolen including a valuable watch I was given on my retirement. It can't be replaced exactly, because styles have changed. I feel anything different just wouldn't have the same sentimental meaning for me. I asked the insurance company if I could just have the cash value instead. The company has agreed, but has reduced the amount it will pay out. Can it do this?*

A Your insurance policy probably contains a clause giving the insurance company the option either to give you the cost of a lost, damaged or stolen item or to replace it. Replacing items direct is one way in which insurers can reduce the amount they pay out in claims, because they can often negotiate discounts with local suppliers. If you opt for cash instead, the insurance company will sometimes reduce the payout by the amount of the discount. Keeping down the cost of claims should help to keep premiums down, benefiting all policyholders, so this practice is not unreasonable if the items you are claiming for are readily obtainable. But it may be quite inappropriate for more unusual items which a supplier is unlikely to be able to replace exactly, and, therefore, it seems unreasonable also for the company to reduce the alternative cash payout. If you are not satisfied with the cash or replacement offered, complain (see page 170).

Q *I'm about to book a holiday and I've been looking through a survey of travel insurance policies. One thing that strikes me is that they all have baggage cover, but the clothes, camera and so on I'll take with me are already covered by my house contents insurance. Why should I pay twice for insurance and if I do can I claim twice if anything does get lost or stolen?*

A It is quite common for there to be an overlap between different insurances: for example, travel and household insurance as in this case or belongings covered by both household and car insurance. But you cannot claim twice. The principle of insurance is that you should be put back into the position you were in before you suffered the loss or damage giving rise to the claim but that you should not be able to profit from it. Therefore, most insurance policies contain a clause stating that, if the loss is covered by other insurance, the policy will pay only a proportion of the claim. The rest would be paid by the other insurance.

However, it is galling to be paying twice for the same cover. In the case of travel insurance, a few companies will let you cancel sections of the policy which are duplicated by other insurances you have and will reduce the premium accordingly. Shop around for an insurance company which allows this.

Inland Revenue

Q *My tax is deducted direct from my pay through the PAYE system, but the amount I'm paying seems too high. Could it be wrong?*

A Certainly it is a possibility, though mistakes are less common under PAYE than in non-PAYE cases. The amount of tax deducted under PAYE hinges on your tax code. The code tells your employer how much free-of-tax pay you are allowed each week or month and tax tables tell him how much tax is due on the remainder. Before the start of the tax year, you should have been given a Notice of Coding telling you your tax code and explaining how it has been worked out. You should check this notice carefully. Errors can arise because, for example, you have not claimed all the allowances to which you are entitled or you have not told the Revenue about all your sources of income. To help you check the correct tax position, use a guide, such as the *Which? Tax-Saving Guide.*★

Q *I've just had a tax assessment which says that I will have to pay £8,600 tax on profits from my business. This is way too high – the tax office has estimated my profits based on last year, but they are a lot lower this year. Presumably I don't have to pay the excess, do I?*

A Write to your tax office within 30 days of the date on the Notice of Assessment, saying that you wish to appeal against the assessment and stating your reasons for doing this. At the same time, you must apply to postpone payment of the amount of tax in dispute. You can make the appeal and application to postpone tax on the form in the booklet accompanying your assessment or in a separate letter. If you have already missed the 30-day deadline, you can still appeal, provided you have a good reason for the delay: for example, you were away from home on holiday or business. If you and your tax office cannot agree on the correct amount of tax due, your case can be referred to the Tax Commissioners – a sort of tax tribunal which will decide on the amount due. Their decision is generally final, but if you disagree on a point of law you could challenge it in court.

Q *I'm a pensioner and, because I have several sources of investment income including some shares held overseas, I fill in a tax return every year. Am I right in thinking that from April 1997 I will have to work out my own tax bill as well as giving the Inland Revenue details of my income? The thought appals me – I'm no tax expert and I really don't think I'll be able to calculate my own bill.*

A You are correct that from April 1997 the new system of self-assessment is being introduced. It will apply to everyone who does not pay all his or her tax through the PAYE system. However, at present the new system is voluntary. Provided you send your completed tax return to your tax office by 30 September following the end of the tax year, the Inland Revenue will work out your tax bill for you just as they do now. If you decide to work out your own tax, you will not have to send in your tax return until the following 31 January.

Q *The tax laws seem to be so comprehensive and precise. I find it hard to believe that there are any loopholes left to allow significant amounts of tax to be saved. How can there be?*

A The tax laws have grown up over centuries and often changes to them have been responses to the way people behave, and new products and practices developed, rather than as part of a structured plan. As a result, although the tax laws are voluminous, there are in fact many gaps and oddities which open the way for tax-saving ruses. In addition, the tax laws treat income in different ways depending on its source. Some of the rules give more scope for tax-saving than others: for example, if you are self-employed you have more opportunities to offset expenses against your income than if you are an employee. There are numerous books about tax-saving, including *Which? Way to Save Tax,*★ on the market to guide you through these opportunities. If your income is substantial or your tax affairs complex, you might also consider enlisting the help of an accountant or other tax specialist. A word of warning, however: tax *avoidance* is the legitimate saving of tax by lawful use of the tax rules; tax *evasion* is illegally failing to pay tax, for example, by not declaring all your income.

Department of Social Security

Q *I'm on income support. My neighbour has offered me a six-week contract to work for his building firm. Given the temporary nature of the work, can I carry on claiming benefit? What would the position be if I didn't tell the Benefits Agency about the contract?*

A Unless you are caring for a family, to be eligible for income support you must be available for work. You are considered to be available provided any work you currently do is for less than 16 hours a week. You must, by law, declare any earnings which will reduce your benefit on a £1-for-£1 basis. If you are working 16 hours a week or more, you are not eligible for income support. However, if you have children, you may be eligible for family credit instead – a benefit designed to supplement low earnings. Unfortunately, the benefits system is cumbersome and makes it hard for people to slip on and off benefit as temporary work becomes available.

If you do not tell the agency about your earnings, you will be guilty of fraud and could be fined and/or sent to jail. Some people do see 'moonlighting' (working in the black economy without declaring their earnings for tax or benefit reasons) as a way of beating the system, but it is illegal.

Q *My husband, who has been a groundsman for the local council for many years, has been unable to work for eight months now because of an injury to his back. Initially, he was claiming incapacity benefit. But the Benefits Agency says he's no longer entitled to this because, it claims, he could take on some other type of work. He can't lift anything, he can't sit for long periods, he can't stand for hours on end and he needs a stick to walk with. How can I get the Agency to change its mind?*

A The rules for incapacity benefit are much stricter than the rules for sickness benefit, which it replaced from April 1995. In particular, from the 28th week of illness or disability, you must be able to show that you are incapable of any work, not simply your normal job. However, if your husband considers that he is not able to carry on any work at all, he should ask the Benefits Agency to review its decision (see page 172). There are three main grounds on which you can apply for a review:

- the initial decision was wrong in law
- some relevant facts were either unknown or mistakenly interpreted
- there has been a relevant change in your circumstances.

If none of these applies, you can take your case straight to the appeal tribunal.

Q *I worked in Germany for many years before I retired on ill-health grounds. I have a small pension paid from Germany, but I know I am also entitled to some pension from the DSS in Britain. However, it has consistently refused my claim. The arguments have gone on for 18 months now and I am desperate. What can I do?*

A You could invoke the complaints procedure as outlined on page 172. Since your case is clearly complex, you might also seek independent advice from, for example, your local Citizens Advice Bureau or your Member of Parliament.★

Q *I've recently retired on my state pension of £60-odd a week and a company pension of £23 a week. It's not a lot, but I manage and at least I'm paying my own way – something I've done all my life. What beats me, though, is that a friend – same age – is claiming benefits and getting £131 a week plus full rent relief and doesn't have to pay council tax. Where's the justice in this?*

A The benefits system is complex with a variety of different benefits available under slightly different rules. One of the biggest problems is the shift from being on benefit to managing on your own income where that income is low. Often the loss of additional benefits, such as housing benefit, free NHS treatment or free school meals can mean that the person making his (or her) own way on a low income can overall be worse off than he (or she) would be on benefit. However, some benefits are available to people on low incomes and you should certainly check whether you are missing out on any benefits to which you are entitled. Seek advice from your local Citizens Advice Bureau★ or local branch of Age Concern.

CHAPTER 6

THE LEGAL SYSTEM

ONE MESSAGE of the book you are currently reading will by now have become clear: the key to beating the various 'systems' described in this book is often a matter of using the legal system to your own advantage. And the same is true of the legal system itself. The paradox is that 'beating' it requires a good understanding of its language, the courts, procedures and your rights. It is therefore essential to acquire the relevant information promptly – and ideally without having to pay legal fees. Whether you obtain this by researching the law and procedures yourself, or by getting access to free or cheap expert knowledge, the result is the same – access to a system that can help you in many different ways. Various sources of free or cheap legal advice are available, depending on the type of claim you have (see 'Sources of help', page 205).

Regular research carried out by *Which?* magazine shows that people with a legal problem who make the system work for them by getting good advice from the right source at an early stage have an excellent chance of getting redress, and may not need to take any significant financial risks. But still far too many people are put off by the cost. Many worry about the solicitors' bills they will have to pay and that they might be liable for the other side's costs. In short, they are thwarted by the system instead of using the system to their advantage.

How the legal system works

The legal system comprises the whole raft of laws passed to regulate our society. In Britain this has developed over several centuries, and the result is a system, administered by the courts and the lawyers, of considerable complexity that can be costly to access.

The law itself aims to be fair and to provide the boundaries for acceptable behaviour. If anybody steps outside those boundaries, by committing a crime, breaking a contract, selling unsafe goods, or simply not providing what the law says is expected of him (or her), the law is the means to punishment or redress.

Often the problems with the system spring from the practitioners, notably solicitors and barristers, who have everything to gain by sustaining its traditions and procedures and by keeping the detail of what they do shrouded in mystery.

The law that offers consumers protection is supposed to exist for the benefit of consumers. But very few of us, when we encounter a problem, are prepared for the archaic language, puzzling procedures and expense that confront us when we attempt to exert our rights. So why is the law such a maze? Why is it so difficult to understand? And why does the system put so many barriers in the way of the layperson? It need not be so. Yet the lawyers and others who work in the cosseted confines of the system, including some unscrupulous ones who feed off its hapless victims, can rightly be accused of maintaining the barriers.

In fact, one of the best ways to beat the system is to avoid using the courts wherever possible; and if doing so becomes unavoidable, to avoid seeking advice in the traditional way.

Both the civil justice system and Legal Aid funding are undergoing major changes. But as with many aspects of the law change has been a long time coming and is a slow process. In 1994, Lord Woolf was appointed by the Lord Chancellor to review the civil justice system and his interim report was published in June 1995. His view was that the civil justice system was too slow, too expensive, too complex and unfair (no surprises there). His aim is to increase access to justice by making the system cheaper, simpler, quicker, and fairer: whether he succeeds, we will have to wait and see. But improved access to justice, with the provison of easier and more understandable court procedures, more efficient courts and friendlier buildings and staff, is now the official goal. What is proposed, if implemented, will change at least the civil justice system beyond recognition, but the changes will be introduced over a fairly lengthy timescale, and how radical the overhaul turns out to be in reality will depend on political will and money.

One of the proposals in the review has already been introduced. In January 1996 the limit for the county court to hear 'small claims' (see page 202) was increased from £1,000 to £3,000 (in England and Wales: the limit remains at £750 for Scotland and £1,000 for Northern Ireland), opening up the courts to many more consumers with claims within these limits.

Consumer protection legislation

The rules that offer protection to consumers come from a wide variety of sources. However, if used properly, they can help you overcome the problems the system presents you with. Some of these laws are made by Parliament in the form of statutes, some by judges in the form of cases argued out by lawyers in the court room (known as common law), and some direct from the European Union in the form of directives. Some operate in the realm of criminal law, others in the realm of the civil law. The first hurdle in the system is finding out what your rights are. Then you have to enforce them. Here is a short guide to where consumer rights come from:

- **statute law** (such as the Sale of Goods Act 1979) is enshrined in Acts of Parliament and in Regulations and Orders under the general authority of Acts of Parliament; it sets out the rights and duties of specified people in specified circumstances
- **common law** is based on the decisions of the courts in actual cases which also set out the rights and duties of people in different circumstances. These are recorded in law reports and form precedents for the future. In this way the courts can adapt the law to new situations without having to wait for Parliament to introduce legislation. The interpretation and definition of the words in various Acts of Parliament form the basis for the judgments made in many cases that come before the courts
- **civil law** is the branch of the legal system which is of most use to individuals who wish to take positive action themselves by seeking redress in the form of compensation. The Sale of

Goods Act 1979 (as amended) and Part I of the Consumer Protection Act 1987 are two examples of Acts of Parliament which offer civil protection. The civil law is concerned with rights and duties that relate to individuals in their dealings with other individuals (including companies and other groups of people). If you suffer loss because someone else breaches civil laws, you have a right to redress and are entitled to take that person to court if need be. The main areas of civil law are tort (which includes nuisance and negligence) and contract. The courts which deal with civil claims are the county court (which includes the small claims court) and the High Court.

- a **contract** is any agreement that can be enforced by law. It gives the parties who have made the contract certain rights and obligations. Contracts can be made in writing, by word of mouth or even without a single word being spoken or written. Every day people make contracts without putting them in writing – by buying food in shops or travelling by bus, for example. These contracts have the same standing as written contracts and, like all contracts, are governed by the law of contract

- **negligence** is the breach of a legal duty to take reasonable care, resulting in damage to someone else. Unlike a contract claim there is no need to show any formal relationship other than one of care. Perhaps the most common example of negligence is a car driver causing an accident. The driver owes a duty to all other road users and pedestrians to take care. If that duty is breached then he must answer for the consequences and pay compensation

- **nuisance** is the unlawful interference with someone else's enjoyment of his home. So if you have noisy neighbours, for example, this law will help you

• **criminal law** is the branch of the law which is concerned with offences against the public, such as the Trade Descriptions Act 1968 and Part II of the Consumer Protection Act 1987. Criminal law is generally enforced by the police, but the specific criminal law affecting consumers is enforced by public authorities such as Trading Standards Departments and Environmental Health Officers (both based at local council offices – see 'Sources of help', page 205). You cannot obtain compensation directly by reporting a criminal offence such as a false trade description, but evidence of such wrongdoing will lend weight to your complaint and sometimes a compensation order may be made as part of the prosecution. The courts which deal with criminal matters are the magistrates' courts and the crown courts.

The courts

If we find ourselves caught up in the court system, most of us as consumers will gain direct experience of the civil courts, either as plaintiffs or defendants, claiming against a trader for compensation for shoddy work or goods, or fending off claims for unpaid bills, or perhaps for compensation arising out of a traffic accident, for example.

An important way to beat the system is to fight your own case without using lawyers. The small claims procedure in the county court is the simplest and most accessible way to do this. But you can represent yourself in any court at any level if you feel confident enough. As a 'litigant in person' you can take a friend to the court with you to take notes, quietly make suggestions and give advice. Alternatively, if you have a friend who is prepared to represent you, you may opt for this course of action provided you ask the court's permission first.

Many of the procedures – for example, in the small claims court, the full county court and the High Court – are the same, as will now be explained.

DIY justice

As long as you have a genuine dispute with a company or trader you can claim through the courts. However, it should always be as a last resort. Avoid having to get tangled up in the court system if possible. Try to sort the matter out by getting advice from reliable sources (see 'Sources of help', page 205) and by using alternative methods. Contact any relevant trade association or governing body and ask if it will conciliate, or refer the matter to an ombudsman if appropriate. If that proves unsuccessful, you will then have to decide between arbitration and court. If you choose the small claims court, this is often referred to as 'small claims arbitration'. But this is different from real arbitration, as explained later (see 'An alternative system', page 212).

Generally, the term 'arbitration' is used to refer to an informal means of arriving at a decision on a dispute which is binding on both parties. But 'arbitration' operated by the courts is completely different from arbitration schemes organised by bodies like the Chartered Institute of Arbitrators. When you start proceedings in the county court, claims of £3,000 or less (in England and Wales) are automatically referred to as 'small claims arbitration', and the whole procedure is more popularly known as the small claims court. In Scotland claims of £750 or less are dealt with in the small claims part of the sheriff court. The procedure is operated by the courts and the case is heard by the district judge.

Arbitration schemes run for trade associations are operated by independent bodies such as the Chartered Institute of Arbitrators. The arbitrators appointed are independent of the trade association and are usually qualified professionals: for example, surveyors, architects, engineers or lawyers.

If you do choose to start legal proceedings (issue proceedings) you need to send one last letter to your opponent stating that if the matter is not settled within a reasonable time, usually seven to 14 days, you will issue a county court summons. During the negotiating process take some tips from the 'Tricks of the trade' section, page 220. If you do not hear from your opponent, or if the response is not satisfactory, you can issue proceedings.

You can start the claim (issue proceedings) in your local county court. But if the company (or person) you are suing defends the case, it will automatically be transferred to a county court nearer its place of business. Many cases are settled out of court, but often only once proceedings have been issued or even at the door of the court. So do not give up: persistence pays. Free leaflets explaining what to do are available from county courts. You can also obtain a default summons from your local county court. There are two forms: N1, which you should use when claiming a fixed amount, and N2, which you should use when you are not claiming a specific amount (for example, in holiday cases in which the claim is for disappointment and loss of enjoyment), but make sure you keep your claim within the small claims limit.

The court forms have been simplified so you should not have too much trouble filling them in. If you do need any assistance the court staff, your local Citizens Advice Bureau or Consumer Advice Centre will help you. Otherwise:

- complete the summons by inserting the your own full name and address (you are the plaintiff) and those of the other side (the defendant) and set out briefly the details of your claim. Finish by stating the remedy you require on the particulars of claim
- it is important to sue the right person or company – the name on the letterhead may, for example, be only the trading name, not the name of the registered company
- check that the trader is still in business by contacting the Trading Standards Department for the area local to the trader, or, if it is a company, phone Companies House★
- once you have completed the summons, take it plus a copy to the court, or send it by first-class post. Also, ensure you keep a copy for yourself. You will have to pay an issue fee (£10-£80 for claims up to £1,000)
- a few days later you should receive a note ('Notice of Issue of Default Summons') from the court telling you the number of the case. The court will send a copy of the summons to the defendant.

Defending a claim

If, on the other hand, *you* receive a summons and you wish to dispute the amount claimed, you should send a defence to the court within 21 days from the date of the postmark by completing form N9B; if not, you risk having judgment entered against you. This form and full instructions should be sent to you with the claim. The court will then send the defence to the person making the claim (the plaintiff). If a defence is not filed with the court within the time limit the plaintiff can apply for judgment to be given automatically ('in default').

At this point you must decide whether you have or want to make a counter-claim against the plaintiffs for any losses you may want to claim against them. Whatever you do, always:

- read very carefully everything the court sends you: court forms and language are not as clear as they could be and mistakes could cost you dear. If in doubt, ask the court staff for help
- put your evidence and arguments together carefully and avoid including irrelevant statements or remarks
- keep receipts for all expenses you intend to claim and make sure you have all the evidence you need to support your arguments, such as estimates, bills and written reports.

Guaranteeing your rights in the system

The Courts Charter

The Court Service is now an executive agency of the Lord Chancellor's Department providing administrative support to the High Court, Crown Court and the county courts. Magistrates' courts, which have their own charters, are administered by local magistrates' courts committees (MCCs). An MCC inspectorate examines the performance of these courts and reports to the Lord Chancellor. Magistrates' courts are not covered by the Charter for Court Users (the 'Courts Charter').

The Courts Charter covers you in your role as a juror, a witness or defendant in criminal cases, and has special standards for divorce cases and family disputes. Most important for consumers, it also spells out what you can expect if you have anything to do with the county court (including the small claims court) or High Court. For example, if you are appearing in a county court, you can expect:

- to have your case heard in court within a maximum of 40 days once you have told the court you are ready for trial
- to be sent a copy of the court's decision no more than 10 days later
- when you write to the court, a response within 10 days.

The courts have many leaflets available, so make use of them: they can work to your advantage. For example, there are leaflets explaining each stage of the small claims procedure as well as family and probate matters. This information is an invaluable guide to the system.

Complaints about any aspect of the service you receive from the courts (but not the outcome of your case) should be made to the customer service manager of the court at the time it arises. Further complaints should be made in writing to the Chief Clerk and if you are not happy with the reply you are given you should write to the Courts Administrator.

The name of the Chief Clerk and the name and address of the Courts Administrator are displayed in every court office. Leaflets contain all the information and addresses you need, as well as describing the complaints procedure in detail. The Courts Charter says that your written complaint will be acknowledged within two working days and you will receive a reply within 20 working days from the date your letter is received.

If you are not happy with the Courts Administrator's investigation you can write to the Court Service Customer Service Unit for an independent investigation. If you have lost money or incurred costs as a result of a mistake by a member of the court staff the Chief Clerk is your point of contact. You must provide proof of your financial loss. The Clerk will assess the claim and send a report to the Courts Administrator. Large claims will be passed on to the Customer Service Unit.★

If you have a complaint about the way a judge has treated you personally in court (apart from decisions made in your case) you should write to the Judicial Appointments Group.★ Quote the name of the court you attended, your court case number, the date of your hearing, if possible the name of the judge concerned, and your reasons for making the complaint.

Sources of help

Where to get advice

Beating the system ideally means settling disputes without going to court; as a starting point, you should try to get clued up about your rights without going to the expense of using lawyers. This includes knowledge of the alternative ways to solve disputes, such as watchdog and trade arbitration schemes, and ombudsmen (see 'An alternative system', page 212).

The right advice is crucial if you are to make the best of your case, but the secret is to go to the right people for help without incurring unnecessary expense. A survey published in *Which?* magazine in January 1994 showed that nearly half of those with legal problems consulted solicitors, who often charge even for initial advice. Only a fifth used the free services of a Citizens Advice Bureau (CAB). Even fewer used their legal expenses insurance (see 'Alternative Funding') or asked Trading Standards Departments for help. And even though a large proportion of readers took legal advice from a solicitor, relatively few then went on to use the more cost-effective ways of getting redress (such as the small claims court).

This could have been due to nervousness about using the legal system without formal legal advice and assistance, or because solicitors were basing their advice on what was profitable for them, or, as other research in *Which?* magazine has shown, because even lawyers themselves did not know of other, low-cost, alternatives. This confirms that where beating the system is your aim you have to know what is available – but you should not rely on the professionals telling you.

Future reforms to the Legal Aid system may allow Citizens Advice Bureaux, Law Centres and other advice centres to offer wider-ranging services on Legal Aid: for example, not only to offer advice but also to take your case to court.

Citizens Advice Bureaux comprise the largest and best-known national network of centres providing free, independent and non-judgemental information and advice to people on any issue which they raise. There are about 1,000 CABx all over Britain; their addresses and telephone numbers are listed in local telephone directories.

They have grouped together as Associations, one in England and Wales, and one in Scotland. Although most of the staff members are not legally qualified they all undergo basic training. They have an extensive information base which is regularly updated. They will refer individuals to solicitors who take part in a fixed-fee interview scheme, or who give initial advice free of charge; or to a law centre if they need representation and Legal Aid is not available, and they cannot afford to pay a solicitor.

Trading Standards Departments are part of the local authority services. They are provided by county councils, metropolitan districts and London boroughs, by regional or islands councils in Scotland, and by area Trading Standards Offices of the Department of Commerce in Northern Ireland. Their work can be divided into two categories: helping consumers and enforcing the criminal law.

The extent to which they can offer help to consumers varies a great deal from area to area, and they may not be as accessible to the public as local advice centres. However, the help available should include advice on all aspects of consumer problems, including information on the law and how to take action.

However, the main job of Trading Standards Departments is enforcing the criminal law as it applies to consumer matters. These include the law on trade descriptions, misleading prices, weights and measures, unsafe or dangerous goods and so on.

Environmental Health Departments are also part of the local authority and exist to enforce the criminal laws on health-related issues which may affect consumers. These include environmental protection, unfit food, lack of hygiene in restaurants, hotels and other eating places, and housing which is not being maintained in a condition fit for habitation.

Legal Advice Centres are informal, non-profit-making legal offices set up by CABx, local authorities and various charitable organisations. They are staffed by volunteer lawyers who give their services free on a part-time or rota basis. They offer free legal advice but do not generally handle any casework or act for you in court.

Law Centres are rather like Legal Advice Centres but can take on the whole case and often represent individuals in legal proceedings.

Which? Personal Service★ The Consumers' Association operates this legal advice line at a cost of £7.75 a quarter. Subscribing gives you access to impartial legal advice from a team of highly qualified consumer lawyers, plus greatly reduced charges for more complicated written legal help with cases.

Other sources of cheap or inexpensive legal advice Among these is a range of community advice centres, often affiliated to the Federation of Independent Advice Centres, which can assist with consumer problems. In some cases specialist advice centres deal with a particular subject area. For example, Shelter, the housing charity and campaigning group, runs a network of Housing Advice Centres which can assist with a wide variety of problems involving housing, including difficulties over mortgages or with the service provided by estate agents.

It is also increasingly common for individual firms of solicitors to offer free legal advice at certain times, usually one evening each week. Although these are not legal advice centres, properly speaking, the situation is similar. Such firms hope that you will then return to consult the solicitor on a fee-paying basis. Of course, the choice is yours.

For other specific areas of the law there are organisations which can put you in touch with lawyers who offer free or cheap initial advice. For example, it is not practical to try to handle a personal injury claim yourself unless the amount involved is very small and your injury very minor; in any event you will need some advice to find out what compensation you should claim, perhaps from:

- the Law Society, which has a panel of personal injury specialists★ and an Accident Line★
- the Association of Personal Injury Lawyers★
- the Motor Accident Solicitors Society★
- other solicitors offering low-cost initial interviews: consult the *Solicitors Regional Directory* in your library, town hall or advice centre
- Action for Victims of Medical Accidents (AVMA),★ which can advise on cases of injury suffered through medical negligence
- the Solicitor's Family Law Association.★

Trade and professional associations Important areas covered by codes of practice include holidays (the Association of British Travel Agents★), mail order (the Mail Order Traders Association), cars (the Society of Motor Manufacturers and Traders), and dry cleaning (the Textile Services Association). The Law Society imposes strict disciplinary rules of conduct on solicitors, breach of which may result in withdrawal of the right to practise. However, not all trade associations manage to embrace all traders operating in their field, and the extent to which they can exercise collective discipline varies considerably.

Some codes of practice specifically include provision for arbitration as a means of solving a consumer complaint ('code arbitration': see 'An alternative system'). This is a method of settling a dispute which avoids any court proceedings: both sides put their case to an independent arbitrator who considers the evidence and the law before making a decision, known as an award, which is binding in law.

Alternative funding

Legal Aid

In brief, most people in the UK now do not qualify for Legal Aid. They are what Consumers' Association has dubbed the MINELAs (Middle Income Not Eligible for Legal Aid). The qualifications for free Legal Aid have been tightened in recent years and it is now available only to people with income at income support levels. Although the Legal Aid budget will probably continue to grow it will not match the rises in legal costs and the number of cases, which means that fewer people are eligible for help. Proposals have been made to improve the system, but it is not yet clear whether these will be implemented or how much difference they will make.

An increasing number of people will have to think even more carefully about taking legal action in the future.

Legal expenses insurance

The legal system is designed to provide a means of getting justice, yet the system itself conspires against many consumers, who are effectively denied access. In short, the cost of the system can stop people getting justice. But legal expenses insurance – which you may have already without even realising it – can cover these costs. Insurance against the possibility of future legal expenses is still a fairly new concept in the UK but has existed in Europe since the beginning of the twentieth century. The cover can pay for a lawyer to claim compensation on your behalf in a wide range of circumstances.

Some house and car insurance policies include legal expenses insurance; others let you buy it as an extra for £10 or so. Car add-ons generally cover compensation for car accident injuries and other uninsured losses, such as hiring a car while yours is off the road. Household add-ons usually cover consumer disputes, legal problems connected with home ownership, personal injury and employment. Some car breakdown services and travel insurance policies help with legal expenses, too, and some policies cover the many problems which can arise from a specific event, such as moving house.

'No win, no fee'

A great number of people are effectively denied justice and access to any system of exercising their legal rights. Those who do not qualify for Legal Aid (see page 209), or who, being just above income support level, would qualify only if they could contribute to legal expenses (in practice, most cannot) constitute 40 per cent of households in Britain; add to these those people who have no legal expenses insurance, who cannot use the small claims court and have no alternative method of resolving their dispute, and it becomes obvious that a huge section of the population has little chance of getting legal redress if wronged, unless those concerned are rich enough to take the financial risk of legal action.

One of the keys to giving consumers access to justice is the development of further alternative ways of funding court cases and paying lawyers' bills. The Courts and Legal Services Act 1990 paved the way for a 'no win, no fee' system in England and Wales (similar arrangements had long been allowed in Scotland). Since July 1995 solicitors have been allowed to offer conditional fee arrangements in the following types of cases:

- personal injury claim. This includes claims of medical negligence and all situations where you have suffered any kind of injury. It also permits claims where the injury is only part of the case: for example, a housing case with a claim for injury to health

- certain bankruptcy/insolvency-related proceedings
- human rights cases.

In these types of case clients are now free to agree with lawyers that the lawyer will take on a legal case on the understanding that, if it is lost, the lawyer will not receive any payment. Conditional fee arrangements remove the uncertainty and financial risk of going to law. Potential clients need not fear that if their case is unsuccessful they will have to pay their own lawyer's bill. If they lose, they pay their own lawyer nothing, although disbursements, counsel's fees etc. will still have to be paid. But this is simply a contract between client and lawyer, so it has no effect on the costs incurred by the client's opponent in the case. If the client loses he (or she) will still have to pay the opponent's costs. However, for a relatively small insurance premium he can insure against having to pay his opponent's legal costs.

There is no doubt that this arrangement provides access to justice for the increasing number of people who are too well off to be entitled to Legal Aid, but not well off enough to go to court at their own expense. So where's the catch?

If lawyers agree to losing their fees when a case is unsuccessful, it seems fair that there should be some *quid pro quo* for taking on this risk. The conditional fee arrangement allows your lawyer to agree with you, in advance, an 'uplift' on his or her normal bill, up to a maximum of 100 per cent (note that in Britain these arrangements are not linked to the amount of compensation awarded to a client, as happens in the USA). If you lose, you pay your lawyer nothing. If you win, you pay what would be his 'normal' fee assessed in the 'normal' way (based on his hourly rate) plus up to the same amount again for winning the case.

Again, as for any other service, you must shop around to find a lawyer prepared to take on your case at the lowest percentage uplift.

The choice is yours. You need to decide whether to take the risk of losing and paying both your own and your opponent's costs *or* of making a conditional fee contract. If you win, a larger part of your compensation will go to your lawyer to pay the increased fees. It may be a risk worth taking as it is often far better to have the opportunity to use the legal system than have no access to justice at all.

Contact the Law Society for a copy of its model conditional fee agreement and details of its insurance policy to cover opponents' costs.

An alternative system

Ombudsman schemes

It is always worth considering making your complaint through the relevant ombudsman scheme to try to settle the dispute before going to court. Britain has a wide range of ombudsman schemes. Some are statutory and cover everyone operating within that industry (for example, the Legal Services Ombudsman); others are voluntary and cover only those companies which have joined the scheme (for example, the Insurance and Banking Ombudsmen). So if you have a complaint against a company that is not a member of a voluntary scheme you cannot take your case to the ombudsman.

You will find specific schemes referred to elsewhere in this book as appropriate. Generally, however, the following criteria apply to all schemes:

- before approaching the ombudsman you must first have exhausted all other means of sorting out the dispute with the company or firm in question (for example, by writing to the head office or person in charge of handling complaints)
- ombudsman schemes are completely free and aim to be less complex and time-consuming than legal proceedings, in many cases going beyond the letter of the law
- there are time limits for complaining, usually six months (as with the Insurance Ombudsman) or 12 months from reaching deadlock with the company or trader. Check with the relevant scheme
- some ombudsmen can award compensation; others can only recommend that the company or trader pays up. Some have a maximum of £100,000 but most are unlimited
- ombudsman schemes are designed to be independent, accessible and, compared to going to court, quick
- an ombudsman's decision is usually binding on the organisation or firm you have complained about, but it is not

binding on you, the person with the complaint, so you can still go to court or to arbitration if you are unhappy with the decision.

Arbitration schemes

Any dispute can be sorted out by arbitration, whether through a scheme operated under a trade association code of practice (code arbitration) or arranged by you independently of any association. Usually you can refer complaints to arbitration only if both sides agree. For some trade associations, such as the Association of British Travel Agents (ABTA), arbitration is obligatory for members if the consumer wishes to use it.

You can request it from the Chartered Institute of Arbitrators★ (Arbiters in Scotland). If you are not using a code arbitration scheme, the loser will be paying for the arbitrator's time, charged at an hourly rate, so it could be costly, depending on the complexity of the problem.

Generally, you and the trader will have to sign a joint application form, an application for arbitration, which you can get from the relevant trade association and/or the body that administers the scheme (for example, the Chartered Institute of Arbitrators). The signed form together with relevant registration fee must be returned to the Institute. If the case is considered appropriate for arbitration, the Institute will send you (as the claimant) a statement of claim and an information sheet, detailing the process. Remember:

- if you have a small claim, you cannot be forced to go to arbitration. The Arbitration Act 1996 outlaws unfair contract terms which state that disputes below the small claims limit must be referred to arbitration: these terms are unlikely to be legally binding
- arbitration schemes are offered as alternatives to court, not in addition, so you have to choose which route to follow
- arbitration schemes generally use written evidence only, so you cannot present your case in person, and it is not always easy to put your problem clearly in writing. Court gives you the chance to put your side of the case personally

- once you have made your choice, the decision of the arbitrator is binding, so you cannot have the case re-heard using the other option if you are unhappy with the decision.

Mediation and conciliation

Some trade associations will try to sort out the dispute between you and their member through conciliation. Mediation schemes are designed to get both sides together to talk through the issues in an attempt to resolve the dispute without it escalating. Look for local initiatives on mediation or contact Mediation UK★ or the Centre for Dispute Resolution.★

Lawyers

There is an important difference between hiring professional services and paying for normal consumer goods. If you buy a washing-machine, you shop around for the best bargain and you know how much you will have to pay; it is usually obvious if it does not work properly and you can ask the shop where you bought it to take it back, to replace it or to repair it. But when it comes to professional services the exact amount to be paid is not always established – or even possible to establish – in advance; sometimes you cannot even get an estimate of the amount. It may simply not be feasible to provide clear instructions as to what is actually required, and often the client has no option but to rely heavily on the discretion of the professional. Poor service is often less easy to identify immediately and you cannot take it (the service) back once it has been provided (although you could in some cases challenge the bill or refuse to pay).

The consequences, should things go wrong, can be much more serious – even ruinous, in the case of poor service from lawyers. Two regulatory bodies represent the two main branches of the profession: the Law Society representing solicitors and the Bar Council representing barristers. If you feel you have had poor service from a lawyer, you will probably need to deal with one of these organisations. First, however, you should be aware of your rights and the lawyers' obligations.

Solicitors

A solicitor's duties in law to provide a service with reasonable skill and care are laid down in various statutes and the rules of common law. In addition solicitors must abide by the set of rules and standards published by the Law Society in its *Guide to the Professional Conduct of Solicitors*. It is not easy reading but it sets out a variety of practice rules, accounting rules, guidance statements and directions which are laid down by the Council of the Law Society.

Breach of legal duties gives the client a right to sue for compensation. Breaches of the rules of professional conduct on the other hand give no legal right to sue, but the client may report the matter to the Office for the Supervision of Solicitors (OSS),★ which will take appropriate action. In many cases a breach of the professional rules will also amount to a breach of legal duties.

A serious breach of the code of professional conduct could lead to disciplinary action by the Law Society and the solicitor may be reprimanded, fined or banned from practising any more. Important areas covered are as follows:

- every solicitors' practice must have an internal complaints-handling procedure and if you wish to complain you must be told whom to approach
- if you have not agreed a fee with the solicitor or no estimate has been given, the solicitor should tell you how the fee will be calculated: for example, on an hourly rate plus mark-up (see 'The costs of the system', page 217)
- on taking instructions the solicitor should give you the best information possible about the likely cost of the matter
- if you are not legally aided the solicitor should tell you that you may set a limit on the costs which may be incurred without further reference and inform you every six months of the approximate amount of the costs to date
- you should receive a 'client care letter' confirming your instructions and giving information on charging and likely costs.

Discipline

The Disciplinary Tribunal of the Law Society will deal with serious matters. Anybody can apply to the Tribunal without going through the OSS although it is more sensible to contact the OSS. The Tribunal cannot order your solicitor to pay compensation but it can reprimand or fine the solicitor, or suspend him from practice, or order his name to be struck off the Roll of Solicitors.

Quality within the profession

The Office for the Supervision of Solicitors (OSS) cannot consider cases of negligence although you would be wise to refer your complaint to it anyway. In theory, if you believe your solicitor has not carried out his duty with reasonable care and skill, including not carrying out the work within a reasonable time, and you have suffered loss as a result, you need legal advice. But that means relying on the system.

If you have a complaint against a solicitor, for example, there are set routes to follow, notably the OSS and the Ombudsman. However, if you feel confident enough to argue your own case and your complaint involves negligence which has caused you financial loss, go direct to the Solicitors Indemnity Fund (SIF). This body, the insurer for the solicitors' profession, will negotiate direct with you over your complaint. As long as you bear in mind that the SIF is acting for the solicitor and not you, you may well short-circuit the unnecessary delays.

Under the Solicitors' Indemnity Rules all principals in a law firm – that is, partners or sole practitioners – are required to be insured for the risk of professional negligence claims against the firm. This means that they are covered whether the negligence was their own or that of their employees or former employees. So you can negotiate direct with the insurance company responsible for insuring the profession, the Solicitors' Indemnity Fund. You may need the help of a Citizens Advice Bureau or Law Centre or Which? Personal Service to do this and perseverance may sometimes be necessary, but if you have all your evidence and arguments worked out persistence is likely to pay. Out-of-court settlements are reached in many cases.

A crucial part of beating any system is to be armed with information on our rights. If we discover that the people we have asked to guide us through the legal maze have got it wrong it compounds the problem. We simply do not expect to have to question legal advice: we desperately want to assume that it is right.

One *Which?* reader bought her home with the help of a solicitor. She checked that ownership rights to a concrete area at the bottom of her garden were included. Her solicitor received an assurance from the seller's solicitor that it was, but did not double-check. When the new owner decided to replace the concrete with grass she discovered that it was designated as a car park and several of her neighbours had the right to use it. She believed that her solicitor had been negligent in not checking this out. The firm denied liability but offered £2,500.

However, this was not enough to compensate her: she had evidence that the value of the property without exclusive use of the area was much less than what she paid. Bizarrely, the solicitor then tried to argue that the new owner had saved money by not being able to dig up the concrete area. She went straight to the Solicitors' Indemnity Fund, but it also offered far less than she expected. It was only after she issued a writ against her solicitor that the SIF made a more realistic offer of £12,500 plus costs; this she accepted.

Within the realm of the law, unlike the NHS, the local council and the banks, for example, there is a great deal you can do yourself to solve life's problems if you have the inclination and a little time. Traditional areas where people used to turn to legal professionals are on the decline – making wills, conveyancing, divorce, to name but three. Moreover, many disputes fall within the scope of the small claims court, so using the courts without a lawyer is even easier.

The costs of the system

Beating the system in terms of the legal profession and the law is no easy task. Even getting free legal advice is difficult in a system that is geared to charging on the basis of time and where the professionals account for nearly every minute spent on a client's problem, then send bills that are rarely itemised and often incomprehensible.

But it is important to remember that as with any other trade or profession you are quite free to shop around to see who will do the job you want for the lowest cost; solicitors are no exception.

In particular, house conveyancing has become very much cheaper in real terms (to the extent that doing-it-yourself is hardly worth it any more) and it is certainly well worth contacting a number of solicitors to find out what the charges will be. Remember, too, that solicitors no longer have the monopoly on such services: you can also use a licensed conveyancer.

The results of another survey for *Which?* magazine (October 1995) were very worrying. Although solicitors have a reputation for high charges the research found that costs vary significantly depending on which firm you use and solicitors too often did not volunteer information about the likely cost of an appointment before the meeting. In some cases clients had no idea of what they would have to pay until they had been given the advice and received the bill. The research also found that many solicitors either gave the wrong advice or failed to give the best advice.

As in most trades or professions, it is possible to ask for a quote or an estimate, the first being binding and the second no more than an indication of the likely amount. Solicitors can agree to do a particular piece of work for a fixed quoted price, called an agreed fee. Whether a solicitor is prepared to agree a fee depends mainly on the type of work involved, because once the fee is agreed that is all he or she can charge regardless of how difficult and time-consuming the case may turn out to be. For that reason you would be extremely unlikely to find a solicitor who will agree a fee in a personal injury claim, for example, because no one knows how quickly it will be settled, if at all, or whether it will go to a trial.

On the other hand, you might be able to agree a fee for a solicitor to represent you on a careless driving charge at a particular magistrates' court on a particular day. More commonly, however, solicitors will be prepared to give an estimate of their likely charges only on the assumption that the matter goes as expected with no surprise complications.

If you think that local solicitors are part of an agreement not to charge less than each other, this could be illegal and should be referred to the Office of Fair Trading. Any kind of price-fixing not in the public interest can be challenged in this way. Prices should be set by the market, by demand, not by an arbitrary agreement between professionals to bolster their profits artificially.

Find out the likely costs in advance by asking the solicitor:

- how much he/she charges
- how many hours' work are likely to be involved: get a written estimate if you can, and set a provisional ceiling on the costs
- when will you have to pay
- what the solicitor is going to do next
- what timescale is involved
- to confirm advice in writing
- to give you regular bills (make this part of the contract with the chosen firm): remember, you are the customer.

A solicitor's bill reflects the cost of the time spent on a case. You can challenge it by asking for a remuneration certificate or having the bill taxed. These are explained later. The bill may also include an 'uplift' – a percentage of that cost – which solicitors may charge if they think the case was particularly complex or needed specialist knowledge, say. This is sometimes called a 'mark-up', 'profit element' or 'care and conduct'. Solicitors must tell you in advance whether they are likely to charge an 'uplift' and what the likely percentage will be. However, very often it is not separately identified, even though it can increase the bill by as much as 100 per cent.

If the matter were not so serious, some of the pronouncements made by judges attempting to set out the rules that permit solicitors to charge 'uplift' fees would be laughable. One judge stated that 'No professional man, or senior employee of a professional man, stops thinking about the day's problems the minute he lifts his coat and umbrella from the stand and sets out on the journey home. Ideas, often very valuable ideas, occur in the train or car home, or in the bath, or even whilst watching television. Yet nothing is ever put down on a time sheet, or can be put down on a time sheet adequately to reflect this out-of-hours devotion of time.'

An old joke illustrates the point. The following appeared on a solicitor's bill to his client: 'Fee for time spent crossing the road to greet you and to discuss your case, and, on discovering that it was not you, crossing back again: 10 guineas.'

What can make matters worse is the fact that you may be paying the charge-out rate for a partner (i.e. a senior person) in the firm but someone else, possibly not legally qualified and hence of far lowlier status and probably rather less experience, may be doing the routine work. Check who will be doing the work and whether you will be paying a different rate for different parts of the work.

If you have time you can do a lot of the routine work yourself, especially the legwork necessary to prepare the grounds for your case. Getting evidence together and photocopying documents yourself saves you having to paying a professional to do this non-legal work. Be businesslike about your relationship. Also, look around for schemes that can give you free or cheap legal advice.

Barristers

There is simply no way to beat a system that says that somebody is not legally accountable for his or her actions in a specific situation. So when the law says (and it does) that advocates, whether barristers or solicitor-advocates, are immune from any claim for negligence arising from their actions in the court room, the innocent consumer who has suffered at the hands of the incompetent lawyer can have no claim. But then, when 'the system' is the law of the land, and the law of the land makes this immunity clear, what can consumers expect?

Barristers too can make a 'no win, no fee' arrangement with your solicitor. So if you have a personal injury case and cannot afford to take the risk of losing and paying out your own legal fees and those of your opponent, raise this with the lawyers you contact before you decide whom to instruct (see 'No win, no fee', page 210).

A complaint system will soon be in place for the bar. Contact the Bar Council (General Council of the Bar)★ for details.

Tricks of the trade

Negotiating is the key to what lawyers do for you. And the strength behind the negotiating depends on how good your position is. So knowing the law and what you are entitled to is the first step to doing your own negotiating successfully. In addition, there are some important procedural points with which it pays to be familiar.

'Without prejudice' letters

To avoid committing yourself by mistake when negotiating settlement terms, write 'without prejudice' at the top of that part of your letter (but do not use it on all your letters as this may cause problems). Any letter which is 'without prejudice' may not be used against you and may not be revealed if you finally have to go to court to fight the claim. For example, a trader may be asking for £2,000 from you; you may feel you owe him only £1,500 at the most, but would be prepared to argue that you should pay nothing. If you make an offer of £1,500 'without prejudice' and this is not accepted by the trader, in the event of the dispute going to court you can still refuse to pay and the judge will never learn that you were prepared to pay anything. If you want to make an offer, or if you are responding to an offer from the trader, you could send two letters, one 'without prejudice' which mentions the offer, the other open, ignoring the offer completely and pursuing the main basis of your claim. Either party in a dispute may make a 'without prejudice' offer in an effort to reach a settlement.

Time limits for claims

How long you have in which to start a claim or for somebody to bring a claim against you depends on the type of claim. The Statute of Limitations puts a time limit on starting a formal claim. Once a claim falls foul of the time limit it is said to become statute barred. If the claim is not begun (by issuing a court summons or writ) within a certain time, the person wanting to bring the claim will lose the right to do so. The most common periods are:

- six years for claims for breach of contract from the date of the breach: this covers any dispute arising from a claim under a contract (for example, those arising under the Sale of Goods Act 1979, or the Supply of Goods and Services Act 1982)
- six years for claims of negligence from the date of the negligent act: this covers any claim for damage, say, to your property where there is no contract between you and the person who caused the damage. Such claims would include, for example, damage caused to your car by another driver
- three years in the event of personal injury, whether the claim is for breach of contract or negligence. This would include claims

for personal injury under the Consumer Protection Act 1987 as well as medical negligence and claims for mental distress

- if you could not have known you had a claim until some time later, then the date of 'knowledge' is important. This means time does not start to run until there is knowledge that you might reasonably have been expected to acquire from facts you could have seen for yourself or with the help of appropriate expert advice.
- defective design or building work may not become apparent until long after the design or work was done. In some cases the Latent Damage Act 1986 can extend the time period for a claim up to a maximum of 15 years from the date of the work. If your claim is complex, legal advice on this may be essential.

Full and final settlement

You may be sent a cheque in 'full and final settlement' or you may want to offer a figure and bring an end to your dispute. The use of these words makes the matter final, so be very careful: even if you do not consider the amount you have been sent to be enough, if you cash the cheque you will have accepted it in settlement of your claim, so you will not be able to claim more. If you do not consider the amount offered to you to be enough, it is best to send it back. If you are unsure whether an offer is fair and are having difficulty working it out yourself, get independent advice from a CAB or law centre. Never allow yourself to be pressurised into accepting less than you are entitled to. If, during negotiations:

- the other side hassles you, write saying that you are seriously considering the offer but are seeking expert or legal advice before you finally decide whether to accept. Most traders will be reasonable and will understand that you need time to make a decision. However, you should remember that an offer can be withdrawn at any time before it is accepted, so do not leave it too long before getting back to the other side
- you receive a cheque in 'full and final settlement', do not bank it, because to do so may be interpreted as acceptance. You should either hang on to it or return it with a letter rejecting the offer.

Of course, the 'full and final settlement' ploy can also work in your favour. Use it for putting the other side under pressure. Send a cheque for the amount you consider reasonable along with the letter. If they cash it then that is the end of the matter.

Trying it on

If your negotiations have failed, one final attempt to make the other side see the light could do the trick. Get a default summons form from your local county court, fill it in as if you were making the claim proper, take a copy of the completed form and send it to the other side with a letter saying that the form is about to be posted to the court unless you receive the cheque in settlement of your claim by return of post. This often has the effect of concentrating the recipient's mind and making it clear that your threats are very likely to be backed up by positive action.

Questions and answers

Q *I have just received a bill from my solicitor. It seems unreasonable and is way above the original estimate I was given. How can I challenge it?*

A You cannot rely on an 'estimate' as a guarantee of the final bill. But a solicitor's bill must be fair and reasonable, although it is not possible to calculate solicitors' fees exactly as there is no set scale of costs and much will depend on the time spent on the matter. If you feel the charges are too high, write to the head partner of the firm setting out your reasons for dissatisfaction. If that does not work there are formal methods for challenging a bill, but how you go about it depends on the type of work done – that is, whether it was classified as non-contentious or contentious.

Contentious work is any for which court proceedings have been started (even if you never actually got to court):

- you should request a detailed breakdown of the bill. The solicitor is obliged to provide this under section 64 of the Solicitors Act 1974
- if you are still not happy, you can apply for the costs to be taxed by the court. This means that a special bill is drawn up and the court decides whether each item is fair and reasonable.

'Taxation' can be expensive: not only will you have to pay a fee to the court to have the bill assessed, but if the bill is reduced by less than one-fifth, you will lose the court fee and have to pay the solicitor's costs of going to court as well as your own.

Non-contentious work is any work done where the case does not involve court proceedings, such as conveyancing:

- ask the solicitor to apply to the Law Society for a remuneration certificate. This states whether the bill is fair and reasonable, and, if it is not, suggests another sum that would be reasonable. This procedure is free
- if you feel that the certified amount is still too high, you still have the right to apply for the costs to be taxed by the court (as above).

The complaints system for solicitors' charges is broadly the same in Scotland. However, there is no procedure for a remuneration certificate, so regardless of whether there have been court proceedings you will have to go for taxation.

Q *I wasn't happy with the work done by my solicitor and decided to change to another, but the old one is refusing to hand over my papers until his bill is paid. Can he do this?*

A As a general rule, a client can change solicitors whenever he or she wishes to do so. If you are already involved in court action, there may be formalities involved which your new solicitor should complete for you. But if you do owe a solicitor any fees for work done, he has the legal right to hang on to your property if it came into his possession as part of his professional employment, and that includes all documents, money, deeds, etc. The principle involved is the same as that which applies when work has been done on your property away from your premises; for example, a garage has the right to hold on to your car if it has done work for which money is owed. There are circumstances in which you can get the papers back without paying the disputed bill:

- the Law Society can recommend that the papers should be released subject to a satisfactory undertaking on your part to pay the outstanding fee

- your new solicitor may agree an undertaking with the original solicitor as to payment once the dispute is resolved
- it may be possible to make a payment of the disputed amount into an 'escrow' account, which will be paid out, in part or in full, only when the dispute over the bill is settled
- if the papers are vital for your case and you would be prejudiced by the solicitor withholding them, you may get a court order for their release: your new solicitor should advise on this.

CHAPTER 7

THE EMPLOYMENT SYSTEM

BECOMING an employee, or an employer, gives us certain rights and confers upon us certain obligations. Most of us take on our status of employee/employer without any specialist knowledge of the employment system, so when a problem arises we may be unsure of our ground. And without knowing where we stand – in other words, what our rights and obligations are – it can be difficult to resolve disputes or settle differences.

This chapter looks at the employment system from both viewpoints, considering the sorts of problems that can arise and the mechanisms that exist to help employees and employers resolve them. Bear in mind that many organisations have their own internal grievance and appeals procedures, which would normally be brought into play long before a dispute was brought to the attention of any external agency (such as ACAS or an industrial tribunal). Apart from that, knowing how the system works, what legislation is there to protect employees from unfair treatment and what steps employers can take to protect themselves against claims, is the best way to 'beat' it.

The legal framework

The main Acts which relate to employment rights are the Disability Discrimination Act 1995; the Employment Act 1989; Employment Protection Act 1975; Employment Protection (Consolidation) Act 1978; Equal Pay Act 1970; Race Relations Act 1976; Sex Discrimination Act 1975; Trade Union and Labour Relations (Consolidation) Act 1992; Trade Union Reform and

Employment Rights Act 1992; Transfer of Undertakings (Protection of Employment) Regulations 1981; and the Wages Act 1986. These are referred to throughout the chapter where relevant. In addition, there is 'good practice', which, though it may not have the backing of legislation, indicates a stance on all employment matters from recruitment to relocation, and from pay negotiations to redundancies.

Problems between employer and employee may arise from misunderstandings about the job, pay and benefits (e.g. that they are different from what was thought to be on offer), or unfair treatment during the course of the employment (e.g. an accusation by an employer of misconduct on the part of an employee; employer finding that the employee is not 'up' to the job; or discrimination against the employee on the grounds of gender or race). Employees may well have the right to challenge decisions within their organisation through its own disciplinary and grievance procedures, and advice can be sought from external bodies such as ACAS.

Advisory, Conciliation and Arbitration Service (ACAS)

This body is independent of the government and controlled by a council of nine members. These include a chairperson, three members appointed after consultation with the TUC and three more appointed after consultation with the CBI.

ACAS★ aims to improve employee/employer relations, by providing specialist codes of practice (including those for disciplinary and dismissal procedures), advice on a wide range of employment matters, and a range of booklets; and by helping to resolve conflicts, in which capacity it offers three different routes – conciliation, arbitration and mediation.

Requests for assistance and advice can be made by both employers and employees.

Industrial tribunals

If an employee feels that he or she has been unfairly dismissed, he or she can take the case to an industrial tribunal, a group of experts brought together to deal specifically with employment issues.

To claim unfair dismissal, the employee must have given at least two years' continuous service. In the case of dismissal on the grounds of sex or race, however, there is no such time qualification.

As well as racial and sexual discrimination, industrial tribunals tend to deal with such issues as breach of contract; deductions from wages; equal pay; guaranteed payments (see below under 'Pay'); health and safety; itemised pay statements (see below under 'Pay'); maternity rights; occupational pensions; redundancy; trade union membership and non-membership rights; transfer of undertakings (employees' rights in the event of a transfer or merger of the organisation); unfair and wrongful dismissal; and written statements of particulars (details of main terms and conditions of service, which employers must provide to employees within two months of joining).

A complaint to an industrial tribunal will be heard by a panel of three people. Each tribunal comprises a chairperson who is a lawyer and two lay members. In certain situations the chairperson may sit alone.

An ACAS conciliation officer will read the documentation and sometimes meets both parties before a complaint to an industrial tribunal is heard. He or she will try to obtain a voluntary settlement if there is a reasonable chance of success.

An industrial tribunal may decide itself or at the request of the employee or employer to hold a pre-hearing review. This occurs where it appears that one of the parties has an unreasonable case, a very technical one, or one that could certainly not succeed.

Complaints to industrial tribunals should be made within three months of the alleged occurrence. A booklet outlining industrial tribunal procedures and an application form (IT1) are available from any Employment Service Office (see local telephone directory), and there is also a helpline.★

Employment Appeal Tribunal (EAT)

The EAT, comprising both judges and lay members, hears appeals based on questions of law resulting from industrial tribunal decisions. Such appeals may relate, for example, to the Employment Protection Consolidation, Equal Pay and Sex Discrimination Acts, in addition to issues concerning trade union membership or non-membership. In cases where a tribunal is thought to have reached a 'perverse decision' from the evidence submitted, the matter can be brought to the EAT.

Court of Appeal

The next level of appeal beyond the Employment Appeal Tribunal is the Court of Appeal (or, in Scotland, to the Court of Session to the Inner House). The judgments of these courts are important, because they guide decisions made by industrial tribunals. The EAT must follow decisions of the Court of Appeal or the Court of Session on statements of law. Appeals on points of law can be made by permission of the judges to these courts and thence, by permission, to the House of Lords. It is the judges' prerogative to decide whether or not it is appropriate that the appeal be referred to them.

The European Community (EC)

EC law can override national legislation (on, for example, changes to maternity protection rights) in the event of inconsistency between national (UK) law and EC law.

Recruitment advertising

When an employer places an advertisement, or instructs an agency, with a view to securing the services of an employee, he or she will want to present the organisation concerned in as good a light as possible and will hope to attract candidates with suitable qualifications and experience. The criteria against which candidates will be measured need to be made clear in the advertisement (or agency brief) to ensure that selection is made fairly and to protect the employer against later claims of unfair treatment, certain types of which are in fact illegal. All the information given in the advertisement – and later at the interview and in the letter of appointment and subsequent contract of employment – should be clear, consistent and unambiguous.

Discrimination

The Sex Discrimination and Race Relations Acts, supported by codes of practice from the Equal Opportunities Commission (EOC)* and the Commission for Racial Equality (CRE),* make it illegal to discriminate against job applicants on the grounds of race or sex.

Advertisements should not have a racial or sexual connotation. Employers should avoid the use of gender-oriented titles such as 'stewardess' or 'salesman'.

There are exceptions where being a man, woman or a person of a particular racial group is a genuine occupational qualification for reasons of decency or privacy or the provision of personal services to persons of a particular racial group. For example, it could be legitimate to advertise for a woman if the job involved working in a woman's prison.

Whilst the media may refuse to carry an advertisement which is potentially discriminatory, any which *do* appear can be referred to the EOC or CRE, and it would be up to one of these bodies to take action.

Applying for a job

Once a candidate has applied for a job, he or she has the right to be considered for it on equal terms to other applicants.

It is illegal not to interview (or recruit) an individual on the grounds of gender, race or disability, as laid down in the Sex Discrimination, Race Relations and Disability Discrimination Acts. Additionally there is an EC Directive – the Equal Treatment Directive – that states that discrimination on the grounds of sex, marital and family status is unlawful in respect of access to jobs. Employers following 'best practice' recommendations will not discriminate on the grounds of age or sexual orientation, either, although there is as yet no legislation to back this stance. Nor should trade union membership, or non-membership, influence the recruitment process.

Discriminatory behaviour would be demonstrated by, for example, an employer asking a female applicant about her career plans over the next five years but not asking the same question of men. Refusing to appoint a woman because she was pregnant would be discriminatory. Discrimination can also take more subtle forms: for example, if the employer were to specify a maximum age of 35 he or she could be excluding women who have had career breaks for maternity reasons and have therefore taken longer to attain the qualifications and experience outlined in the job requirements.

Employers should also avoid asking questions on application forms that could be regarded as discriminatory: for example, asking for the candidate's place of birth. This would in theory make it possible to screen out people of a particular ethnic origin.

Appointments should be made on the basis of objective criteria against which all candidates are assessed. However, if an employee feels he or she has suffered discrimination, redress can be achieved via an industrial tribunal. It is for the applicant to demonstrate that discrimination has taken place. The employer, on the other hand, must show that the decision was made for sound and justifiable reasons. If the tribunal upholds the complaint, the employer will be ordered to pay compensation, which is set by the tribunal and is not subject to any financial limit. The EOC and CRE sometimes offer assistance to individuals in such cases.

Whilst discrimination against job applicants is notoriously difficult to prove, because the burden of proof is on the individual, it can be costly for the employer – not just in money terms, but also in respect of damage to the firm's image.

Interviews

Statements made at the interview should be consistent with information given in the preceding job advertisement. Generally, it is unwise to make a job offer or salary offer, or to promise special arrangements, to the applicant at an interview.

Employers should take care not to ask questions that could be construed as discriminatory, and in particular never to ask a woman whether she is intending to start a family (or contemplating having more children).

Job offers and contracts of employment

A job offer can be made verbally or in writing or both. Verbal offers can be binding. Employees should expect confirmation of a verbal offer in writing (i.e. a letter of appointment). This letter can be accompanied by a statement of the main terms and conditions of service (good employers will send this as a matter of course), otherwise known as the 'written statement of particulars' (see below).

Conditional offers of employment

Employers may make offers of employment conditional on the receipt of satisfactory references or a medical report following examination. If these are unsatisfactory the employer may withdraw the offer of employment. (The offer can also be withdrawn for other reasons, for example, circumstances suddenly changing at the organisation concerned, but notice must be given in accordance with the contract.)

If the job offer is withdrawn owing to an unsatisfactory reference, the employer does not need to reveal the content or the source of it. However, if the source of a reference is known and the reference is defamatory, the applicant (or employee) may sue the writer for defamation of character.

The employee may have started the job before the employer is in possession of references or the medical information. If the information is unsatisfactory the employer can dismiss the employee by giving the required notice. Unless the employee is 100 per cent sure that nothing untoward will be revealed by references or the medical report he or she should avoid putting at risk the job just started until the offer of employment is unconditional.

'Written statements of particulars of employment'

Letters in which a job offer is made are often backed up by a document outlining the main terms and conditions of employment ('written statement of particulars'). It is important for employees to have this, so that they know what they are signing up for. Employees are entitled to receive this statement within eight weeks of starting the job, and many employers issue it with the letter of appointment. These two items often constitute the contract of employment, although technically the contract also embodies custom and practice at the organisation in question.

The supporting legislation for contracts of employment is the Employee Protection (Consolidation) Act. The contract/written statement outlines the main terms and conditions of employment, but will not contain every detail of the job.

Employers should take care that the information given in the written statement/contract is clear, non-contradictory and consistent with what has been said in the advertisement, at the interview, and in the letter of appointment.

The written statement should contain the following information:

- names of employer and employee
- job title and a brief summary of the job
- place(s) of work
- date of joining
- whether any previous employment with the same or another employer counts as continuous service (i.e. length of service for the purposes of pensions, holiday entitlement, claims of unfair dismissal, etc.)
- the pay, including method of calculating overtime and bonuses
- date when paid
- hours of work
- holiday entitlement and pay
- entitlement to accrued holiday pay on leaving.

The employer should also refer the employee to the following information or explain how to access it:

- sick leave and pay
- information on pensions
- whether a contracting-out certificate in respect of the state pension exists
- notice period for employer and employee
- whether collective agreements (e.g. those agreed by a trade union/staff consultative body and employer) will subsequently vary, and form part of, the main terms and conditions

- disciplinary rules and how to challenge a disciplinary decision. (Employers with fewer than 20 people do not need to supply this information)
- how to progress a grievance relating to employment.

If an employer refuses to provide this information the employee has redress to an industrial tribunal, which will order that it be supplied.

The written statement of particulars of employment should be kept up to date by the employer and employees should be notified of changes within one month of the change being implemented (but see below).

Changes to terms and conditions of employment

An employer may from time to time wish to vary the terms and conditions of employment to suit changing circumstances. Generally this can be done if the employee consents to the change; if the change is part of a collective agreement; or the right to vary a particular term or condition was specified in the original written statement of particulars.

If an employer unilaterally varies the terms and conditions, and the employee does not accept the change, this may constitute a breach of contract. In this situation the employee may resign with redress to an industrial tribunal for wrongful or constructive dismissal. ('Constructive dismissal' means that by breaching the contract of employment the employer has effectively dismissed the employee: for example, an employer's behaviour may be such that the employee has to terminate the employment; to claim constructive dismissal the employee must indicate that he or she is terminating the employment.)

Whether or not the tribunal decides the dismissal is fair or unfair will depend on a number of factors. The tribunal will consider whether the employer consulted with the employee and acted reasonably in wanting to make the change in the first place. Employers wishing to introduce changes to their employees' terms and conditions should therefore be aware of the importance of consultation beforehand.

Probationary or trial periods

It is common for employers to take on employees initially for a trial period – say, for three or six months – to establish their suitability for the job. During this time, it is the employer's responsibility to tell the employee where there are deficiencies in performance or conduct. Also during this period the employee is entitled to the statutory notice period or the notice stated in the offer of employment and written statement of particulars, whichever is the longer (the statuory period of notice during a six-month trial period would be one week; however, the contractual period of notice may be longer – two weeks, for example).

It is important that the employer makes it clear that employment during the trial period can be terminated by notice. If this is not explicit the individual could be entitled to be employed for the duration of the probationary/trial period.

Pay

The Wages Act and Employment Protection Consolidation Act governs issues relating to pay. Each employee must be given an itemised pay statement on or before the date of being paid. This should show the gross pay; fixed and variable deductions and reasons why these have been made; and the net pay.

Deductions

Apart from statutory deduction such as income tax (PAYE) and National Insurance, deductions from pay can be made if there has been an overpayment of salary or expenses; to satisfy a court order or tribunal decision; as a result of a disciplinary decision arising from legislation; due to participation in a strike or industrial action; or for statutory reasons to pay an amount to a statutory authority, e.g. attachment of earnings. In addition, the Child Support Agency can force employers to make deductions direct from pay to cover child maintenance.

Any other deductions must have been provided for and agreed by the employee in the written statement of particulars; or agreed to in advance in writing by the employee.

Employees within the retail sector are protected from excessive deductions for till or stock deficits: deductions cannot be more than one-tenth of pay.

Sick pay

Employers are responsible for paying, as a minimum, Statutory Sick Pay (SSP) for up to 28 weeks. SSP for employees with average weekly earnings of £61 or more is £54.55. For further information on SSP telephone the Freeline Social Security number.★

Guaranteed payments

Employers who have insufficient work available to keep employees occupied full-time and need to restrict their costs may offer 'short-time working'. An employee on short-time working and with one month's service is entitled to a payment based on normal daily pay up to £14.50 a day and not exceeding 5 days in any period of 3 months.

There may be more favourable provisions in the contract of employment but where no contractual obligations exist the payment will be calculated as outlined above.

Guaranteed payments are not payable if there is a strike, lockout or other industrial action involving the employer and employee. Employees will not have the right to guarantee payments if they refuse suitable alternative work or do not comply with reasonable requirements as to their availability.

A week's pay

The term 'a week's pay' is used in all fields of employment for purposes such as the calculation of redundancy, sick pay and so on.

In many cases pay does not vary from week to week. In this case 'a week's pay' is for *normal* working hours including contractual overtime (but excluding non-contractual overtime). It also includes regular bonuses and allowances which do not vary.

Where pay does vary week by week 'a week's pay' is pay for the *normal* working hours at the average hourly rate. This is calculated on the hours worked and the payment received in the previous 12-week period.

Periods of notice

An employee is required to give the employer at least one week's notice after one month's service.

An employee is entitled to 1 week's notice after 1 month; 1 week for each year of continuous employment for 2–12 years' employment; 12 weeks' notice for 12 or more years of continuous employment.

These are the minimum periods of notice applicable. Employers and employees may agree longer periods, which should be referred to in the written statement of particulars.

Payment in lieu of notice

An employee and employer may agree to waive the period of notice where there is provision in the contract of employment to do this. Pay in lieu of this should be the gross amount due, less deductions for tax and National Insurance.

If the employer *imposes* pay in lieu of notice the contract will have been breached. Employers may therefore offer to compensate the employee, to discourage the employee seeking redress through an industrial tribunal. The employer is advised to make a gross payment to which the employee would have been entitled had he or she remained employed until the end of the notice period and to explain this in writing. As the payment is compensation for immediate dismissal it can be paid without deductions for tax and National Insurance.

Discipline and dismissal

Discipline

For matters of discipline in the workplace, the legislation is the Employment Protection (Consolidation) Act. The ACAS code of practice, *Disciplinary Practice and Procedures in Employment*, is an important reference document.

A good employer will have a sound disciplinary procedure to ensure that employees are treated fairly. Procedures which follow the ACAS code of practice will normally be regarded as fair and reasonable by an industrial tribunal.

Although no employer can cover every eventuality, employees should know what sorts of behaviour would be regarded as disciplinary matters.

A criminal offence which occurs away from work is not an automatic reason for dismissal. The consideration is whether the offence makes the person unsuitable for the job.

Whilst there should be consistency of treatment (for example, theft by one individual is completely overlooked but results in summary dismissal for another), other factors and mitigating circumstances should be taken into account. A long-serving employee with a good performance record may have a lesser penalty imposed than an employee with a poor performance record.

In summary, the ACAS code of practice for disciplinary procedures recommends that:

- the complaint against the employee should be in writing
- the employee should be told what actions can be taken and by whom
- the employee should be told of the complaint against him/her and given the opportunity to respond before a decision is made
- no disciplinary action should be taken until there has been a thorough investigation
- the employee has the right to be accompanied by a trade union representative or colleague
- except in the case of gross misconduct no employee should be dismissed for the first breach of discipline
- the employee is given an explanation of what penalty has been imposed
- the employee may appeal against the decision.

The procedure itself should include the following provisions:

- the manager should establish the facts promptly and obtain statements from any witnesses
- where the matter is serious the employee may be suspended from work with pay

- for less significant incidents an informal oral warning may suffice
- for minor issues a formal oral warning may be given
- for more serious issues a written warning should be given setting out the facts and what will happen in the case of a recurrence. The employee should be told that this is the first stage of the formal disciplinary procedure
- the employee should be informed that further disciplinary offences may result in a final written warning being given. Again, this should set out the facts and what will happen in the case of a recurrence. The employee should be told that this is the final stage of the formal disciplinary procedure
- the employee should be made aware that further recurrence could lead to dismissal.

Dismissal

The majority of employees have the right not to be unfairly dismissed. Redress is to an industrial tribunal. The main exceptions are those who do not have two years' continuous employment with their employer; are beyond normal retiring age; or normally work outside Great Britain.

If someone is dismissed because he or she refuses to join a trade union or conversely *is* a member of a trade union he or she can claim unfair dismissal without having two years' continuous employment. The two–year rule does not apply to a dismissal relating to an employee's pregnancy, nor does it apply if an employee took action to avoid danger at work or carried out recognised health and safety duties.

Employees who are eligible to claim unfair dismissal are entitled to a written statement of the reason for their dismissal within 14 days of making the request. A complaint can be made to a tribunal if this is not supplied or the reasons given are inadequate or false.

Reasons for dismissal

A dismissal will be regarded as fair if the employer acts reasonably and the reason for the dismissal falls within one of the following categories:

- capability and qualifications
- conduct
- contravention of a statutory requirement
- some other substantial reason
- redundancy (see page 244).

Capability and qualifications

'Capability' means competence in the job; lack of it results in unacceptable performance. The employee should be given the opportunity to improve by being warned that his/her performance is not to an acceptable standard. He or she should be given training and support to become competent. If alternative employment exists which the employee is capable of undertaking, this option should be considered. Only if these steps do not lead to improvement should dismissal take place, for the reason of capability.

There is a difference between 'can't do', which is a matter of capability, and 'won't do', which relates to conduct and is discussed below.

'Qualifications' means a degree, diploma or other qualification necessary for the job. If a qualification is a requirement for doing the job (for example, medical qualifications for a doctor, legal qualifications for a solicitor or barrister), a dismissal (disbarring in the case of a barrister) for giving false information would be fair.

Job application forms often carry a statement to the effect that falsehood could lead to dismissal, so if an applicant has claimed to have a degree and this is subsequently found to be false when the applicant is in employment he or she could be dismissed.

If on the other hand an employee is appointed on the clear condition that he or she *will obtain* a particular qualification and does not meet the condition within a reasonable time frame, the failure to do so could be ground for dismissal owing to inadequate qualifications.

Dismissal for ill health falls into the category of capability. An employee who is incapable of doing the job for health reasons, including injury and physical incapacity, may be subject to dismissal. However, industrial tribunals will want to ensure that the employer acted with consideration before dismissing the employee. This means considering alternative employment;

consultation with the employer about his or her health and potential for improvement; assessing the 'fit' with the employer's business needs – the employee's capabilities and the work available; and taking advice from a medical adviser about the employee's health and prognosis.

Often a contractual entitlement to sick leave and pay exists. This should normally expire before the employee is dismissed.

Conduct

This reason for dismissal is more commonly referred to as misconduct. Examples include persistent lateness, and not following required procedures and instructions ('won't do'). An employer does not have to show beyond reasonable doubt that the misconduct happened. For example, if an employer honestly believes that a shop manager has been taking goods home, he or she does not have to prove that the theft took place if the evidence is not available.

A first instance of misconduct may result in a warning but should not normally result in dismissal unless it is gross misconduct.

The definition of gross misconduct is an action by an employee which fundamentally repudiates the contract of employment and justifies the summary dismissal of the employee. Before coming to the decision that as a result of the conduct it is intolerable to continue to employ the individual, the employer should have carried out an investigation to establish the facts and listened to the employee's response.

It may be appropriate to suspend the employee whilst undertaking such an investigation. Suspensions for this reason are normally on full pay.

Disciplinary rules often provide examples of gross misconduct, although they may include a rider to the effect that the list is not exclusive or exhaustive. Some examples are:

- theft and dishonesty
- falsification of timesheets or expense claims
- fighting
- malicious damage to company property
- sexual harassment
- racial or sexual discrimination.

Contravention of statutory requirements

These would include, for example, the expiry of a work permit, or loss of a driving licence where driving is an integral part of the job. The employer must be sure that to continue employing the person would result in a statutory requirement or duty being contravened.

Some other substantial reason

This is not a useful catch-all for employers to use: the reason must be sufficient to justify the dismissal. Examples include:

- a personality clash between two employees. It should be noted that when this occurs it is often difficult to apportion responsibility. If one employee rather than both is dismissed the dismissal may be regarded as unfair by the industrial tribunal
- a re-organisation for economic or efficiency reasons following which the employee does not want to accept the new arrangements. It is important that the employer acts reasonably and that there are sound efficiency and economic reasons for the change
- failing to disclose important information (or falsifying it) when applying for a job: for example, being asked on the application form to give details of any serious illness and not supplying it
- the expiration of a fixed-term or temporary contract of employment which is dependent on an end date or an event happening: for example, an employee on maternity leave and returning to work, or external funding from a third party ceasing.

Unfair dismissals

Where a dismissal is found to be unfair a tribunal can make various 'awards' to the employee concerned, as described below.

Reinstatement or re-engagement order

This can be made in cases where the employee is willing to return to work. The industrial tribunal will ascertain whether it is practicable for the person to return to his/her old job (reinstatement) or to return to a comparable job with the same employer (re-engagement). However, these remedies are rarely used.

In the case of reinstatement the person is treated as if he or she had not been dismissed and does not lose any accrued benefits. Re-engagement is slightly different as the employee can return on terms that are similar terms to those that applied previously, as far as is reasonably practicable, though possibly in a different capacity.

Compensation

There are three types of award: basic, compensatory and additional.

The basic award is the same calculation as for redundancy, apart from the fact that service from age 16 onwards counts (see below). The maximum payable is £6,300.

On top of the basic award a compensatory award can be made, in order to compensate for loss experienced by the employee as a result of the dismissal, e.g. loss of earnings, other benefits and pension rights. The maximum award is £11,300.

An additional award applies where the employee has asked for an order of reinstatement or re-engagement but the employer has not complied with such an order. It is paid in addition to a basic and compensatory award.

It should be noted that the industrial tribunal will reduce any compensation if it is thought that the individual has contributed to the dismissal or has not taken reasonable steps to mitigate loss.

Wrongful dismissal

This normally occurs where the employee has no redress for unfair dismissal, e.g. less than two years' service and/or has been dismissed in breach of the contract of employment. A common example would be dismissal without notice. The employee can sue through the courts or take the breach of contract claim to an industrial tribunal. The upper limit for compensation through an industrial tribunal is £25,000.

Compromise agreements

This is a solution employers may offer if they do not want a complaint to go to an industrial tribunal. It tends to happen where the employer knows the dismissal to be unfair; is uncertain of the strength of his/her case; or wants the complaint to go away quickly and quietly. Under a compromise agreement the non-observance of employment rights can be settled without going to an industrial tribunal or involving ACAS. The agreement and details of associated payment should be in writing. The employee, for his/her own protection, must receive independent legal advice from a person who is professionally indemnified.

Redundancy

Redundancy occurs where an employer intends, or has ceased, to carry on the business *for which* the employee was employed and is therefore dispensing with the job; or intends or has ceased to carry on the business *where* the employee was employed. Redundancy also occurs where the requirement for an employee to carry out work of a particular kind has ceased or will cease or diminish.

It is worth noting that where such changes in the working pattern take effect it is the post, not the person, that becomes redundant.

Alternative employment

Employees should not be made redundant just because their job has disappeared. An employer must show that no other suitable alternative employment is available. If an employee unreasonably refuses a suitable offer of alternative employment he or she may lose the right to redundancy pay.

Where suitable alternative employment is accepted this will count as continuous service (see above under 'Written statements of particulars of employment'). However, where the job is different, or the same but with different terms and conditions (i.e. alternative as opposed to suitable alternative employment), the employee is entitled to try the job for four weeks without losing the right to redundancy pay.

Redundancy pay

Regardless of hours worked the employee with two years' continuous service is entitled to redundancy pay. Pay is based on length of service up to a maximum of 20 years and is calculated as follows:

For each complete year of service	
aged 41–65	1.5 weeks' pay
aged 22–41	1 week's pay
aged 18–22	0.5 weeks' pay

There is a ceiling for the calculation of £210 per week.

Some employers will pay in excess of the statutory maximum. If an employee suspects redundancies are pending he or she should ask for access to the redundancy policy (if one exists) in order to find out what the general provisions are and to see whether there is any reference to redundancy pay and calculations. In any event employers should give the employee a written statement of how the redundancy pay was calculated when the payment is made.

It is common practice for employees on a fixed–year contract to be asked to sign a clause when they are appointed to waive their right to redundancy pay when the contract expires.

Consultation

Employers must consult with appropriate representatives when redundancies are in the offing. Consultation should have taken place at least 30 days before the first dismissal takes place if 20 or more employees are to be made redundant. If an employer is proposing to dismiss more than 100 employees the consultation period must be at least 90 days.

Even if a trade union is not recognised and there is no staff consultative body the employer has an obligation to consult with 'appropriate representatives' of staff (say, a group of employees selected by staff who come together specifically for this redundancy consultation process).

Consultation includes information on the reasons for the redundancies, the numbers and types of staff involved, selection methods and how redundancy payments will be calculated. Employers must take responses into account before finalising plans.

There is no legal obligation to consult with employees where fewer than 20 redundancies will occur, but employers should still act reasonably and should certainly consult with employees individually otherwise the dismissal could be found unfair.

Time off

Employees who have been given notice of redundancy and who have two years' service or more are entitled to reasonable time off with pay to look for other employment or arrange training for future employment. The tribunal award for paid time off is two-fifths of a week's pay, but this is not a set amount. The important word here is 'reasonable'.

Notice

Employees are entitled to the normal period of notice under their contract of employment. An individual may have found a job before the notice has expired. He or she will be entitled to redundancy pay if the employer has agreed or there are existing provisions to this effect. If the employer objects and asks the employee, in writing, to work the period of notice or otherwise forfeit payment the employee may go to an industrial tribunal to ascertain whether payment should be made.

Transfer of undertakings (takeovers and mergers)

The employer must consult with appropriate representatives in the event of a business changing hands or merging. Employees have certain rights in such situations. First, the contract of employment cannot be terminated by the existing employer. The contract of employment (apart from pension obligations) transfers to the new employer. A dismissal will automatically be unfair if it is connected with the transfer unless it is for economic, technical or organisational reasons: in other words, the reason for the dismissal will be 'some other substantial reason', as described above.

If the employee transfers and finds the terms and conditions less favourable he or she can resign and claim constructive dismissal.

Discrimination in employment

It is unlawful to discriminate in employment either directly or indirectly on the grounds of gender, marital status, colour, race, nationality or ethnic or national origin. New legislation has added disability to this list from December 1996. This relates to *all* employment terms and conditions from training provision to promotion. If an employee suffers discrimination in the workplace, he or she has redress to an industrial tribunal and if the case is proved there is no limit on the compensation that may be awarded. The legislation against discrimination at work is embodied in the Sex Discrimination, Race Relations, Equal Pay and Disability Discrimination Acts, supported by Codes of Practice from the Equal Opportunities Commission (EOC) and the Commission for Racial Equality (CRE).

The employer may have an Equal Opportunities policy but the existence of one does not necessarily guarantee good employment practice. It needs to be monitored to ensure it is effective.

To date no legislation exists for sexual orientation or age.

Equal Pay Act

The Sex Discrimination and Equal Pay Acts cover different aspects of discrimination. The Equal Pay Act applies to pay and less favourable terms under the contract of employment being applied to employees of the opposite sex in the same employment; or to those who undertake broadly similar work or are doing work of equal value.

The Sex Discrimination Act applies to less favourable treatment (in general) of employees and job applicants.

Disability Discrimination Act

This new legislation, effective from the end of 1996, makes it illegal to discriminate against disabled people in employment or when applying for jobs. It replaces the quota system and does not apply to employers with less than 20 employees.

Maternity rights

If a woman is dismissed on maternity-related grounds this is automatically deemed to be unfair dismissal.

All employees who become pregnant are statutorily entitled to 14 weeks' maternity leave and the right to return to work regardless of length of service and hours worked. The employee can choose to begin her maternity leave at any time during the 11 weeks before the expected week of childbirth. Within the 14 weeks' entitlement is two weeks' compulsory leave following the date of birth.

Pay apart, the employee is entitled to benefit from the terms and conditions of employment that would have applied had she not been away on maternity leave, e.g. accrued holiday entitlement.

To be entitled to maternity leave and associated rights the employee should notify her employer when she intends to start her leave and the expected week of the birth. This notification should be in writing and within 21 days of her starting the leave. If the employer requires it she should also produce a certificate from a doctor or midwife which states the expected week of childbirth.

At the end of the maternity leave the employee has the right to return to her original job. If she wishes to return before the 14 weeks are up she should give her employer seven days' notice. If she is unable to return to her job because it is has become redundant, she must be offered suitable alternative employment on equivalent terms and conditions, if this exists.

Women with two years' unbroken service at the eleventh week before the expected week of confinement are entitled to maternity absence beyond the 14 weeks: they can return to work at any time from the end of the statutory maternity leave period up to 29 weeks counting from the beginning of the week in which childbirth occurs.

The calculation of statutory maternity pay (SMP) is complex. The employee's payroll or personnel department should be able to explain maternity pay and leave entitlement. Information is also available from the DSS. Some employees have provisions in excess of the statutory entitlements. Pregnant employees should look at such provisions at the earliest opportunity.

A pregnant woman is entitled to paid time off for antenatal care and should produce an appointment card or medical certificate if the employer asks to see evidence of such absence.

If a woman wants to return to work on a part-time or jobshare basis – say, after returning from maternity leave – she has the right to make this request. The employer must consider the request taking into account the size of the organisation, work involved, and whether part-time working or a jobshare is feasible. There is now an assumption among industrial tribunals that many jobs can be shared, and if the employer unreasonably turns down such a request he or she is at risk of having acted discriminatorily.

However, jobshares do involve employers in extra costs, in recruitment and training at the very least, and possibly in overlapping working hours for handover/continuity purposes.

Health and safety at work

The Health and Safety at Work Act 1974 exists to promote improvement of health and safety at work. Both employees and employers have obligations under the Act.

It is the duty of every employer to ensure, as far as is reasonably practicable, the health, safety and welfare at work of all employees. For their part, employees should take reasonable care of themselves and others, co-operate with the employer in health and safety requirements and not interfere with or misuse anything provided for their safety and welfare.

Breaches of the Act can result in prosecution. Penalties for offences can be imposed through the criminal courts. Claims against employers for compensation for injury or industrial disease would be taken as a civil action.

Trade union duties and activities

If an employer 'recognises' an independent trade union he accepts that its members have the right to take time off for union activity. Trade union officials such as shop stewards are entitled to paid time off to carry out duties relating to pay or other negotiations and other defined matters. Members of the union are entitled to take time off to participate in defined union

249

activities e.g. workplace meetings or voting in ballots (but *not* industrial action).

Dismissal of an employee for being a member of and taking part in union activities would be deemed 'unfair'. Likewise, It would be 'unfair' if it resulted from the employee refusing to join a trade union (the 'closed shop' is now illegal).

Note

The information provided in this chapter relates to England and Wales; whilst the employment system in Scotland and Northern Ireland is broadly similar, it will differ in some respects.

Please note that all monetary amounts quoted in this chapter are those known at the time of writing and are subject to amendment.

Questions and answers

Q *My employer has asked me to work at other premises which are three miles down the road. Can he do this?*

A You should refer to your offer of employment and written statement of particulars. If there is a clause (known as a mobility clause) to which you have agreed that states that you are required to work, as required, at any of the company's premises, then it is a reasonable request. Even if there is no such clause, the request may be deemed reasonable if there is a convenient and frequent public transport service. Otherwise, you might be able to claim redundancy if the need for you to do the job at that workplace has ceased or diminished; or to claim constructive dismissal as the employer has unilaterally changed your contract of employment (but you would need to resign to do this). In considering your claim for redundancy or constructive dismissal an industrial tribunal would look at the reasonableness of the request in terms of additional travelling time and costs and the discussions which took place between you and your employer.

Q *I have lost my driving licence. Can I be dismissed?*

A It depends on whether or not driving is essential for you to do your job. If it is and you cannot make equivalent and alternative arrangements then you can be dismissed, although your employer should first consider alternative employment. If it is not, dismissal on this ground would be potentially unfair.

Q *Two months ago I received a first formal oral warning allegedly for 'refusing to carry out a reasonable instruction'. I have now been given a final warning for 'unauthorised absence'. This isn't in line with the ACAS code of practice, is it?*

A It seems not to be, but you need to look at your organisation's disciplinary rules and procedures. Some provide for the stages of the ACAS code of first formal oral warning, first formal and then final written warning to be 'jumped', though usually only when the misconduct is serious. Often they also provide for unrelated misconduct from the first and subsequent incident to be taken into consideration.

Q *I have had a series of temporary contracts as opposed to fixed-term contracts. The first two were for a year, the next one for six months. I have now been told that my employment has ended. Do I have any rights?*

A You may well have, depending on the length of breaks between contracts. If the employment has been continuous the you will have employment rights including unfair dismissal and redundancy provisions.

Q *I work part-time and have been told that I have few rights. Is this the case?*

A No. For employment protection purposes, if you have two years' service you have the same statutory rights as a full-time employee.

CHAPTER 8

PUBLIC TRANSPORT

THE PUBLIC transport system has undergone many changes in recent years. Privatising the various transport bodies has dramatically altered the way the system operates. From the privatisation of British Airways and buses in the 1980s to the privatisation of British Rail in the mid–1990s, massive public ownership in the transport sector has given way to a myriad of private transport operating companies. Supporters say that the competition resulting from privatisation has and will continue to improve services for users. Opponents say that the search for profit can be at the expense of some of the things that really matter to users, such as the continued provision of benefits that are available to users of large systems (for example, national railcards and other network benefits available under British Rail), access to unbiased information, regular services, general standards of service and, crucially, safety.

The need for passengers to have a strong voice seems more important than ever before but, at least as far as bus services are concerned, passenger representation seems woefully inadequate. In general terms, passengers often have just cause for complaint, whether to private or public companies. But knowing the best route to take is often far from easy. And even when you do take it, you may not be happy with the outcome. This chapter highlights some of the main issues affecting public transport users and looks at what can be done about them.

Rail

Privatisation in brief

The 'big issue' that has dominated the rail industry over the past few years is the process of privatisation of British Rail. The government hopes that privatisation will result in an improved rail service for users. Critics think it will not. Privatisation has meant a major shake-up of rail services nationwide. Twenty-six train-operating companies (TOCs) form the basis of the new privatised structure (this figure includes EuroStar). Each is to be privately run as a franchise. Each company has to negotiate access to track, depots and stations from Railtrack, a separate company which owns and maintains the whole of the rail network. In some cases, negotiations take place with separate private companies: private companies will, for example, own and run 14 large metropolitan stations.

Rail users' interests

The industry has two regulatory bodies which oversee the running of the rail service: the Office of Passenger Rail Franchising (OPRAF) and the Office of the Rail Regulator (ORR).★ The Office of the Rail Regulator is the main body responsible for the protection of rail users' interests and an important part of its remit is to try to make sure competition and market forces have a positive effect on services. But a more direct link with users is provided by the eight regional Rail Users' Consultative Committees★ and the London Regional Passengers Committee.★ These are responsible for dealing directly with users' concerns and complaints. The committees have a wide brief covering all aspects of rail users' interests and a special responsibility for assessing the effect on users if stations or lines are proposed for closure. They have to report to the Regulator on potential hardship caused by closure and may make recommendations to lessen the impact of any proposed closure.

Local RUCCs keep a watch on matters such as punctuality and reliability of train services, overcrowding, cleanliness, fares, train design and station facilities. The London-based Central Rail Users' Consultative Committee (CRUCC) co-ordinates the work of the RUCCs and deals with matters that affect rail users nationally.

Competition and ticket sales

An important issue concerning the ease with which passengers can get appropriate tickets for travel when rail companies are competing against each other has been raised by the difficulties passengers have been experiencing in obtaining accurate and unbiased information. It should be fairly simple to find out the best price for your journey: you should be able to ask for the cheapest ticket to your destination and assume that the information you are given is correct. One of the Regulator's rules by which the train-operating companies must abide is that they should give unbiased information on their rivals', as well as their own, ticket prices. Journey times for cheaper tickets may be longer, but you should still be given information on cheaper fares.

However, research by Consumers' Association has highlighted problems in this area. In a report on rail fares published in *Which?* magazine in January 1996, researchers made over 250 ticket enquiries at 28 stations and enquiry points nationwide asking for the price of the cheapest tickets to a range of destinations. All the routes had more than one TOC operating on them. In nine out of ten cases, the answers the researchers were given were not the cheapest available for the service needed. On average, where an incorrect price was given, the TOCs overpriced by £24.

When the research was repeated a few months later (and the results highlighted in the BBC television programme *Panorama*) there was no improvement in the provision of information from ticket offices.

So, if the TOCs are giving out the wrong information, how can you be sure you are getting the best deal? It can be difficult, but you can improve your chances by doing a little research in advance or by asking your question at the booking office more specifically. All fares, no matter what company has set them, are listed clearly in the National Fares Manuals and this information is also automatically downloaded to station ticket machines. TOC staff possess the Fares Manuals and a number of libraries also take them: indeed, it is possible for members of the public to purchase them, but they run to many thousands of pages and are inevitably expensive, so this is unlikely to be a money-saving ploy for the majority of rail travellers. However, the *ABC Rail Guide* (published monthly, currently at £6.60, and available in many libraries) lists all fares from London to most stations in Britain and even if your journey is not from London it will give a good idea of the types of fares available (whether by time of travel, advance purchase, or whatever).

When you make an enquiry about a ticket, as well as specifying when you want to travel (outward and return if necessary), ask whether setting out at a different time would allow you to buy a cheaper ticket. Next, ask whether other TOCs operate between the same points (not necessarily by the same route) and state that you want to know the prices for the company that offers the cheapest tickets, even if the journey time is longer. Note that travelling between the same points might imply not just a different route but different stations in the same town: for example, the two principal ways of travelling from London to Birmingham are from London Euston to Birmingham New Street and from London Marylebone to Birmingham Snow Hill, but both these fares are listed under London-to-Birmingham in the Fares Manuals. Putting the salesperson 'on the spot' should greatly improve your chances of an accurate answer, but bear in mind that on many lines there will be no difference between operators. It is also important to complain to the Regional RUCC and the TOC if you find out you have been given biased information: TOCs are breaking regulations and could have their licences revoked for doing this.

Passengers' charters

The effectiveness of passengers' charters is another area of concern to users. The British Rail Passengers Charter sets target standards and also explains under what circumstances passengers can get compensation if something goes wrong. Now the private rail companies are required to produce their own charters, which will include performance targets at least as demanding as BR's existing ones. Each type of rail service (InterCity, inter-urban, rural, commuter, etc.) has its own targets for punctuality and reliability. Targets may vary from one company to the next. Passengers can claim refunds if trains are delayed for more than an hour, as long as the delay was caused by something within the company's control. Passengers holding monthly or longer-term season tickets can claim discounts if the company fails to achieve the standards set for punctuality and reliability by more than a short margin.

Performance figures should be on display at all staffed stations and should be updated at monthly intervals. However, station staff may fail to display updated information – or indeed, to display any information at all. In a survey in *Which?* magazine published in 1995, of 29 stations checked, only eight had punctuality standards and targets on display.

If you find this problem at your station, ask station staff if they have the information: if they cannot or do not seem able to help you, contact the customer service section of the head office of the rail company operating the service you want to find out about. Staff there will have this information and are obliged to provide you with it.

As for actually making a claim under the terms of the charter, posters should be on display at stations telling you how to go about it. Again, however, the *Which?* survey found that only 16 of the 29 stations checked had displayed this information.

In fact, you need to ask at the station for a refund claim form, which you can either fill in at the time or send on later. If a specific journey has been delayed by more than an hour, you can claim for vouchers to the value of a certain percentage of the price paid for the journey. Again, a member of staff should be able to provide you with a claim form. However, it is worth bearing in mind that if you are not satisfied with the figure offered – perhaps you have missed an important appointment, for instance – you can and should ask for more. Wording in the charter should not be viewed as being set in stone and companies can be flexible. Discretion should always be allowed and something as broad as a charter can never cover all the eventualities.

An important issue that has been raised by RUCCs and others concerning charters is that, depending on the details and how they are interpreted, they need not always be to the benefit of passengers. For example, standards and targets may be deliberately set so low that they are easily achievable and the company looks good on paper. Users inevitably lose out.

Taking a complaint further

If you are not happy with the way a train-operating company has dealt with a complaint, or if you are generally concerned about some aspect of the service and want a separate body to deal with a particular matter, you can contact your local Rail Users' Consultative Committee (RUCC)★ or, in London, the London Regional Passengers Committee.★ Members of the Committees represent a wide cross-section of rail users, including commuters, leisure travellers, senior citizens and people with disabilities. General issues including fares, quality of service and policy issues affecting the area concerned are regularly discussed with train and station operators at Committee meetings, which are also open to the public. The Regulator can refer matters to the RUCCs for investigation and the RUCCs can ask the Regulator to use his powers to take action where necessary.

As well as dealing with individual complaints and, where necessary, putting companies under pressure to reverse decisions, the RUCCs bring to the attention of the regulators (ORR and OPRAF) overall successes or failures of local services. They represent the passengers' view to the Regulator and can refer individual complaints to the Regulator, particularly when these complaints highlight wider issues of significance to rail users in general.

For individual complaints, write to the relevant operating company first; its name and address is shown on notices at the station or in the telephone directory. Put your complaint in writing. If you are not satisfied with the response, contact the Secretary of your local RUCC in writing. Enclose copies of any correspondence you have had with the company.

Getting involved in broader issues

Rail users' groups have been set up by rail users in many parts of the UK and are run on a voluntary basis. Some of these groups have a high profile and are closely involved with RUCCs. One of the best ways of getting involved in the wider rail issues is to join one of these. To find out whether there is a local group in your area, ask your regional RUCC for contact details. If, having been a member of one of these groups for a while, you wish to volunteer for an RUCC, you can enquire about vacancies.

Rail safety

Privatisation has raised important matters concerning rail safety. Concerns centre on levels of safety investment in the rail system and the fact that a private company may be inclined to put profit before safety. For example, the Railway Inspectorate, which is part of the Health and Safety Commission, has an important independent role to play in safety and accident investigation but it gets involved only with serious accident cases. Railtrack deals with the rest. There are worries that it will be hard for Railtrack to remain impartial in these investigations. This system is in contrast to the aviation industry where the Air Accidents Investigation Branch of the Department of Transport deals with all accident investigations.

RUCCs are closely involved with safety matters. As well as helping to highlight safety issues in the broader sense, they can bring pressure to bear in areas such as the provision of improved lighting, the introduction of closed-circuit TV at stations and better coach design. On the latter topic, for example, better design would incorporate corridor connections that allow passengers to move from any part of the train to another, for improved passenger security; unfortunately, at present, many peak-hour trains are formed of several units joined together, and whilst all modern rolling-stock has connections between the coaches that make up each unit, many are now being built with no end-corridor connection that allows people to pass between the units, which is a nuisance not only for staff carrying out ticket checks and for catering trolleys, but for individual passengers needing to move for their own safety and also for any evacuation of the train in the event of an emergency – especially in a tunnel.

If you are concerned about any aspect of rail safety, the RUCC can help voice your concerns.

The safety measures pertaining in the Channel Tunnel in the event of fire or terrorist activity have long been a source of concern to organisations like Consumers' Association. CA would have preferred, from the safety standpoint, passengers to be separated from their cars while they are travelling on Le Shuttle. But above all it wants the information on which the decision not to segregate cars and passengers was based to be released.

Eurotunnel is still keeping secret all the safety information that would make it possible for independent evaluation of safety in terms of design and operation of the tunnel. No independent external organisations have been allowed to evaluate the tunnel, so passengers cannot be sure that safety is being put before profit.

There is an element of crossover between different organisations in relation to Channel Tunnel safety. Basically, passengers concerned about safety en route to the tunnel should complain first to Eurostar, which operates the passenger train service, and then to either the London Regional Passengers Committee or the RUCC for Southern England, depending on where the problem is occurring (for example, following initial contact with Eurostar, concerns about security measures such as baggage checks at the Waterloo terminal should be addressed to the LRPC while concerns relating to the Ashford terminal should be addressed to the local RUCC). The LRPC and RUCC for Southern England liaise closely with each other and can redirect complaints to each other if necessary. However, their responsibilities to do not extend to inside the tunnel. If your concerns are about safety actually within the tunnel (for example, evacuation procedures), take them up with Eurotunnel, the company which owns and runs it and is responsible for safety procedures.

Complaints and concerns about safety can also be addressed to the Channel Tunnel Safety Authority,* a government body responsible for overseeing tunnel safety which is able to raise issues with Eurotunnel as appropriate.

Major change of land use for new road or rail route

Proposals for any new road or rail route always involve widespread consultation with all the interested parties, especially those directly affected by the change in land use. Nothing can happen without the granting of planning permission. Initially, an application is made by the developer(s) wishing to build the road or rail link to the planning authority, or authorities, responsible for the land. The application is made available to the public and individuals likely to be affected may be directly informed. Often opposition to the scheme is considerable, generating huge publicity and likely to lead to a public enquiry. (In the case of the new private-sector rail link between London and the Channel Tunnel, a private bill – private because it was private to specific interests, rather than a matter of public policy – had to be introduced in Parliament before its construction could be approved.)

Anyone opposing a new road or rail route should try to get support from others and to set up a pressure group: group opposition is always more effective than individual efforts. Try to get support from other organisations, such as environmental bodies, that may share your attitude, and to get local councillors and MPs on your side. Collect signatures for a petition, setting out your concerns and objections and explaining how it affects you or your immediate area specifically (take advice from an MP on the language you use), but without going into great detail.

If you want to find out what other petitions exist and what they say, the clerk of the Private Bills Office in the House of Commons should be able to help you.

At the enquiry, opposition groups have the opportunity to express their views, as do the developer and the planning authority. Be sure to collect as much evidence as possible to fight your cause: for example, a survey of the number of people using the land affected, and for what purposes. You may wish to employ professionals, such as lawyers or planners, to help you present your case. At the end of the enquiry, the enquiry inspector considers all the evidence and produces a report. It can be many months before a decision is made. If the decision goes against you, you may be able to appeal; and as a last resort the case may be taken to the High Court for a judicial review, although this would be a rare occurrence.

If blight is a problem in the case of your area, it is likely that your MP will be prepared to fight on your behalf. With an MP's help you can exercise the option of accusing the Department of

Transport of maladministration, in not carrying out its duties properly and hence causing your property to be blighted. (MPs whose constituencies were on the Channel Tunnel rail link have been fighting on their constituents' behalf for such compensation, and the Ombudsman has recommended that the Department of Transport should pay selected compensation; although the DoT refuted the claims it is considering blight payments of the type recommended.)

Buses and coaches

Almost all bus services in Britain are provided by private companies, ranging from large groups with thousands of buses in different regions of the country to small, localised operators with fewer than five. Outside London, buses have been deregulated – in other words, bus companies can provide a service largely without restrictions, although there may be controls on the number of vehicles operating if this would otherwise cause congestion. Bus companies have to register with the regional Area Traffic Commissioner, who ensures that companies run services as registered and that they are operating safely. Local authorities may subsidise the provision of services which are not commercially viable but may be socially necessary. In London, London Transport no longer has its own buses but organises about 650 bus routes through private-sector companies operating under contract. Deregulation of London buses has been on the cards, but the London Regional Passengers Committee, in alliance with other organisations, has persuaded the government to put its plans into cold storage.

Long-distance coaches are provided by private companies. There are no restrictions on the routes served or the number of vehicles operated. A national network of routes is maintained by the National Express (operating in England and Wales) and Scottish Citylink companies, largely through franchised operations.

Getting your voice heard

A major issue concerning official consumer representation is the lack of it. In contrast to rail users, bus users are poorly organised as consumers. It could be argued that rail passengers, unlike bus users, are seen by politicians as a group to be placated because so many opinion-formers commute into central London. Unlike the rail industry, the bus system has no regulator, although calls have repeatedly been made by opposition parties and pressure groups for the setting up of an 'OFBUS'-type regulatory body. The government and industry view, however, is that there is no need for this additional layer of bureaucracy.

In the same way that there is no overall regulator, there are no official regional bodies representing user interests, apart from in London where the London Regional Passenger Committee looks after user interests for buses as well as trains. This is in contrast to the national network of Rail Users' Consultative Committees, which were set up by the government specifically to represent the views of rail users. Area Traffic Commissioners are meant to make sure timetables are not detrimentally changed without agreement, but have been criticised as being incapable of enforcing the rules covering this.

Consumer representation outside London is largely left to a pressure group, the National Federation of Bus Users (NFBU).★ This was established in 1985, in the run-up to deregulation, to bring together various organisations and concerned individuals with an interest in bus services. The Federation negotiates with the Department of Transport, with major operators and with local authorities. It also seeks to encourage the establishment of local bus users' groups and has close links with other pressure groups with an interest in transport issues – for example, Transport 2000,★ which is an environmental organisation pressing for an environmentally sensitive transport policy that takes into account the access and social needs of all travellers. The NFBU can take up individuals' complaints about bus services with companies which have not been resolved with the company concerned.

For complaints or suggestions relating to bus services outside London, the general procedure is to write to the customer services section of the company first (or the company and the local authority if a bus route is threatened with cuts), and to contact the NFBU as the next stage. Larger companies are likely to have their own charter and/or leaflets explaining complaints procedures.

The other main organisation with an interest in bus users is Buswatch.* This is a charity which carries out research into the provision of bus services and the views of users, but the NFBU is the main campaigning organisation.

If you have a complaint about a tendered bus service, take it in the first instance to the local authority responsible for tendering the service: this is the body which sets the service standards bus companies should meet as part of the tender, and if a bus company is not meeting these standards the local authority may decide to award the tender to another company. Bus timetables usually carry details of the authority which is ultimately responsible for tendered services. See also page 269.

The impact of deregulation

When local bus services were deregulated in 1986 and the process of privatisation started, competition was expected to stimulate more and better services at keener prices. But things have not quite worked out like this. Although in some areas services have certainly improved, in others standards have fallen. Fares have not dropped and bus usage has declined. And where more than one company operates on a route, rather than opting to run a different service, passengers have been tending to take the first bus that comes along even if it is a more expensive one.

The theory of market forces stimulating price and quality competition does not, therefore, work in practice. The end result is sometimes simply more and more buses clogging up the roads, competing for passengers by aiming to be the first at the stop. Some companies have been known to use over-aggressive and anti-competitive practices to get their passengers: for example, a larger company may run a free bus service for a while to squeeze other companies out, then it can 'claim' the route as its own.

When matters such as this are referred to the Office of Fair Trading or the Monopolies and Mergers Commission, both of which have a special interest in anti-competitive practices, slow-moving bureaucracy means that by the time judgments are made it is often too late for the 'squeezed-out' companies. Another problem has been the condition of bus fleets. It seems that many companies have failed to invest in new buses, preferring to run existing vehicles into the ground. An ageing fleet may lead to poorer passenger standards, including the potential for unreliability and increased safety risk, unless the vehicles are meticulously maintained. There have been drawbacks with ticket usage too. Because separate bus companies operate in the same area, in many instances companies refuse to accept tickets issued by another company. This does not make travelling any easier for passengers. What matters to users is not the ideology of competition and deregulation but the existence of decent, cheap, easily usable and regular public transport.

The Labour party has proposed the re-regulation of buses through an extended network of passenger transport authorities, which will be given new powers to plan and contract for buses in their areas. The present government has put the deregulation of London buses on hold. As a result of deregulation problems, some form of re-regulation looks more and more likely.

Coach safety

This has been a major issue of the last few years. Concerns about the lack of seat belts on coaches, and about speeding, have resulted in increasing pressure on the government to tighten up the safety rules.

It is generally accepted that seat belts would save lives and reduce injuries in coach accidents. The government's own report in 1994 acknowledged this. But seat belts are still not compulsory on coaches, other than those used primarily to transport children, although some coach companies may have fitted them voluntarily. Consumers' Association and other groups have criticised the government for this, claiming that it has bowed to pressure from the coach industry not to burden coach companies with the extra expense. In CA's view, if belts cannot be fitted to coaches immediately, those coaches should not be on the road. It has also advocated that three-point belts should be fitted in mini-buses too.

If you are concerned about coach safety, ask the company with which you are planning to travel if it has fitted belts. The more people ask, the greater the pressure on coach companies to provide them.

As for speeding, although all coaches must be fitted with a device that restricts the maximum speed to 70mph, or 65mph for new coaches, the police, many car users and even the Department of Transport have noted that coaches break this speed limit. The problem is that tampering with speed limiters takes place, and is relatively easy to do. Tachographs, the devices which record journey time and speed, are also tampered with. Consumers' Association has urged that fiddling with tachographs should be made an endorsable offence leading to loss of licence.

If you think you have seen a speeding coach, report the company, and ideally the registration number, to the police as soon as you can. If you are travelling on a coach that is speeding, report this to the company operating the coach. After all, it is human life that the driver is putting at risk.

Airlines

Structure and organisation

British airlines are all private companies, as are a number of the major airports. The Civil Aviation Authority (CAA) is a statutory body which oversees the airline industry and is responsible for its economic and safety regulation. Its board members are appointed by the Secretary of State for Transport but it is funded by the aviation industry. A primary objective of the CAA is to ensure that British airlines provide air services at competitive prices consistent with a high standard of safety and that they meet passenger demand.

As well as responsibility for airlines, the CAA has important regulatory powers over the larger airports and can take action against unfair practices, in particular any abuse of the airports' monopoly position. All airports used for public transport must also have a safety licence from the CAA. This covers such matters as the provision of fire-fighting and medical services.

Airline safety and security

British airlines generally have a good safety record. Every aircraft company must have an Air Operator's Certificate before it can fly.

This is granted by the CAA, after inspection and when it is satisfied that the operator is competent to operate its aircraft safely. CAA flight operations inspectors check that safety standards are maintained. All aircraft registered in Britain must be granted a Certificate of Airworthiness by the CAA before being flown.

Security measures at airports were tightened in 1994 with the introduction of regulations requiring airlines to account for and authorise for travel every item of hold baggage placed on board international flights originating in Britain. This should cut down on mis-routed baggage as well as improving security.

Although the CAA has strong powers, its dual role – namely, protecting the industry and also setting and monitoring safety standards – has come under fire. It has been criticised by Consumers' Association, amongst others, for failing to introduce certain safety measures, such as compulsory smokehoods. Progress towards safety improvements can be slow, as there is no one to regulate the CAA – it decides its own methods, objectives and timescales. There have been calls for a new independent UK public transport safety commission with powers to regulate and control safety, leaving the CAA to concentrate on other matters.

Passenger representation

The Air Transport Users Council* operates as the official passenger representation organisation. It deals with complaints made by consumers concerning individual airlines and airports and is involved in issues concerning safety, overbooking, flight delays, airports and a whole range of other air transport matters that are of concern to users. Though funded by the Civil Aviation Authority, it views itself as an independent body. Safety is a particular concern and all reports of apparently unsafe practice are investigated, and subsequently brought to the attention of the CAA and the airline concerned if there is sufficient evidence. The Council is always in close contact with the CAA's Safety Regulation Group and has an important role to play in bringing passenger concerns about safety to the CAA's attention. It also pushes for higher compensation limits for death or injury occurring as a result of aircraft accidents.

Legal protection

When your booking is accepted by an airline, a legally binding contract is made between you and it. Under the Warsaw Convention, airlines are obliged to compensate you if they fail to get you to your destination within a 'reasonable' amount of time of your scheduled arrival. On long-haul flights, a reasonable amount of time is considered to be about six hours. But the strength of your claim depends on what caused the delay: bad weather, for instance, is beyond the airlines' control, so you are unlikely to be able to claim substantial compensation if this was responsible for the hold-up.

If you are a victim of overbooking you are also entitled to compensation. Airlines deliberately overbook some scheduled flights because they presume that some people will not turn up. But sometimes more people than the plane can carry arrive for the flight. If you turn up on time and are 'bumped' – in other words, there is no seat for you on the flight – under EC regulations covering scheduled flights from European airports you will be entitled to a full refund or a seat on the next available flight. The airline must also offer you immediate cash compensation of £120 for flights up to 3,500 km, and £240 for longer flights (these amounts are halved, however, if the airline can get you to your final destination within two hours of the original scheduled arrival time, or within four hours for flights over 3,500 km). Your claim in such instances is against the airline: talk to a member of the airline booking staff at the airport.

For air travel from a US airport, if you are 'bumped' involuntarily owing to overbooking and the airline arranges substitute transportation that is scheduled to arrive at your destination more than one hour but less than two hours (four hours on international flights) after your original arrival time, the airline must pay you an amount equal to the one-way fare to your final destination. If the substitute transportation is scheduled to get you to your destination more than two hours later (more than four hours on international flights), or if the airline does not make any substitute travel arrangements for you, the compensation doubles (i.e. you receive 200 per cent of the fare). You are always allowed to keep your original ticket, which you can use on another flight or have refunded. The 'denied boarding' compensation is essentially a payment for your inconvenience.

In the past, it was generally the view that to book a flight with a 'bucket shop' could mean putting your money at risk. Although many were perfectly reputable, some have been known to disappear after taking customers' money but before issuing tickets. Now, regulations from the Civil Aviation Authority that came into force in 1995 require any agent selling discounted flights to be covered by an Air Travel Organiser's Licence (ATOL). This means that if an agent goes bust after you have paid for your ticket, you will get a full refund. If you do not get a ticket immediately from the agent, you should by law be given an Atol receipt. Make sure you get one as this confirms that your contract is with the Atol-holder.

Paying less for your fare

Distance is largely irrelevant when it comes to setting air fares. The fare-fixing policies of national governments and competition between airlines affect fares more than distance. It is not hard to get cheap fares – you just need to know where to look.

When buying plane tickets, it is worth knowing about the differences between different types. The cheapest tickets tend to be charter fares or consolidated fares (but never make assumptions: airline special offers or other types of tickets can sometimes be cheaper). Charter flights are sold by airlines to tour operators, who then try to fill them with 'package' holidaymakers. Flights from unsold packages are sold as 'seat-only' fares. Consolidated fares are available on scheduled flights – flights run by airlines to a published timetable. A consolidator (more commonly known as a 'bucket shop') negotiates favourable prices with airlines by guaranteeing to sell a certain number of tickets. It puts its own mark-up on the tickets and sells them on. Such deals are often found in newspaper classified ads, but travel agents should also be able to find them for you. Apex, Pex, Super Apex and Super Pex are the airlines' 'official' discount fares. Most of the above airfares have certain restrictions or drawbacks, such as having to book two weeks in advance or having to stay over a Saturday night.

To get the cheapest fare, put the high-street travel agents or flight agencies to work. They have access to vast databases containing the current deals available. By shopping around, the chances are that you will cover more databases, because some agents will have negotiated special deals. Be persistent: you may not be offered the cheapest deal straight away. You can phone tour operators direct to get information on seat-only deals. Check the small ads too for 'last-minute' deals from consolidators and agents. Remember that to get the cheapest fares you also need to be flexible about when you fly and which airline you fly with. For child reductions, on scheduled flights you may be better off paying for an unofficially discounted adult fare than for an officially discounted fare with a child reduction.

Questions and answers

Q *My local bus company is planning to cut a service running through my village that I and other villagers use regularly. Is there anything I can do to stop this happening?*

A Private bus companies are entitled to cut any service they consider to be unprofitable: as companies trying to make a profit, they cannot be forced to run a service on which they are losing money. However, public concern about communities, especially rural ones, becoming isolated as a result of lack of public transport can persuade local authorities to step in to save threatened services. Bus companies can maintain unprofitable services under contract to the local authority if the local authority feels there is a social need for that service. The local authority subsidises the service so that it becomes profitable for the company (the contract is allocated through a system of competitive tendering).

To find out whether this would be possible in your case, contact your local authority – the Public Transport Co-ordinating Officer tends to be a good starting point. Help is not automatically given: the local authority makes a decision as to how necessary the service is and availability of financial resources can of course affect the final decision (although local authorities can apply for aid from the Rural Development Commission). It is in your interests to show how important the service is to the community and it is worth forming a bus users' group to show how many people depend on it: the National Federation of Bus Users can provide advice.

Q *I've recently witnessed a deterioration in the standards of the rail service I use to get to work. What can I do about it?*

A Your regional Rail Users' Consultative Committee (or London Regional Passengers Committee in and around London) is specifically designed to help provide a strong user voice for concerns about falling standards and will take up issues with both the train operator concerned and the rail regulator, if necessary. The RUCCs regularly discuss fares, quality of service and policy issues with local train and station operators. You can approach your RUCC directly with your concerns but the standard procedure is to contact the train operator first to see what it says: it may, for instance, already be aware of problems and have plans to improve the situation. If, however, you are not happy with the train operator's response, you should contact the RUCC in writing and it will take up the issues on your behalf. Remember, too, that rail users' groups can provide a strong collective voice. Check with your RUCC to find out whether there is one in your area. If there is not, your RUCC should be able to give advice on setting one up. Organised user pressure can have a powerful impact on train operators

Q *I travel through the Channel Tunnel regularly in my car and although I've never experienced problems I'm concerned about what would happen if there were a fire or an explosive device on the train when it is going through the tunnel. How do I know if I'm safe?*

A Unfortunately, it is impossible to be sure. There has been a lot of controversy over certain aspects of Channel Tunnel safety. Eurotunnel and the Channel Tunnel Safety Authority say it is safe. The problem is that despite repeated requests from organisations such as Consumers' Association, Eurotunnel has not made public all the safety information that would allow independent external organisations to evaluate whether the design and operation of the tunnel is as safe as it could be. Without this evidence, it is impossible to be completely confident that travelling in the tunnel is safe. Of particular concern is the fact that the design of the train used in the Tunnel puts cars, passengers and fuel together in an enclosed space, which creates a fire risk and makes evacuation more difficult. It is worth your registering your concerns with Eurotunnel and with the Channel Tunnel Safety Authority.★ The Authority will take up individual complaints about safety with Eurotunnel if necessary.

Q *I was unhappy with the service I received from the airline with which I flew on holiday. The ground staff were inefficient, the flight was overbooked and my young son ended up sitting in a separate part of the plane from me. How do I complain?*

A The general advice from the Air Transport Users Council when you have a complaint is in the first instance to try to sort it out by speaking to someone on the spot (many complaints can be sorted out straight away). If you are still not satisfied, try to identify who is responsible for what has gone wrong: it may not always be the airline. Make a note of staff names, times and any other relevant information. Your complaint is more likely to succeed if you have all the facts. It might be useful, too, to ask for the names and addresses of other passengers who saw what went wrong. Put your complaint in a letter, briefly explaining what happened and, if you want, what you expect to be done about it. Keep a copy of your letter. Send the letter to the customer relations department of the airline, or, if you travelled on a package, address it to the tour organiser or operator. If the complaint concerns one of the airport's services, write to the customer services department of the airport. If, after you have made a written complaint, you are not satisfied with the outcome, contact the Air Transport Users Council,★ which can follow up the complaint and put pressure on the airline if appropriate. Alternatively, contact the Association of British Travel Agents★ or the Association of Independent Tour Operators.★

Q *I've heard that smokehoods on planes could save lives in an accident. So why aren't planes fitted with them?*

A Smokehoods are designed to allow airline passengers to see and breathe more easily in smoke. They range from simple transparent bags with a filter to special masks with sophisticated filters or pressurised air bottles. The Air Accidents Investigations Branch has recommended that they should be introduced on planes.

The Civil Aviation Authority has refused to make the carrying of passenger smokehoods mandatory for a number of reasons, including the fact that they could slow down evacuation and that they would save few lives. However, other experts have rejected these arguments. The CAA also claims that improvements to cabin seat materials to make them more fire-resistant have cut the need for smokehoods.

Consumers' Association has long pushed for the introduction of smokehoods, but to no avail. It has also called for the separation of *all* public transport accident investigation from bodies which are responsible for safety enforcement or, indeed, promotion of the industry concerned.

If you have any concerns about safety on a flight, you should contact the airline concerned and, if you do not get a satisfactory response, the Air Transport Users Council, which has regular consultations with the CAA about safety.

Addresses and Further Reading

Accident Line
Law Society of England and Wales
0500 192939

Action for Victims of Medical Accidents (AVMA)
Bank Chambers, 1 London Road,
Forest Hill, London SE23 3TP
0181–291 2793

Advisory Centre for Education (ACE)
1b Aberdeen Studios, 22 Highbury
Grove, London N5 2DQ
0171–354 8321 (2–5 p.m.)

Advisory, Conciliation and Arbitration Service (ACAS)
Head Office, Brandon House,
180 Borough High Street, London
SE1 1LW
0171–210 3000

Air Transport Users Council
5th Floor, Kingsway House,
103 Kingsway, London WC2B 6QX
0171–242 3882

Anti-Bullying Campaign
0171–378 1446

Association of British Insurers (ABI)
51 Gresham Street, London
EC2V 7HQ
0171–600 3333

Association of British Travel Agents (ABTA)
55–57 Newman Street, London
W1P 4AH
0171–637 2444

Association of Independent Tour Operators
133a St Margaret's Road,
Twickenham, Middlesex TW1 1RG
0181–744 9280

Association of Personal Injury Lawyers (APIL)
0115 9580585

Bank of England
Threadneedle Street, London
EC2R 8AH
0171–601 4444

Banking Ombudsman
70 Gray's Inn Road, London
WC1X 8NB
0171–404 9944

Benefits Agency Chief Executive
Quarry House, Quarry Hill, Leeds
LS2 7UA
0113–232 4000

Benefits Agency
(see local telephone directory under 'Benefits Agency' or 'Social Security, Department of')

Boarding Schools Association
Ysgol Nant, Valley Road,
Llanfairfechan, Gwynedd LL33 0ES
01248 680542

The British Acupuncture Council
0181–964 0222

The British Association for Counselling
1 Regent Place, Rugby, Warks
CV21 2PJ
01788 578328

British Bankers Association
Pinners Hall, 105–108 Old Broad
Street, London EC2N 1EX
0171–216 8800

The British Chiropractic Association
29 Whitley Street, Reading
RG2 0EG
01734 757557

The British Complementary Medicine Association
39 Prestbury Road, Cheltenham,
Gloucestershire GL52 2PT
01242 226770

British Dyslexia Association
01734 668271

The British Medical Acupuncture Society
01925 730727

British Medical Association
BMA House, Tavistock Square,
London WC1H 9JP
0171–387 4499

Building Societies Association and Council of Mortgage Lenders (CML)
3 Savile Row, London W1X 1AF
0171–437 0655

Building Societies Commission
15 Great Marlborough Street, London
W1V 2LL
0171–437 9992

Building Societies Ombudsman
Millbank Tower, Millbank, London
SW1P 4XS
0171–931 0044

Buswatch (as for NFBU, below)

Careers and Occupational Information Centre
0117 977 7199

Careers Resource and Advisory Centre (CRAC)
c/o Hobsons Publishing plc, Bateman
Street, Cambridge CB2 1LZ
01223 354551

Centre for Dispute Resolution
0171–481 4441

Centre for Information on Language Teaching
20 Bedfordbury, London WC2N 4LB
0171–379 5131

Centre for Studies on Inclusive Education (CSIE)
Redland Close, Bristol BS6 6UE
0117–923 8450

Chartered Institute of Arbitrators
24 Angel Gate, City Road, London
EC1V 2RS
0171–837 4483

Citizens Advice Bureaux
(see local telephone directory or
advertisements in local newspaper)

The Commission for Racial Equality
Elliot House, 10–12 Allington Street,
London SW1E 5EH
0171–828 7022

Companies House
01222 380801

Contributions Agency Chief Executive
Room C 1837, DSS, Benton Park
Road, Longbenton, Newcastle upon
Tyne NE98 1YX
0191–213 5000

The Council for Dance Education and Training
Riverside Studio, Crisp Road,
London W6 9RL
0181–741 5084

Council for the Registration of Schools Teaching Dyslexic Pupils
9 Elgy Road, Gosforth, Newcastle upon Tyne NE3 4UU

The Customer Service Unit
The Court Service, 6th Floor Southside, 105 Victoria Street, London SW1E 6QT
0171–210 1775; 210 2009; 210 2200

Department for Education and Employment
Mowden Hall, Darlington, Co. Durham DL3 9BG
01325 392156
(information on assisted places)

Department for Education and Employment Publications Centre
Sanctuary Buildings, Great Smith Street, London SW1P 3BT
0171–925 5555

Department of Education for Northern Ireland
Rathgael House, Balloo Road, Bangor, County Down BT19 2PR
01247 279279

Department of Health
PO Box 410, Wetherby, LS23 7LN

Department of Social Security
Newcastle upon Tyne NE1 4QN
01232 524292

Department of Trade and Industry (Headquarters)
Ashdown House, 1 Victoria Street, London SW1H 0ET
0171–215 5000

DSS offices
(see local telephone directory under 'Social Security, Department of' or 'Benefits Agency')

DSS Pensions and Overseas Benefits Directorate, Newcastle upon Tyne NE98 1BA

DVLC
Swansea SA99 1BR
0792 772151

The Dyslexia Institute
01784 463851

Education Otherwise
32 Carey Park, Looe, Cornwall PL13 2JP
(send s.a.e. for information)

Employment Service Helpline
0345 959775
(industrial tribunal enquiries)

The Equal Opportunities Commission
Overseas House, Quay Street, Manchester M3 3HN
0161 833 9244

Freeline Social Security
0800 666 555
(Statutory Sick Pay queries)

Gabbitas Educational Trust
Carrington House, 126–130 Regent Street, London W1R 6EE
0171–734 0161

General Council of the Bar
3 Bedford Row, London WC1R 4DB
0171–242 0082

The General Council and Register of Osteopaths
56 London Street, Reading, Berks RG1 4SQ
01734 576585

General Dental Council
37 Wimpole Street, London W1M 8DQ
0171–486 2171

General Medical Council
178–202 Great Portland Street, London W1N 6JE
0171–580 7642

General Optical Council
41 Harley Street, London W1N 2DJ
0171–580 3898

Health Information Service
0800 66 55 44

Health Literature Line
0800 555 777, or via Internet,
http://www.open.gov.uk./doh/tables
96.htm

Health and Safety Executive
Rose Court, 2 Southwark Bridge,
London SE1 9HS
0171–717 6000

**Health Service Commissioner
(Ombudsman)**
England
11th Floor, Millbank Tower,
Millbank, London SW1P 4QP
0171–217 4051
Wales
4th Floor, Pearl Assurance House,
Greyfriars Road, Cardiff CF1 3AG
01222–394621
Scotland
Ground Floor, 1 Atholl Place,
Edinburgh EH3 8HP
0131–225 7465
Northern Ireland
Parliamentary Commissioner for
Administration
Freepost, Belfast BT1 6BR
01232–233821
(Freephone 0800 282036)

House of Commons
London SW1A 0AA
0171–219 3000

**House of Commons Public
Information Office**
0171–219 4272

House of Lords Library
0171–219 3107

Independent Adjudicator
3rd Floor, Haymarket House, 28
Haymarket, London SW1Y 4SP
0171–930 2292

Independent Healthcare Association
22 Little Russell Street, London
WC1A 2HT
0171–430 0537

**Independent Schools Information
Service (ISIS)**
56 Buckingham Gate, London
SW1E 6AG
0171–630 8793

Institute for Complementary Medicine
PO Box 194, London SE16 1QZ
0171–237 5165

**Insurance Brokers Registration
Council (IBRC)**
15 St Helen's Place, London
EC3 6DS
0171–588 4387

Insurance Ombudsman
Citygate One, 135 Park Street,
London SE1 9EA
0171–928 7600

**Investment Managers Regulatory
Organisation (IMRO)**
Lloyds Chambers, 1 Portsoken Street,
London E1 8BT
0171–390 5000

Investment Ombudsman
0171–796 3065

Judicial Appointments Group
6th Floor Southside, 105 Victoria
Street, London SW1E 6QT

Kidscape
Parents' Bullying Line 0171–730
3300, Tuesday & Wednesday,
10 a.m.–4 p.m.

Law Society of England and Wales
0171–242 1222 (personal injury
lawyers 01602 580583)
(see also Accident Line, above)

Legal Services Ombudsman
22 Oxford Court, Oxford Street,
Manchester M2 3WQ
0161 236 9532

Local Government Ombudsman
21 Queen Anne's Gate, London
SW1H 9BU
0171–915 3210

London Regional Passengers Committee
Clements House, 14–18 Gresham Street, London EC2V 7PR
0171–505 9000

Mediation UK
01179 241234

Members of Parliament
(see House of Commons)

Mental Health Act Commission
Maid Marion House, 56 Houndsgate, Nottingham NG1 6BG
0115–943 7100

Mental Health Commission for Northern Ireland
Elizabeth House, 118 Hollywood Road, Belfast BT4 1NY
01232 651157

Mental Welfare Commission for Scotland
25 Drumsheugh Gardens, Edinburgh EH3 7RB
0131 225 7034

Money Management National Register of Independent Fee-Based Advisers
c/o Matrix Data Ltd, FREEPOST 22 (SW1565), London W1E 7EZ
0117 976 9444

Motor Accident Solicitors Society
0117 9292560

National Association for Gifted Children
Park Campus, Boughton Green Road, Northampton NN2 7AL
01604 792300

National Blood Service
0345 711711

National Federation of Bus Users (NFBU)
18 Little Southsea Street, Southsea, Hants PO5 3RS
01705 814493

National Waiting List Helpline
(College of Health)
0181–983 1133

NHS Policy and NHS Executive Boards
Quarry House, Quarry Hill, Leeds LS2 7UE

Nursery Voucher Scheme information line
0345 543 345 (charged at local rates)

Occupational Pensions Advisory Service (OPAS)
11 Belgrave Road, London SW1V 1RB
0171–233 8080

Occupational Pensions Regulatory Authority (OPRA)
[not available at time of going to press]

Office of Fair Trading
Field House, 15–25 Breams Buildings, London EC4A 1PR
0171–242 2858

The Office of the Rail Regulator
1 Waterhouse Square, 138/142 Holborn, London EC1N 2ST
0171–282 2000

Office for the Supervision of Solicitors
Victoria Court, 8 Dormer Place, Leamington Spa CV32 5AE
01926 820082

Open and Distance Learning Quality Council
27 Marylebone Road, London NW1 5JS
0171–935 5391

Open University Central Enquiry Service
PO Box 200, Walton Hall, Milton Keynes MK7 6AA
(01908) 653231

Optical Consumer Complaints Service (OCCS)
PO Box 4685, London SE1 8YH
0171–261 1017

Osteopathic Information Service
PO Box 2074
Reading, Berks RG1 4YR
01734 512051

Parliamentary Commissioner for Administration (Ombudsman)
Church House, Great Smith Street, London SW1P 3BW
0171–726 3000

Patient's Charter and NHS Performance Tables
Health Literature Line
0800 555 777

Pensions Ombudsman
11 Belgrave Road, London SW1V 1RB
0171–834 9144

Personal Insurance Arbitration Service (PIAS)
(see Chartered Institute of Arbitrators)

Personal Investment Authority (PIA)
7th Floor, 1 Canada Square, Canary Wharf, London E14 5AZ
0171–538 8860

PIA Ombudsman
3rd Floor, Centrepoint, 103 New Oxford Street, London WC1A 1QH
0171–240 3838

Primary Care and Practising Development Directorate
Dundonald House, Upper Newtonards Road, Belfast BT4 3TL

Rail Users' Consultative Committees
Scotland
249 West George Street, Glasgow G2 4QE
0141 221 7760
North East
Hilary House, 16 St Saviour's Place, York YO1 2PL
01904 625615
North West
5th Floor, Boulton House, 17–21 Chorlton Street, Manchester M1 3HY
0161 228 6247
Wales
St David's House, East Wing, Wood Street, Cardiff CF1 1ES
01222 227247

Midlands
77 Paradise Circus, Queensway, Birmingham B1 2DT
0121 212 2133
East
Midgate House, Midgate, Peterborough PE1 1TN
01733 312188
West
13th Floor, Tower House, Fairfax Street, Bristol BS1 3BN
0117 926 5703
South
4th Floor, 35 Old Queen Street, London SW1H 9JA
0171–222 0391

Royal Institution of Chartered Surveyors
12 Great George Street, Parliament Square, London SW1P 3AD
0171–222 7000

School Curriculum and Assessment Authority
Newcombe House, 45 Notting Hill Gate, London W11 3JB
0171–229 1234

Scottish Legal Services Ombudsman
2 Greenside Lane, Edinburgh EH1 3AH
0131 556 5574

The Scottish Office, Education and Industry Department
Victoria Quay, Edinburgh EH6 6QQ
(National Curriculum 0131–556 8400; assisted places 0131 244 0953)

Securities and Investments Board
Gavrelle House, 2–14 Bunhill Row, London EC1Y 8RA
0171–638 1240

Sheed & Ward Ltd
14 Cooper's Row, London EC3N 2BH

SIB Register enquiries
0171–929 3652

The Society of Homoeopaths
2 Artizan Road, Northampton
NN1 4HU
01604 21400

Solicitors Family Law Association
01689 850227

Solicitors' Indemnity Fund
100 St John Street, London
EC1M 4EH
0171–566 6000

Tax Enquiry Centre
(see local telephone directory under
'Inland Revenue')

Transport 2000
Walkden House, 10 Melton Street,
London NW1 2EJ
0171–388 8386

*United Kingdom Central Council for
Nursing, Midwifery and Health
Visiting*
23 Portland Place, London W1N 4JT
0171–637 7181

UK Council for Psychotherapy
Regent's College, Inner Circle,
Regent's Park, London NW1 4NS
0171–487 7554

*Universities and Colleges Admissions
Service (UCAS)*
Fulton House, Jessop Avenue,
Cheltenham, Gloucestershire
GL50 3SH

The Welsh Office
Schools Administration Division
Cathays Park, Cardiff CF1 3NQ
01222–826080

Which? Personal Service
For details of how to subscribe
write to:
Which? Ltd, Castlemead, Gascoyne
Way, Hertford SG14 1LH or
telephone 0171–830 6000

Publications

Health Advice for Travellers
(Department of Health booklet T5)
0800 555 777

Which Subject? Which Career? (£12.99)
is published by and available from
Which? Ltd (see below)

The *Which? Tax-Saving Guide* is an
annual free supplement to *Which?*
magazine

Which? Way to Save Tax (£14.99) is
an annual guide published by and
available from Which? Ltd,
Castlemead, Gascoyne Way, Hertford
SG14 1LH (or order, p&p free, on
Freephone 0800 252100), or from
bookshops

INDEX